Noël Coward

COLLECTED PLAYS: EIGHT

'I'LL LEAVE IT TO YOU', THE YOUNG IDEA,
'THIS WAS A MAN'

'I'll Leave It To You' and The Young Idea, the first of Coward's plays ever
to be produced, were, as he said, 'enthusiastically acclaimed by the
critics and ran five weeks and eight weeks respectively. In both of
them I appeared with the utmost determination.' Of 'I'll Leave It To
You', the Daily Mail wrote in 1920: 'Freshly written and brightly acted,
the piece betrays a certain striving after ultra-comic effect. Mr. Noël
Coward, the author, who is not yet twenty-one, is almost too
successful in making the younger nephew a most objectionable boy.'

In his review of The Young Idea in 1923 James Agate wrote in the
Saturday Review: 'There is something in the make-up of this young
playwright beyond the mere farceur . . . I look to him not for "heart
interest" but for the gentle castigation of manners. Let Mr. Coward go
on to give us closely observed people babbling of matters of general
interest and not, sempiternally, of their green passions.'

In his Preface, Coward wrote of 'This Was A Man' (1926): 'Many first
nighters complained that the dinner scene in the second act was the
longest meal they had ever sat through. The play failed in spite of
some patches of expert acting and also, I hasten to add, some patches
of expert writing.' It was originally banned from performance in
Britain 'for facetious adultery', 'because the Lord Chamberlain took
exception to the fact that when, in the last act, the husband learns that
his wife, who is unscrupulous, has seduced his best friend, who is
unintelligent, he goes off into gales of laughter.'

Noël Coward

COLLECTED PLAYS

EIGHT

'I'LL LEAVE IT TO YOU'

THE YOUNG IDEA

'THIS WAS A MAN'

Introduced by Sheridan Morley

Methuen Drama

METHUEN WORLD CLASSICS

3 5 7 9 10 8 6 4 2

This edition first published in Great Britain in 2000
by Methuen Publishing Ltd
215 Vauxhall Bridge Road, London SW1V 1EJ

'I'll Leave It To You' was first published in 1920 by Samuel French Ltd
and republished by Heinemann in 1950 in *Play Parade* Vol. 3
The Young Idea was first published in 1924 by Samuel French Ltd and
republished by Heinemann in 1950 in *Play Parade* Vol. 3
'This Was A Man' was first published in 1928 by Martin Secker in a
volume entitled *Three Plays with a Preface* and republished by
Heinemann in 1950 in *Play Parade* Vol. 3

Copyright in all the plays is by the Estate of the late Noël Coward
Introduction copyright © 2000 by Sheridan Morley
Chronology copyright © 1987, 1999 by Jacqui Russell

The right of the authors to be identified as the authors of these works
has been asserted by them in accordance with the Copyright, Designs
and Patents Act, 1988

ISBN 0 413 75510 X

Methuen Publishing Limited Reg. No. 3543167

A CIP catalogue record for this book
is available from the British Library

Typeset by Deltatype Ltd, Birkenhead, Merseyside
Printed and bound in Great Britain by
Cox & Wyman Ltd, Reading, Berkshire

CAUTION

CONTENTS

INTRODUCTION

In this, the eighth volume of the Coward Collection, we offer a trio of real rarities, which have not been in print since the original (1950) edition of Coward's *Play Parade* Volume Three. Though even the most fervent of Coward admirers would have to admit that these are not major works – essentially juvenilia, in that all were written in Noël's and the twentieth century's early to mid twenties – and they have seldom been professionally revived since their first nights (often closely followed as these were by their last nights), nevertheless all contain the seeds of his later writing and all have a certain biographical fascination. They also inevitably contain the interest of 'lost' works which are often more revealing than the familiar classics.

'*I'll Leave It To You*' and *The Young Idea* were the first two Coward plays ever to be produced; they were, wrote Noël later, 'enthusiastically acclaimed by the critics, and ran five weeks and eight weeks respectively. In both of them I appeared with the utmost determination.'

'*I'll Leave It To You*' owes its origin to the Broadway producer Gilbert Miller, who had taken an early interest in Noël and (in 1919, when Coward himself was still on the verge of his twentieth birthday), given him the outline of a light comedy which Miller wanted written for the leading light comedian of the West End stage, Charles Hawtrey, the man whom as a child actor Noël had most admired and even tried to emulate and imitate. 'I was always extremely wary,' wrote Noël later, 'of writing based on someone else's idea, but I was hardly in any position, as an unproduced playwright and out-of-work actor and failed song-writer, to turn down Gilbert's suggestion. In three days I completed this amiable, innocuous and deeply unpretentious little comedy.'

Miller seemed reasonably pleased, negotiated a few minor changes, and agreed that he would finance a trial production at the Gaiety, Manchester, in April 1920, after which (all being well) it would go on to London and Charles Hawtrey.

As usual, Noël himself proved the play's most astute critic: 'The dialogue on the whole was amusing and unpretentious, and the construction was not bad; but it was too mild and unassuming to be able to awake any really resounding echoes in the hearts of the great public. I was naturally entranced with it, and had the foresight to write myself a wonderful part, and, at least in Manchester, my youth seemed to attract some attention in the press.'

Writing in the *Manchester Guardian* the morning after that 1920 opening night, Noël's first as playwright and actor, Neville Cardus thought that 'Mr. Coward's new play is perhaps the neatest thing of its sort we have lately had in Manchester – and a vast amount of that sort we have recently had.' Other local reviews were good, and one ran the first-ever profile of the young Noël: 'There is something freakish, Puck-like about the narrow slant of his grey-green eyes, the tilt of his eyebrows, the sleek backward rush of his hair. He is lithe as a fawn; and if you told him, with perfect truth, that he was one of the three best dancers in London, his grieved surprise at hearing of the other two would only be equalled by his incredulity.'

At the end of a successful first week in Manchester, however, Mrs. Gilbert Miller and Mrs. Charles Hawtrey appeared in Noël's dressing-room to announce that, on reflection, the play didn't have a hope of being a hit in London and they were off to cable their husbands accordingly. Noël, undefeated and enraged, found a rival management, that of Lady Wyndham (the actress Mary Moore, widow of Sir Charles Wyndham who had built up the theatre chain of that name), who agreed to stage it in the London summer. Noël, still six months away from his twenty-first birthday, had to have his father sign the contract on his behalf.

'*I'll Leave It To You*' duly opened at the New (now Albery) Theatre on 21 July 1920 to reviews that were generally good and clearly impressed by Noël's announcement that he had written the whole thing in three days, 'whereas often my plays take me a whole week'. The notices were not selling ones, however, and at the start of the summer doldrums the play survived a mere thirty-seven performances; but it did Noël considerable good. He managed to sell amateur rights to Samuel French for 'a comfortable sum', and American rights were also sold for a production (Noël's first in the US) which opened in Boston in 1923, only to disappear somewhere on the road to Broadway.

Nevertheless, the play gave Noël a rough draft for the characters of Simon and Sorel Bliss who were to appear five years later in his much more successful *Hay Fever*; it also led to several 'Boy Author Makes Good' press profiles, in one of which Lady Wyndham described Noël as 'Britain's Sacha Guitry'. Her enthusiasm waned, however, when she saw the weekly box-office returns, and the gloom of the final week was deepened by her money-saving decision to cut the stage lighting to half.

But Noël was now well established in the press; the *Scotsman* called him 'an amazing youth', the *Sunday Chronicle* wrote of 'an infant prodigy' and Noël himself admitted to the *Globe*: 'The success of it all has been a bit dazzling. This may be an age of youth, but it does not always happen that young people get their chance of success. I have been exceptionally lucky; I made up my mind I would have one of my plays produced in London by the time I was twenty, and I hope soon to be my own manager as well.'

For the record, he didn't go into management for another ten years, but he did give the *Daily Mail* a detailed glimpse of his writing technique: 'With *"I'll Leave It To You"*, I wrote the first and last acts within a day, working from nine to five with, of course, a short lunch break. The second act took me two days – it was very much harder. I roughly schemed out the plot, and then I let the play take its own way. I find all the technical details, of entrances and exits and so on, just work themselves out as I write at white heat . . . I hardly alter a line of a play once it is written.'

The only major revival of 'I'll Leave It To You' was by the Noël Coward touring company (one dedicated to his plays and led by a young James Mason) at Malvern in 1932, though a decade earlier, when Noël found himself in New York and short of funds, he turned it into a short story and sold it to the Condé Nast magazine empire.

The Young Idea, described as 'a comedy of youth in three acts', was written a year later, when in 1921 Noël found himself playing an unrewardingly small role in a long-running comedy called *Polly With a Past*. As he wrote later, '*Polly* bored me early in the run, but I was already working on a lot of other things. Songs, sketches and plays were bursting out of me far too quickly, and without nearly enough critical discrimination. My best effort during this period was a comedy in three acts, *The Young Idea*, which was primarily inspired by Bernard Shaw's *You Never Can Tell*. I felt rather guilty about the plagiarism, but sent it to Shaw and received back my script, scribbled all over by GBS with alterations and suggestions . . . He said I showed every indication of becoming a good playwright, provided that I never read in my life another word that he, Shaw, had written . . . He said that unless I could get clean away from him, I would always be a back-number, and be hopelessly out of date even before I was forty.'

Noël took the advice to heart, and *The Young Idea* went on a long and fruitless round of managers' offices in London and New York until eventually Robert Courtneidge, father of the Cicely who was to end her career in Noël's *High Spirits* forty years later, agreed to a trial production in Bristol in the September of 1922.

Once again Noël had written himself one of the best roles, and (as with '*I'll Leave It To You*') the regional reviews were good; one Bristol paper wrote of 'sparkling dialogue, abounding humour and unexpected situations', but even so it was to be another six months before *The Young Idea* could be found a London home at the Savoy. Noël was now on twenty pounds a week as actor and author, and again the overnight reviews were excellent. For the *Observer*, however, St John Ervine, himself a playwright of note, expressed some early doubts: 'Mr. Coward has not quite conquered his habit of writing plays as if they were charades, but he has wit and invention, and if only he can restrain the enthusiasm of his many friends and acquire a sense of fact, he will probably one day write a very good comedy.' To balance Ervine, the *Sunday Chronicle* called *The Young Idea* 'the best farcical comedy to hit London since *The Importance of Being Earnest*', while the *Sunday Pictorial* hailed Noël as 'the best-dressed young wit in London' without revealing the runners-up.

Nevertheless, *The Young Idea* survived only seven weeks at the Savoy, teaching Noël yet again that reviews, good or bad, did not necessarily have the last word on success or failure. The only two professional revivals of *The Young Idea* since the war in Britain have been at Guildford in 1989, and in Chester as part of the Coward Centenary celebrations in November 1999.

The last play in this volume, 'This Was A Man', dates from 1926 and has a curious production history in that, banned by the Lord Chamberlain, it has only ever been seen in New York and then widely in France and Germany during the late 1920s, since when it has disappeared without a trace.

Written in the autumn of 1925 while on holiday in Palermo, and dedicated to his first great manager and lover Jack Wilson, 'This Was A Man' was a comedy which Noël himself considered to be 'primarily satirical and on the whole rather dull . . . when it was first seen on Broadway' (in 1926, albeit briefly). He wrote:

> Many first nighters complained that the dinner scene in the second act was the longest meal they had ever sat through. The play failed in spite of some patches of expert acting and also, I hasten to add, some patches of expert writing; but these alas were not enough to relieve the general tedium. It was not at that time produced in England because the Lord Chamberlain [then the theatrical censor] took exception to the fact that when, in the last act, the husband learns that his wife, who is unscrupulous, has seduced his best friend, who is unintelligent, he goes off into gales of laughter. Some years later the official ban on 'facetious adultery' was lifted and the play was produced by a repertory company – I think at Malvern – with distinguished lack of success. The fundamental error in the play is the second act which is a long drawn out duologue between the wife and the ultimately seduced friend, both of whom are tiresome characters. If it had been written with less meticulous veracity and more wit it might have succeeded but even so I doubt it. Bores on the stage however ironically treated invariably bore the audience. Perhaps it will be more interesting to read than to see.

'This Was A Man' had its major success in the Christmas season of

1927/28 when produced by the English Players in Paris, a company which specialised in staging banned British plays in the safety of France. It has never had another major production, or indeed, so far as can be checked, even a minor one.

The Lord Chamberlain's veto did however lead Noël to write for the *Sunday Chronicle* a stirring attack on stage censorship:

> I protest with all the energy I can summon up against this fantastic state of affairs. Almost every day, the law courts and police courts reveal the details of some unorthodox human alliance or intrigue. Yet no one makes a shout about it. But let a variation of these circumstances be translated to a stage play that even sets out to show the wickedness of the thing, and see what an uproar they evoke. See how the Censor will arise in his wrath to smite with his blue pencil . . . what I am calling for is a freer stage, but at the same time I am not advocating licence for anyone to come along and produce a play whose only point is its indelicacy . . . If we must have a Censor, at least let us have one who is able to discriminate between vulgarity and wit.

Regardless of Noël's attacks, and those of many of his playwriting contemporaries, the Lord Chamberlain was to survive in the office of plays censor for almost another forty years, and it was to him that Noël had to make the case in 1930 for *Private Lives* being, despite all appearances, a 'strictly moral' comedy.

Sheridan Morley
2000

1899   16 December, Noël Pierce Coward born in Teddington, Middlesex, eldest surviving son of Arthur Coward, piano salesman and Violet (*née* Veitch). A 'brazen, odious little prodigy', his early circumstances were of refined suburban poverty.

1907   First public appearances in school and community concerts.

1908   Family moved to Battersea and took in lodgers.

1911   First professional appearance as Prince Mussel in *The Goldfish*, produced by Lila Field at the Little Theatre, and revived in same year at Crystal Palace and Royal Court Theatre. Cannard, the page-boy, in *The Great Name* at the Prince of Wales Theatre, and William in *Where the Rainbow Ends* with Charles Hawtrey's Company at the Savoy Theatre.

1912   Directed *The Daisy Chain* and stage-managed *The Prince's Bride* at Savoy in series of matinées featuring the work of the children of the *Rainbow* cast. Mushroom in *An Autumn Idyll*, ballet, Savoy.

1913   An angel (Gertrude Lawrence was another) in Basil Dean's production of *Hannele*. Slightly in *Peter Pan*, Duke of York's.

1914   Toured in *Peter Pan*. Collaborated with fellow performer Esmé Wynne on songs, sketches, and short stories – 'beastly little whimsies'.

1915   Admitted to sanatorium for tuberculosis.

1916   Five-month tour as Charley in *Charley's Aunt*. Walk-on in *The Best of Luck*, Drury Lane. Wrote first full-length song, 'Forbidden Fruit'. Basil Pycroft in *The Light Blues*, produced by Robert Courtneidge, with daughter Cicely also in cast, Shaftesbury. Short spell as dancer at Elysée Restaurant (subsequently the Café de Paris). Jack Morrison in *The Happy Family*, Prince of Wales.

1917   'Boy pushing barrow' in D.W. Griffith's film *Hearts of the World*. Co-author with Esmé Wynne of one-acter *Ida Collaborates*, Theatre Royal, Aldershot. Ripley Guildford in *The Saving Grace*, with Charles Hawtrey, 'who ... taught me many points of comedy acting', Garrick. Family moved to Pimlico and re-opened boarding house.

1918   Called-up for army. Medical discharge after nine months. Wrote unpublished novels *Cats and Dogs* (loosely based on Shaw's *You Never Can Tell*) and the unfinished *Cherry Pan* ('dealing in a whimsical vein with the adventures of a daughter of Pan'), and lyrics for Darewski and Joel, including 'When You Come Home on Leave' and 'Peter Pan'. Also composed 'Tamarisk Town'. Sold short stories to magazines. Wrote plays *The Rat Trap*, *The Last Trick* (unproduced) and *The Impossible Wife* (unproduced). Courtenay Borner in *Scandal*, Strand. *Woman and Whiskey* (co-author Esmé Wynne) produced at Wimbledon Theatre.

1919   Ralph in *The Knight of the Burning Pestle*, Birmingham Repertory, played with 'a stubborn Mayfair distinction' demonstrating a 'total lack of understanding of the play'. Collaborated on *Crissa*, an opera, with Esmé Wynne and Max Darewski (unproduced). Wrote *'I'll Leave It To You'*.

1920   Bobbie Dermott in *'I'll Leave It To You'*, New Theatre. Wrote play *Barriers Down* (unproduced). *'I'll Leave It To You'* published, London.

1921   On holiday in Alassio, met Gladys Calthrop for the first time. Clay Collins in American farce *Polly With a Past*: during the run 'songs, sketches, and plays were bursting out of me'. Wrote *The Young Idea*, *Sirocco*, and *The Better Half*. First visit to New York, and sold parts of *A Withered Nosegay* to *Vanity Fair* and short-story adaptation of *'I'll Leave It To You'* to *Metropolitan*. House-guest of Laurette Taylor and Hartley Manners, whose family rows inspired the Bliss household in *Hay Fever*.

1922   *Bottles and Bones* (sketch) produced in benefit for Newspaper Press Fund, Drury Lane. *The Better Half* produced in 'grand guignol' season, Little Theatre. Started work on songs and sketches for *London Calling!* Adapted Louise Verneuil's *Pour avoir Adrienne* (unproduced). Wrote *The Queen Was in the Parlour* and *Mild Oats*.

1923   Sholto Brent in *The Young Idea*, Savoy. Juvenile lead in *London Calling!* Wrote *Weatherwise*, *Fallen Angels*, and *The Vortex*.

1924   Wrote *Hay Fever* (which Marie Tempest at first refused to do, feeling it was 'too light and plotless and generally lacking in action') and *Easy Virtue*. Nicky Lancaster in *The Vortex*, produced at Everyman by Norman MacDermott.

1925   Established as a social and theatrical celebrity. Wrote *On with the Dance* with London opening in spring followed by *Fallen*

Angels and *Hay Fever*. *Hay Fever* and *Easy Virtue* produced, New York. Wrote silent screen titles for Gainsborough Films.

1926 Toured USA in *The Vortex*. Wrote 'This Was A Man', refused a licence by Lord Chamberlain but produced in New York (1926), Berlin (1927), and Paris (1928). *Easy Virtue, The Queen Was in the Parlour*, and *The Rat Trap* produced, London. Played Lewis Dodd in *The Constant Nymph*, directed by Basil Dean. Wrote *Semi-Monde* and *The Marquise*. Bought Goldenhurst Farm, Kent, as country home. Sailed for Hong Kong on holiday but trip broken in Honolulu by nervous breakdown.

1927 *The Marquise* opened in London while Coward was still in Hawaii, and *The Marquise* and *Fallen Angels* produced, New York. Finished writing *Home Chat*. *Sirocco* revised after discussions with Basil Dean and produced, London.

1928 Clark Storey in Behrman's *The Second Man*, directed by Dean. Gainsborough Films productions of *The Queen Was in the Parlour*, *The Vortex* (starring Ivor Novello), and *Easy Virtue* (directed by Alfred Hitchcock) released – but only the latter, freely adapted, a success. *This Year of Grace!* produced, London, and with Coward directing and in cast, New York. Made first recording, featuring numbers from this show. Wrote *Concerto* for Gainsborough Films, intended for Ivor Novello, but never produced. Started writing *Bitter-Sweet*.

1929 Played in *This Year of Grace!* (USA) until spring. Directed *Bitter-Sweet*, London and New York. Set off on travelling holiday in Far East.

1930 On travels wrote *Private Lives* (1929) and song 'Mad Dogs and Englishmen', the latter on the road from Hanoi to Saigon. In Singapore joined the Quaints, company of strolling English players, as Stanhope for three performances of *Journey's End*. On voyage home wrote *Post-Mortem*, which was 'similar to my performance as Stanhope: confused, under-rehearsed and hysterical'. Directed and played Elyot Chase in *Private Lives*, London, and Fred in *Some Other Private Lives*. Started writing *Cavalcade* and unfinished novel *Julian Kane*.

1931 Elyot Chase in New York production of *Private Lives*. Directed *Cavalcade*, London. Film of *Private Lives* produced by MGM. Set off on trip to South America.

1932 On travels wrote *Design for Living* (hearing that Alfred Lunt and Lynn Fontanne finally free to work with him) and material for new revue including songs 'Mad about the Boy', 'Children of the Ritz' and 'The Party's Over Now'. Produced in London as

Words and Music, with book, music, and lyrics exclusively by Coward and directed by him. The short-lived Noël Coward Company, independent company which enjoyed his support, toured UK with *Private Lives*, *Hay Fever*, *Fallen Angels*, and *The Vortex*.

1933   Directed *Design for Living*, New York, and played Leo. Films of *Cavalcade*, *To-Night Is Ours* (remake of *The Queen Was in the Parlour*), and *Bitter-Sweet* released. Directed London revival of *Hay Fever*. Wrote *Conversation Piece* as vehicle for Yvonne Printemps, and hit song 'Mrs Worthington'.

1934   Directed *Conversation Piece* in London and played Paul. Cut links with C. B. Cochran and formed own management in partnership with John C. Wilson. Appointed President of the Actors' Orphanage, in which he invested great personal commitment until resignation in 1956. Directed Kaufman and Ferber's *Theatre Royal*, Lyric, and Behrman's *Biography*, Globe. Film of *Design for Living* released, London. *Conversation Piece* opened, New York. Started writing autobiography, *Present Indicative*. Wrote *Point Valaine*.

1935   Directed *Point Valaine*, New York. Played lead in film *The Scoundrel* (Astoria Studios, New York). Wrote *To-Night at 8.30*.

1936   Directed and played in *To-Night at 8.30*, London and New York. Directed *Mademoiselle* by Jacques Deval, Wyndham's.

1937   Played in *To-Night at 8.30*, New York, until second breakdown in health in March. Directed (and subsequently disowned) Gerald Savory's *George and Margaret*, New York. Wrote *Operette*, with hit song 'The Stately Homes of England'. *Present Indicative* published, London and New York.

1938   Directed *Operette*, London. *Words and Music* revised for American production as *Set to Music*. Appointed adviser to newly-formed Royal Naval Film Corporation.

1939   Directed New York production of *Set to Music*. Visited Soviet Union and Scandinavia. Wrote *Present Laughter* and *This Happy Breed*: rehearsals stopped by declaration of war. Wrote for revue *All Clear*, London. Appointed to head Bureau of Propaganda in Paris, to liaise with French Ministry of Information, headed by Jean Giraudoux and André Maurois. This posting prompted speculative attacks in the press, prevented by wartime secrecy from getting a clear statement of the exact nature of his work (in fact unexceptional and routine). Troop concert in Arras with Maurice Chevalier. *To Step Aside* (short story collection) published.

1940   Increasingly 'oppressed and irritated by the Paris routine'. Visits USA to report on American isolationism and attitudes to war in Europe. Return to Paris prevented by German invasion. Returned to USA to do propaganda work for Ministry of Information. Propaganda tour of Australia and New Zealand, and fund-raising for war charities. Wrote play *Time Remembered* (unproduced).

1941   Mounting press attacks in England because of time spent allegedly avoiding danger and discomfort of Home Front. Wrote *Blithe Spirit*, produced in London (with Coward directing) and New York. MGM film of *Bitter-Sweet* (which Coward found 'vulgar' and 'lacking in taste') released, London. Wrote screenplay for *In Which We Serve*, based on the sinking of HMS *Kelly*. Wrote songs including 'London Pride', 'Could You Please Oblige Us with a Bren Gun?', and 'Imagine the Duchess's Feelings'.

1942   Produced and co-directed (with David Lean) *In Which We Serve*, and appeared as Captain Kinross (Coward considered the film 'an accurate and sincere tribute to the Royal Navy'). Played in countrywide tour of *Blithe Spirit*, *Present Laughter*, and *This Happy Breed*, and gave hospital and factory concerts. MGM film of *We Were Dancing* released.

1943   Played Garry Essendine in London production of *Present Laughter* and Frank Gibbons in *This Happy Breed*. Produced *This Happy Breed* for Two Cities Films. Wrote 'Don't Let's Be Beastly to the Germans', first sung on BBC Radio (then banned on grounds of lines 'that Goebbels might twist'). Four-month tour of Middle East to entertain troops.

1944   February–September, toured South Africa, Burma, India, and Ceylon. Troop concerts in France and 'Stage Door Canteen Concert' in London. Screenplay of *Still Life*, as *Brief Encounter*. *Middle East Diary*, an account of his 1943 tour, published, London and New York – where a reference to 'mournful little boys from Brooklyn' inspired formation of a lobby for the 'Prevention of Noël Coward Re-entering America'.

1945   *Sigh No More*, with hit song 'Matelot', completed and produced, London. Started work on *Pacific 1860*. Film of *Brief Encounter* released.

1946   Started writing 'Peace in Our Time'. Directed *Pacific 1860*, London.

1947   Gary Essendine in London revival of *Present Laughter*. Supervised production of 'Peace in Our Time'. *Point Valaine* produced,

London. Directed American revival of *To-Night at 8.30*. Wrote *Long Island Sound* (unproduced).

1948 Replaced Graham Payn briefly in American tour of *To-Night at 8.30*, his last stage appearance with Gertrude Lawrence. Wrote screenplay for Gainsborough film of *The Astonished Heart*. Max Aramont in *Joyeux Chagrins* (French production of *Present Laughter*). Built house at Blue Harbour, Jamaica.

1949 Christian Faber in film of *The Astonished Heart*. Wrote *Ace of Clubs* and *Home and Colonial* (produced as *Island Fling* in USA and *South Sea Bubble* in UK).

1950 Directed *Ace of Clubs*, London. Wrote *Star Quality* (short stories) and *Relative Values*.

1951 Deaths of Ivor Novello and C. B. Cochran. Paintings included in charity exhibition in London. Wrote *Quadrille*. One-night concert at Theatre Royal, Brighton, followed by season at Café de Paris, London, and beginning of new career as leading cabaret entertainer. Directed *Relative Values*, London, which restored his reputation as a playwright after run of post-war flops. *Island Fling* produced, USA.

1952 Charity cabaret with Mary Martin at Café de Paris for Actors' Orphanage. June cabaret season at Café de Paris. Directed *Quadrille*, London. 'Red Peppers', *Fumed Oak*, and *Ways and Means* (from *To-Night at 8.30*) filmed as *Meet Me To-Night*. September, death of Gertrude Lawrence: 'no one I have ever known, however brilliant . . . has contributed quite what she contributed to my work'.

1953 Completed second volume of autobiography, *Future Indefinite*. King Magnus in Shaw's *The Apple Cart*. Cabaret at Café de Paris, again 'a triumphant success'. Wrote *After the Ball*.

1954 *After the Ball* produced, UK. July, mother died. September, cabaret season at Café de Paris. November, Royal Command Performance, London Palladium. Wrote *Nude With Violin*.

1955 June, opened in cabaret for season at Desert Inn, Las Vegas, and enjoyed 'one of the most sensational successes of my career'. Played Hesketh-Baggott in film of *Around the World in Eighty Days*, for which he wrote own dialogue. October, directed and appeared with Mary Martin in TV spectacular *Together with Music* for CBS, New York. Revised *South Sea Bubble*.

1956 Charles Condomine in television production of *Blithe Spirit*, for CBS, Hollywood. For tax reasons took up Bermuda residency. Resigned from presidency of the Actors' Orphanage. *South Sea*

Bubble produced, London. Directed and played part of Frank Gibbons in television production of *This Happy Breed* for CBS, New York. Co-directed *Nude With Violin* with John Gielgud (Eire and UK), opening to press attacks on Coward's decision to live abroad. Wrote play *Volcano* (unproduced).

1957 Directed and played Sebastien in *Nude With Violin*, New York. *Nude With Violin* published, London.

1958 Played Gary Essendine in *Present Laughter* alternating with *Nude With Violin* on US West Coast tour. Wrote ballet *London Morning* for London Festival Ballet. Wrote *Look After Lulu!*

1959 *Look After Lulu!* produced, New York, and by English Stage Company at Royal Court, London. Film roles of Hawthorne in *Our Man in Havana* and ex-King of Anatolia in *Surprise Package*. *London Morning* produced by London Festival Ballet. Sold home in Bermuda and took up Swiss residency. Wrote *Waiting in the Wings*.

1960 *Waiting in the Wings* produced, Eire and UK. *Pomp and Circumstance* (novel) published, London and New York.

1961 Alec Harvey in television production of *Brief Encounter* for NBC, USA. Directed American production of *Sail Away*. *Waiting in the Wings* published, New York.

1962 Wrote music and lyrics for *The Girl Who Came to Supper* (adaptation of Rattigan's *The Sleeping Prince*, previously filmed as *The Prince and the Showgirl*). *Sail Away* produced, UK.

1963 *The Girl Who Came to Supper* produced, USA. Revival of *Private Lives* at Hampstead signals renewal of interest in his work.

1964 'Supervised' production of *High Spirits*, musical adaptation of *Blithe Spirit*, Savoy. Introduced Granada TV's 'A Choice of Coward' series, which included *Present Laughter*, *Blithe Spirit*, *The Vortex*, and *Design for Living*. Directed *Hay Fever* for National Theatre, first living playwright to direct his own work there. *Pretty Polly Barlow* (short story collection) published.

1965 Played the landlord in film, *Bunny Lake is Missing*. Wrote *Suite in Three Keys*. Badly weakened by attack of amoebic dysentery contracted in Seychelles.

1966 Played in *Suite in Three Keys*, London, which taxed his health further. Started adapting his short story *Star Quality* for the stage.

1967 Caesar in TV musical version of *Androcles and the Lion* (score by Richard Rodgers), New York. Witch of Capri in film *Boom*, adaptation of Tennessee Williams's play *The Milk Train Doesn't*

Stop Here Any More. Lorn Loraine, Coward's manager, and friend for many years, died, London. Worked on new volume of autobiography, *Past Conditional. Bon Voyage* (short story collection) published.

1968   Played Mr Bridger, the criminal mastermind, in *The Italian Job.*

1970   Awarded knighthood in New Year's Honours List.

1971   Tony Award, USA, for Distinguished Achievement in the Theatre.

1973   26 March, died peacefully at his home in Blue Harbour, Jamaica. Buried on Firefly Hill.

1999   Major centenary celebrations all around the world.

'I'LL LEAVE IT TO YOU'

To

MY MOTHER

'*I'll Leave It To You*' received its first London production on 21st July 1920 at the New Theatre, with the following cast:

MRS DERMOTT			MISS KATE CUTLER
OLIVER			MR DOUGLAS JEFFERIES
EVANGELINE			MISS MURIEL POPE
SYLVIA	}	*her children* {	MISS STELLA JESSE
BOBBIE			MR NOËL COWARD
JOYCE			MISS MOYA NUGENT
DANIEL DAVIS, *her brother*			MR E. HOLMAN CLARK
MRS CROMBIE			MISS LOIS STUART
FAITH CROMBIE			MISS ESME WYNNE
GRIGGS, *butler*			MR DAVID CLARKSON

———

The action of the play takes place in Mulberry Manor, MRS DERMOTT'S *house, a few miles out of London.*

Eighteen months elapse between Acts I and II, and one night between Acts II and III.

ACT I

SCENE: *The Hall of Mulberry Manor. All the furniture looks very comfortable. Through the window can be seen a glimpse of a snowy garden; there is a log fire. The light is a little dim, being late afternoon. Seated on the table swinging her legs is* JOYCE, *she is attired in a fur coat and goloshes, very little else can be seen, except a pink healthy-looking young face.* SYLVIA *is seated on the Chesterfield R. She is twenty-one and exceedingly pretty. It is about five days before Christmas.*

JOYCE (*brightly*): My feet are simply soaking.

SYLVIA (*sewing*): Why on earth don't you go and change them? You'll catch cold.

    BOBBY *enters R. He is a slim, bright-looking youth of twenty.*

JOYCE: I don't mind if I do. (*Laughs.*) Colds are fun.

BOBBIE: She loves having a fuss made of her, beef tea – chicken – jelly with whipped cream – and fires in her bedroom, little Sybarite.

JOYCE: So do you.

BOBBIE (*comes* C.): No, I don't; whenever my various ailments confine me to my bed, I chafe – positively chafe at the terrible inactivity. I want to be up and about, shooting, riding, cricket, football, ludo, the usual run of manly sports.

SYLVIA: Knowing you for what you are – lazy, luxurious —

BOBBIE (*pained*): Please, please, please, not in front of the child. (JOYCE *kicks.*) It's demoralising for her to hear her idolised brother held up to ridicule.

JOYCE: You're not my idolised brother at all – Oliver is. (*Turning away, pouting.*)

BOBBIE (*seated R. on Chesterfield, sweetly*): If that were really so, dear, I know you have much too kind a heart to let me know it.

3

SYLVIA: What is the matter with you this afternoon, Bobby – you are very up in the air about something.

> JOYCE *takes her coat off, puts on back of chair* R. *of table.*

BOBBIE (*rising and sitting on club fender*): Merely another instance of the triumph of mind over matter; in this case a long and healthy walk was the matter. I went into the lobby to put on my snow boots and then – as is usually the case with me – my mind won. I thought of tea, crumpets and comfort. Oliver has gone without me, he simply bursts with health and extraordinary dullness. Personally I shall continue to be delicate and interesting.

SYLVIA (*seriously*): You may *have* to work, Bobbie.

BOBBIE: Really, Sylvia, you do say the most awful things, remember Joyce is only a schoolgirl, she'll be quite shocked.

JOYCE: We work jolly hard at school, anyhow.

BOBBIE: Oh, no, you don't. I've read the modern novelists, and I *know* all you do is walk about with arms entwined, and write poems of tigerish adoration to your mistresses. It's a beautiful existence.

JOYCE: You are a silly ass. (*Picks up magazine.*)

SYLVIA: It's all very well to go on fooling, Bobbie, but *really* we shall have to pull ourselves together a bit. Mother's very worried, as you know, money troubles are perfectly beastly, and she hasn't told us nearly all. I do so hate her to be upset, poor darling.

BOBBIE: What can we do? (*Sits* L. *end of Chesterfield.* JOYCE *puts down magazine and listens.*)

SYLVIA: Think of a way to make money.

BOBBIE: It's difficult now that the war is over.

SYLVIA: That's cheap wit, dear; also it's the wrong moment for it. (JOYCE *giggles.*)

BOBBIE: It's always the wrong moment for cheap wit, admitting for one moment that it was, which it wasn't.

JOYCE: Oh, do shut up, you make my head go round.

> *Enter* EVANGELINE *downstairs; she is tall and almost beautiful; she carries a book in her hand.*

BOBBIE (*turning*): Oh, Vangy, do come and join us; we're on the verge of a congress.

EVANGELINE: I must read some more Maeterlinck. (*Posing.*)

4

BOBBIE: You mean you must let us see you reading Maeterlinck.

EVANGELINE (*goes to him, back of Chesterfield, touches his hair*): Try not to be so irritating, Bobbie dear; just because *you* don't happen to appreciate good literature, it's very small and narrow to laugh at people who do.

SYLVIA: But seriously, Vangy, we are rather worried (EVANGELINE *moves*) about mother; she's been looking harassed for days.

EVANGELINE (*sitting in armchair*): What about?

SYLVIA: Money, money, money! Haven't you realised that? Uncle Daniel sent a pretty substantial cheque from South America (*all nod*) that helped things on a bit after father's death, but that must be gone by now – and mother won't say how much father left.

JOYCE: Perhaps she doesn't know.

BOBBIE: She must know now, he's been dead nearly six months – inconsiderate old beast!

SYLVIA: Bobbie, you're not to talk about father like that. I won't have it; after all —

BOBBIE: After all what? – He was perfectly rotten to mother and never came near her for four years before his death. Why should we be charming and reverent about him just because he's our father. When I saw him I hated him, and his treatment of mum hasn't made me like him any better, I can tell you.

EVANGELINE: But still, Bobbie, he was *our father*, and mother was fond of him – (BOBBIE: Ha!) – once, anyhow, there's nothing to be gained by running him down.

SYLVIA: The point is, have we enough money to keep on as we are, or haven't we?

JOYCE (*quickly*): The only one who knows is mother, and she won't say.

SYLVIA: We haven't asked her yet; we'll make her say. Where is she?

BOBBIE: Up in her room, I think.

SYLVIA: Go and fetch her down. (*Puts sewing on form.*)

BOBBIE: What, now?

SYLVIA: Yes, *now*.

BOBBIE: Oh, no!

SYLVIA and EVANGELINE: Yes, go along.

5

BOBBIE: Righto! we'll tackle her straight away.

Exit BOBBIE *upstairs.*

JOYCE (*goes to* EVANGELINE): Do – do you think we may have to leave this house?

SYLVIA: I don't know.

JOYCE: I should simply hate that. (*Sits on right end of form.*)

EVANGELINE: So should we all – it would be miserable.

SYLVIA: Think how awful it must be for mother.

JOYCE: I say, don't you think Oliver ought to be here – if anything's going to happen? He's the eldest.

SYLVIA: He wouldn't be any help. He cares for nothing but the inside of motors and the outside of Maisie Stuart; he's not observant enough to know her inside.

EVANGELINE: What a perfectly horrible thing to say!

SYLVIA: Well, it's absolutely true; he thinks she's everything that's good and noble, when all the time she's painfully ordinary and a bit of a cat; what fools men are.

JOYCE (*blasé*): One can't help falling in love.

Enter MRS DERMOTT *downstairs followed by* BOBBIE; *she is a pretty little woman with rather a plaintive manner.*

MRS DERMOTT (*as she descends*): Bobbie says you all want to talk to me! What's the matter, darlings? (*Comes C.*)

SYLVIA: That's what we want to know, Mum; come on now, out with it. You've been looking worried for ever so long.

BOBBIE stays at foot of stairs.

MRS DERMOTT: I don't know what you mean, Sylvia, dear, I —

SYLVIA: Now listen to me, Mother; you've got something on your mind, that's obvious to anyone; you're not a bit good at hiding your feelings. Surely we're all old enough to share the worry, whatever it is.

MRS DERMOTT (*kissing her*): Silly old darlings – it's true I have been a little worried – you see, we're ruined.

SYLVIA
EVANGELINE } Mother!
BOBBIE
JOYCE

The girls rise.

MRS DERMOTT (*shaking her head sadly*): Yes, we're ruined; we haven't a penny. (*Moves to chair below table.*)

SYLVIA: Why didn't you tell us before?

MRS DERMOTT (*sitting*): I only knew it myself this morning, I had a letter from Tibbets; he's been through all the papers and things.

EVANGELINE: Father's papers?

MRS DERMOTT: I suppose so, dear. There wouldn't be any others, would there?

BOBBIE (*coming down*): But Mother, what did he say, how did he put it?

MRS DERMOTT: I really forget – but I know it worried me dreadfully.

> JOYCE *sits on form.*

EVANGELINE: And we literally haven't a penny?

MRS DERMOTT: Well, only fifteen hundred a year; it's almost as bad.

> EVANGELINE *sits in armchair.*

JOYCE: Shall we have to give up the house?

MRS DERMOTT: I'm afraid so, darling; you see there are taxes and rates and things. Tibbets knows all about it – he's coming down to-night.

SYLVIA: Can't Uncle Daniel do anything?

> BOBBIE *sits on table.*

MRS DERMOTT: He's my only hope. I cabled to South America three weeks ago. I didn't know the worst then, but I felt I wanted someone to lean on – after all, his cheque was a great help.

JOYCE: Is he very, very rich?

MRS DERMOTT: He must be, he's a bachelor, and he has a ranch and a mine and things.

BOBBIE: Has he answered your cable?

MRS DERMOTT: No, but of course he may have been out prospecting or bronco-breaking or something when it arrived. They live such restless lives out there – oh, no, I don't think he'll fail me, he's my only brother.

EVANGELINE: I wonder how much he *has* got.

7

MRS DERMOTT: Perhaps Tibbets will know – we'll ask him.

BOBBIE: Why, is he Uncle Daniel's lawyer as well?

MRS DERMOTT: No, dear, but you know lawyers are always clever at knowing other people's business – I shall never forget —

BOBBIE: Yes – but Mother, what will happen if he *isn't* rich, and doesn't help us after all?

MRS DERMOTT: I really don't know, darling. It's terrible upsetting, isn't it?

JOYCE: It will be *awful* having to give up the house.

MRS DERMOTT: Well, Tibbets says we needn't for another two years. It's paid for until then or something.

SYLVIA (*sits on the Chesterfield*): Thank heaven! What a relief!

MRS DERMOTT: But we shall have to be awfully careful. Oh, darlings (*she breaks down*), thank God I've got you. (*Weeps on* BOBBIE'S *knee.*)

SYLVIA: Buck up, Mother, it isn't as bad as all that. After all, we can work.

BOBBIE (*without enthusiasm*): Yes, we can work. (*Moving from table to* R.)

EVANGELINE: I shall write things, really artistic little fragments —

BOBBIE: We want to make money, Vangy.

MRS DERMOTT: But, darlings, you know you can't make money unless you're Socialists and belong to Unions and things.

EVANGELINE: Well, I know *I* should make money in time. There's a great demand for really good stuff now.

SYLVIA: Do you think yours *is* really good?

EVANGELINE: I'm sure it is.

MRS DERMOTT *reads a magazine.*

BOBBIE: Well, God help the bad.

EVANGELINE (*rising*): Look here, Bobbie, I'm tired of your silly jeering at me. Just stop trying to be funny. (*Moves to* L.C.)

BOBBIE (*hotly*): I realise the futility of endeavour when I see how funny others can be *without* trying (*following her*).

EVANGELINE: Ill-bred little pip squeak!

JOYCE (*jumping up; firing*): He's not a pip squeak. Fanny Harris says he's the most good-looking boy she's ever seen.

EVANGELINE: She can't have seen many then. (*Moves to fireplace.*)

BOBBIE: Oh! Don't betray your jealousy of my looks, Evangeline. It's so degrading.

EVANGELINE: I tell you —

MRS DERMOTT: Children, stop quarrelling at once. I think it's most inconsiderate of you under the circumstances.

> BOBBIE *sits on table back to audience. There is silence for a moment. Enter* GRIGGS *from hall with a telegram.*

GRIGGS: For you, madam.

> *All show an interest.*

MRS DERMOTT (*taking it*): Thank you, Griggs. (*She opens it and reads it.*) There is no answer, Griggs. (*Exit* GRIGGS, R.) My dears!

JOYCE: What is it, Mother, quick?

MRS DERMOTT (*reading*): Arrive this afternoon – about tea time, Daniel.

SYLVIA: Uncle Daniel!

EVANGELINE: In England!

MRS DERMOTT: I suppose so. It was handed in at Charing Cross.

BOBBIE: What luck! (*Gets off table.*)

MRS DERMOTT: We're saved – oh, my darlings! (*She breaks down again.*)

JOYCE: He may not have any money after all.

MRS DERMOTT: He'd never have got across so quickly if he hadn't. (*She sniffs.*) Oh, it's too, too wonderful – I have not seen him for six years.

BOBBIE: As a matter of fact it is jolly decent of him to be so prompt.

MRS DERMOTT: Where's Oliver? He ought to be here to welcome him too.

BOBBIE (C.): Oliver has gone for a brisk walk, to keep fit he said, as if it made any difference whether he kept fit or not.

MRS DERMOTT: It makes a lot of difference, dear. He is the athletic one of the family. (BOBBIE *is annoyed.*) I don't like the way you speak of him, Bobbie. We can't all compose songs and be brilliant. You must try and cultivate a little toleration for others, darling. (OLIVER *passes window from* L.) Oliver is a great comfort to me. Tibbets only said —

EVANGELINE (*glancing out of the window*): Here he is, anyhow. Who's going to tell him the news?

MRS DERMOTT (*rising, goes to stairs*): Well, I've no time now, I must change my dress for Daniel. Turn on the lights, Bobbie; make everything look as cosy and festive as you can. (*On stairs.*) Run into the kitchen, Joyce dear, and tell cook to make an extra supply of hot cakes for tea. I'm sure Daniel will love them after being so long abroad and living on venison and bully beef and things. (*Ascending, then turns.*) You will all wash before tea, won't you, darlings? It's always so important to make a good first impression, and he hasn't seen any of you since you've been grown up. (*Glances in mirror.*) Oh! look at my face, I look quite happy now.

> *Exit* MRS DERMOTT *upstairs.*

SYLVIA: I think mother is rather mixing up North and South America; they don't have such awful hardships where Uncle Daniel comes from.

> *Enter* OLIVER *from hall; he is a thick-set, determined-looking man of twenty-five.*

OLIVER: Hallo! (*Crossing to table L.C.*)

JOYCE (*going to him, excitedly*): Something wonderful has happened, Oliver.

OLIVER: What is it?

JOYCE: We're ruined. I've just got to go and order extra teacakes. Isn't it all thrilling?

> *Exit* JOYCE *into hall.*

OLIVER: What on earth's she talking about?

SYLVIA: It's perfectly true. We haven't any money, but Uncle Daniel's coming today, and we're sure he'll help us.

OLIVER (*dazed*): Haven't any money, but —

EVANGELINE (*at fire*): Mother's been rather vague as usual, but we gather that we're practically penniless, and that we shall have to give up the house after two years unless something happens.

SYLVIA: Luckily Uncle Daniel is happening – this afternoon. Mother's just had a wire from him – he's certain to be rich, mother says.

> BOBBIE *leaning against stairs.*

OLIVER: Why?

SYLVIA: Because he's a bachelor, and has been living in South America for five years.

BOBBIE: Six years.

SYLVIA: Five years.

BOBBIE: Six years – mother said so.

SYLVIA: No, she didn't —

OLIVER: Well, it doesn't matter. How does mother know we're penniless?

BOBBIE (*coming C.*): She heard from Tibbets this morning, he's coming down tonight.

OLIVER (*sinking into chair*): By jove, what a muddle!

> JOYCE *re-enters, crosses to chair L.C., takes coat and exits upstairs.*

SYLVIA: It's all quite clear when you think it out.

BOBBIE (*C.*): We've all got to wash and make ourselves look clean and sweet for Uncle Daniel. Your collar's filthy; you'd better go and change it quickly. He may be here at any minute.

SYLVIA: Turn on the lights, Bobbie – and do let's hurry.

> BOBBIE *turns up the lights and goes upstairs followed by* OLIVER. EVANGELINE *goes up slowly after them.*

OLIVER: What a muddle! What a muddle! (*As he crosses to stairs.*)

EVANGELINE (*following him*): What a muddle! What a muddle! (*Turns on stairs.*) Shall I put on my emerald green tea gown? (*To* SYLVIA.)

SYLVIA: No, dear; it's ever so much too old for you.

EVANGELINE (*piqued*): I don't think it's at all too old for me. I shall certainly put it on.

> *She disappears upstairs.* SYLVIA *is left alone. Suddenly there comes a loud peal at the front door bell.* SYLVIA *sees some half-made crêpe-de-chine underclothes on form, takes them, hides them under cushions on window seat L. Draws curtains to window L., then L.C. as enter* GRIGGS, *followed by* UNCLE DANIEL, *in an opulent-looking fur coat – he is a tall, stoutish man of about forty-five.* SYLVIA *shrinks back by stairs.*

GRIGGS (*assisting him off with his coat*): If you will wait, sir, I'll tell Mrs Dermott you are here.

DANIEL: Thank you. (*Goes round to fireplace, warms hands, turns.*)

> GRIGGS *has meanwhile taken his coat into the lobby.* SYLVIA *creeps*

cautiously from behind and goes towards stairs. DANIEL *looks round
and sees her. He watches her in silence for a moment, as she goes up
a few stairs.*

Excuse me – have you been stealing anything?

SYLVIA (*jumping*): Oh, Uncle Daniel – I didn't want you to see
me.

DANIEL: Why not?

SYLVIA: I wanted to change my frock and do my hair.

DANIEL: It looks quite charming as it is – I suppose you are
Evangeline?

SYLVIA: No I'm not, I'm Sylvia. (*Coming to him.*)

DANIEL (*below Chesterfield*): Sylvia! I didn't know there was a
Sylvia.

SYLVIA (R.C., *laughing*): I was having concussion last time you
were here, having cut my head open on a door scraper at
school. Naturally you wouldn't remember me.

DANIEL: Oh, but I do now, you were the sole topic of
conversation at lunch. How foolish of me to have let you slip
my memory. Where are all the others?

SYLVIA: They're upstairs improving on the Almighty's concep-
tion of them as much as possible in your honour; I was just
going to do the same when you caught me.

DANIEL: You looked extraordinarily furtive.

SYLVIA: And untidy. We've just been having a sort of family
conference. It was very heating.

DANIEL: I think you might have waited for me – I'm a most
important factor. What were you discussing?

SYLVIA: Oh – er – ways and means.

DANIEL: I see, it's as bad as that!

SYLVIA: But you wait until mother comes. She'll explain
everything. I'll go and hurry her up. (*She goes upstairs.*)

DANIEL: Don't leave me all alone. I'm a timid creature.

SYLVIA (*turns*): After all that bronco-busting! I don't think!

    Exit SYLVIA *upstairs.*

DANIEL: Bronco-busting! What on earth does she mean? (*He
walks slowly to fireplace and stands with his back to it.*)

    Enter MRS DERMOTT *downstairs. They meet C.*

MRS DERMOTT: Danny! Danny! darling —

DANIEL (C.): Anne! (*He kisses her fondly.*)

MRS DERMOTT: Oh, my dear, you have been away such a long time.

DANIEL (*he turns her round to* R.): Well, this is splendid – you do look fit! Do you know I've often longed to be home. I've imagined winter afternoons just like this – with a nice crackly fire and tea and muffins in the grate. (*Putting her on Chesterfield.*)

MRS DERMOTT: Oh well, they're not in the grate yet, dear, but they will be soon. I ordered a special lot because I knew you loved them.

He sits beside her; she is nearest the fire.

I can never thank you enough for sending the cheque, Danny.

DANIEL: Oh, rubbish.

MRS DERMOTT: It was the greatest help in the world.

DANIEL: I started for home the very moment I heard you were in trouble; has everything been very, very trying?

MRS DERMOTT: Only during the last few days. You see, George hadn't been near me for four years before he died, so it wasn't such a terrible shock as it might have been. Of course, he was my husband, and it was upsetting, but still —

DANIEL: He behaved like a beast to you, and —

MRS DERMOTT: Well, he's dead now – but don't let's discuss my affairs. Tell me about yourself; what have you been doing?

DANIEL: That can wait. Considering that the sole object of my coming to England was to help you, I think we ought to concentrate. Tell me now, has he left you very badly off?

MRS DERMOTT: Well, Tibbets says we're ruined, but you know what Tibbets is. Such a pessimist!

DANIEL: Tibbets?

MRS DERMOTT: Yes, our lawyer, you know.

DANIEL: Do I? How much have you got?

MRS DERMOTT: I think Tibbets said about fifteen hundred; of course we can't keep the house and family going on that, can we?

DANIEL: Of course we can't. What do the children intend to do?

MRS DERMOTT: Well, they don't quite know, poor darlings.

DANIEL: Poor darlings! Is Oliver at home?

MRS DERMOTT: Yes. He's going to be a barrister or an engineer.

He's very vague about it, but has been learning Pelmanism, so I know he's going to be something.

DANIEL: I see. Bobbie?

MRS DERMOTT: Oh, Bobbie, he's so young. Of course, it's not his fault.

DANIEL: Naturally.

MRS DERMOTT: He composes, you know – beautiful little songs – mostly about moonlight. Evangeline writes the words. She is *very* artistic, and —

DANIEL: What does Sylvia do?

MRS DERMOTT: Oh, she helps me.

DANIEL: In what way?

MRS DERMOTT: Oh – er – she – well – she does the flowers, and comes calling with me, and she's *invaluable* at jumble sales, when we have them.

DANIEL: And the youngest?

MRS DERMOTT: Joyce? Oh, she's still at school – she's going to Roedean next year to be finished.

DANIEL: Finished? Oh, I see! Well! They sound a pretty hopeless lot.

MRS DERMOTT: Oh, Danny, how can you be so horrid? Why, they're all darlings! You can't expect them to work. They've not been brought up to it.

DANIEL: I think it's about time they started.

    Enter EVANGELINE *downstairs, followed by* OLIVER, BOBBIE *and* JOYCE. SYLVIA *comes last.*

MRS DERMOTT (*rising, back to audience*): Here they are. Children, this is Uncle Daniel.

    DANIEL *rises, stands L. of Chesterfield.*

EVANGELINE (*gracefully embracing him*): I remember you quite well.

DANIEL: Splendid. Evangeline?

EVANGELINE: Yes, Evangeline. (*Crosses to fire, down stage.*)

OLIVER (*shaking hands*): So do I. (*Moves to above* EVANGELINE.)

BOBBIE (*shaking hands*): I don't remember you a bit, but I may later when we all start reminiscencing. (*Goes* L.)

JOYCE (*kissing him*): We've been simply longing for you to come home.

DANIEL: Little Joyce — (JOYCE *moves to top of table.*)

SYLVIA (*kissing him*): D'you know you haven't changed a bit since I last saw you!

DANIEL *smiles at her.*

DANIEL: May I say that it gives me immeasurable joy to be here once more in the bosom of my family. (*Sits on Chesterfield.*)

BOBBIE: We're not really your family, but never mind.

DANIEL: I don't. But I have looked forward to this moment through the long sun-scorched nights with the great dome of the sky above me – shapes have drifted out of the surrounding blackness and beckoned to me, crying 'Home, home' in depressing voices. I have heard the sand-bug calling to its mate. 'Home', it said, and bit me —

SYLVIA *sits on arm of chair*, R.C.

MRS DERMOTT: Silly old darling, Danny. (*Sits R. of Chesterfield.*)

JOYCE: What did you do out there, Uncle?

DANIEL: Lots of things – gold mining, ranching, auction —

BOBBIE: Auction? (*Leaning on table.*)

MRS DERMOTT: Is it a very wonderful life, Danny?

DANIEL: Occasionally – on good days.

BOBBIE: How do you mean, good days?

DANIEL (*rather embarrassed*): Well – er – just good days.

MRS DERMOTT: Do come and sit down, all of you; you look so terribly restless.

They sit, OLIVER *on arm of Chesterfield,* JOYCE *crosses to form R.,* EVANGELINE *on club-fender,* BOBBIE *chair below table,* SYLVIA *armchair.*

DANIEL: I feel restless. It must be the home surroundings after all these years.

BOBBIE: I should love to go abroad.

DANIEL: It would make a man of you, my boy.

BOBBIE: I should simply loathe that.

DANIEL: So should I between ourselves, but still — Oh, by the way, I – I have something rather important to say to you, you must prepare yourselves for a shock – I – I — (*He dabs his eyes with his handkerchief.*)

MRS DERMOTT: What on earth is it, Danny?

DANIEL: I – I — (*Another dab.*)

SYLVIA: Oh, Uncle, tell us.

DANIEL: I – er – it's this. I consulted my doctor just before I sailed.

MRS DERMOTT: Yes?

DANIEL: He – he gave me just three years to live.

MRS DERMOTT: Danny, what do you mean?

DANIEL (*firmly*): It's true – three years, he said.

MRS DERMOTT: It's the most awful thing. Tell us why – what's the matter with you? (*Quickly.*)

DANIEL (*rather staggered*): The matter with me?

MRS DERMOTT: Yes, of course, you must see a specialist at once.

DANIEL (*pulling himself together dramatically*): No specialist in the world could ever do me any good.

MRS DERMOTT: Well, what is it? For God's sake tell us!

DANIEL (*takes his breath*): Sleeping sickness! (*Smiles broadly at* MRS DERMOTT.)

MRS DERMOTT: What!! (*They all move.*)

DANIEL: Yes, it's frightfully prevalent out there.

MRS DERMOTT: Oh, Danny, I hope it's not infectious.

OLIVER: Sleeping sickness! By jove!

DANIEL: Yes, I simply daren't go to sleep without an alarm clock.

MRS DERMOTT: Danny darling, it's all too dreadful – I can't believe it.

BOBBIE (*rising*): But, Uncle, I thought sleeping sickness polished you off in one night.

DANIEL (*embarrassed*): So it does, but that one night won't happen to me for three years. The doctor says so. He knows. You see I've got it internally or something.

MRS DERMOTT (*firmly*): You must never go back there – you shall stay with us until – until – the end —

> She breaks down, sobs on DANIEL'S shoulder.

SYLVIA (*goes behind Chesterfield*): Oh, Mother darling, don't cry. (*She looks at* DANIEL *rather angrily.*)

DANIEL (*rising*): I'm sorry I have upset you, Anne. But I have told you this today with a purpose in my mind. (*Moving to* C.)

OLIVER: A purpose?

DANIEL (L. *of armchair*): Yes, I have a few words to say to you all

– words which, though they may sound a little mercenary, are in reality prompted by very deep feeling.

MRS DERMOTT: Poor Danny.

DANIEL: Ssh! (*Waves her to silence.*) It may seem to all of you 'banal' in the extreme to talk of money on an occasion such as this, but believe me, it's best to get it over. I came over to England this time, as I have said, with a purpose – one might almost say a double purpose. Firstly, to comfort my sister, your dear mother, in her hour of – er – tribulation. (*He pauses.*) If you would just say 'yes' or 'quite so' whenever I pause, it would help me enormously.

SYLVIA: All right, we will.

DANIEL: Thank you, you are a good girl. Where was I?

BOBBIE: Tribulation.

EVANGELINE: Hour of tribulation (*in his tone*).

DANIEL: — hour of tribulation. (*He pauses.*)

SYLVIA } Yes.
BOBBIE } Quite so.

DANIEL: I thank you. And secondly, to feast my eyes, perhaps for the last time on earth, upon you children – also to talk to you seriously, for after all, you're my only relatives in the world.

SYLVIA } Yes, yes.
BOBBIE } Quite so.

DANIEL: I am as you may have guessed, a wealthy man —

EVERYONE (*eagerly*): Yes, yes! (*Movement from all.*)

DANIEL: And out there (*he nods his head descriptively*) we don't get much chance of spending our money —

BOBBIE } Quite so.
OLIVER } No, no!

DANIEL: And now I come to the point. At the end of three years I shall be no more.

EVANGELINE: Quite so!

OTHERS: Sh!!

    MRS DERMOTT *sniffs*.

DANIEL: Bear up, Anne; we must all die sometime.

MRS DERMOTT: Yes, but not of sleeping sickness. It's so horrible. Anything else – but not sleeping sickness.

DANIEL: I believe it is very comfortable, but that is neither here nor there. What I was going to say was this, I am a firm believer in the old-fashioned laws of entail. I have no patience with this modern way of dividing up legacies between large numbers of people —

SYLVIA (*with interest*): Yes, yes?

BOBBIE (*with equal interest*): Quite so!

DANIEL: When I pass into the great beyond (MRS DERMOTT *sniffs. He is obviously rather pleased with that remark, so he repeats it*) – pass into the great beyond, I intend to leave the whole bulk of my fortune to the one of you who has made good —

OLIVER: How do you mean 'Made good'?

DANIEL: I mean make good your position in the world, justify your existence, carve for yourself a niche in the Temple of Fame — (*Turning R.*)

BOBBIE (*very quickly and brightly*): Yes, yes?

DANIEL (*turns, sharply*): That was entirely unnecessary, I didn't pause.

BOBBIE: Sorry.

They are all self-conscious as he addresses them.

DANIEL: What is the use of idling through life, frittering away your youth, I repeat, frittering away your youth, when you might be working to achieve some great and noble end? (OLIVER *embarrassed.*) You, Oliver, you might in time be a great inventor, and know all about the insides of the most complicated machines. You, Evangeline (EVANGELINE *rises, poses by fireplace, one hand on mantel.* JOYCE *laughs – she pulls her hair*), might develop into a great poetess; your mother tells me that you already write verses about the moonlight. They all start like that, only unfortunately some of them stay like it. (*She sits again.*) You, Bobbie, you are artistic, too, you might without undue strain become a world famed composer, artist, actor. (BOBBIE *rises, moves down L., posing as actor.*) Sylvia, for you I foresee a marvellous career as a decorative designer. You already arrange flowers and jumble sales – and last, but not by any means least, little Joyce (JOYCE *hangs her head, polishes her nails*), now on the very threshold of life. What are you going to do with yourself? Sit at home and wait for a nice husband with mediocre prospects and perhaps an over-developed

Adam's apple? Never, never! You too must rise and go forth –
the world is calling to you. Do what you will. I can't think of a
career for you at the moment, but no matter. I only want to
impress upon you all the necessity of making good at
something – make good, make good, make good! And the one
I consider has done best for himself and the family name, to
him – or her – I will bequeath every penny I possess. (*Goes up
four stairs.*)

OLIVER ⎫ (*rising and all talking at once*): But look here —
EVANGELINE ⎪ Uncle dear, of course —
BOBBIE ⎬ How in Heaven's name are we to —
SYLVIA ⎪ Really I don't quite see —
JOYCE ⎭ It's going to be very difficult —

    All looking towards DANIEL, *the positions are now as follows:* –
DANIEL, *up four stairs.* MRS DERMOTT *extreme* R. SYLVIA *up* R.C.
OLIVER *down* R.C. EVANGELINE *down* C. JOYCE *up* L.C. BOBBIE
down L.

DANIEL (*holding up his hand*): Please – couldn't you possibly speak
one at a time? Sylvia? (*Motions to her.*)

SYLVIA (*stepping forward*): What we want to know, Uncle, is how
on earth are we to start?

    They all nod.

DANIEL (*smiling benignly, arms outstretched*): I'll leave it to you!

    All turn to audience open-mouthed as the CURTAIN *descends.*

ACT II

The SCENE *is the same as Act I. Eighteen months have elapsed. All the windows are wide open. It is a glorious summer day. Alterations in the furniture are noted at the end of the play. At the table L.* EVANGELINE *is seated when the curtain rises, typewriting slowly but firmly. There are a lot of papers strewn about. On the piano there is a sort of pastry board to which is affixed a working model of a motor engine in miniature.* JOYCE *is seated at table L.C. laboriously copying out a sheet of music on to some manuscript paper.*

JOYCE (*showing music*): Is it a crotchet or a quaver that has a waggle on the end of it?

EVANGELINE: I haven't the remotest idea.

JOYCE: I do think Bobbie might write them a little more distinctly, it's awfully difficult to copy.

    JOYCE *hums.*

EVANGELINE: I don't wish to appear surly or disagreeable to my younger sister, but if you don't stop squawking I shall hurl something at you.

JOYCE: Oh, all right. (*She hums louder.*)

EVANGELINE (*after a short pause*): Joyce, you really are maddening; you know perfectly well that I have to revise and retype an entire short story which in itself is a nerve-racking job, and all you do is to burble and sing, and gabble. Can't you be quiet?

JOYCE: Why don't you go and work in your own room?

EVANGELINE: Because it would be neither comfortable nor proper with three inquisitve painters there, running up and down the kitchen steps.

JOYCE: Oh, I'd forgotten.

    JOYCE *hums again.*

EVANGELINE: But if you desire to continue your noises, may I

20

suggest that you do your music in the summer house. There's a nice firm table there.

JOYCE: No thanks, I'm quite comfy here.

EVANGELINE: Well, I'm sorry to hear it.

Enter MRS DERMOTT *from hall. Goes to table and tidies papers.*

MRS DERMOTT: Vangy, dear, I *do* think you might have made the hall look a little tidier. We shall have Mrs Crombie and Faith here soon. It really is tiresome of Bobbie to have made me ask them, specially as Uncle Daniel's coming too. They'll be terribly in the way and we shall have to make conversation instead of listening to Uncle Daniel's thrilling stories. (*Goes to Chesterfield and tidies papers.*)

EVANGELINE: I can't think why you didn't wire and put them off yesterday.

MRS DERMOTT: Because Bobbie would have been miserable and sulky.

EVANGELINE: He's very inconsiderate. I don't think you ought to give in to him so much, Mother; it only makes him worse. What he can see in that tiresome little cat beats me.

JOYCE: She's awfully pretty.

MRS DERMOTT *merely takes papers from one place to another, frequently dropping some, as she is 'tidying up'.*

EVANGELINE: And entirely brainless.

JOYCE: Well, we can be thankful that Mrs Crombie isn't staying over the weekend. One day of her is bad enough.

MRS DERMOTT (*tidying papers on form*): You mustn't talk like that, dear. After all they are our guests and Bobbie's friends, and we must be kind even if we don't like them very much. (*Picking up waste-paper basket from the front of table.*) I'm only worrying because darling Daniel may be hurt at our having strangers in the house when he arrives.

JOYCE: Oh, Uncle Dan won't mind. He's probably used to face polar bears and things in his shack.

EVANGELINE: But it seems hard luck to leave raging bears on one side of the Atlantic and meet Mrs Crombie on the other.

JOYCE *goes into screams of laughter and then chokes.*

MRS DERMOTT (*anxiously*): Darling – do be careful. (*Drops papers and puts waste-paper basket through window* L.C. *Enter* BOBBIE *downstairs.* MRS DERMOTT *continues to tidy up room.*)

BOBBIE: What's the matter?

EVANGELINE: Nothing much, only your crochets and quavers have sent our little ray of sunshine into a rapid decline.

BOBBIE: Have you done it?

JOYCE (*weakly*): The top treble thing's a little wobbly, but I'll ink it over afterwards.

> MRS DERMOTT *is tidying window seat.*

BOBBIE (*kissing her hurriedly and loudly*): Thanks, you're a lamb. I'll try it now.

EVANGELINE: Oh! Bobbie, don't try it now!

BOBBIE: I shall. (*He goes to piano, then turns furiously.*) Well, really it is the *limit*. Why can't Oliver keep his rotten engine in the shed. It will scratch all the polish. (*He takes the model off piano and bangs it on the floor.*)

MRS DERMOTT: Oh, Bobbie, don't break that thing. Oliver's so proud of it. I can't think why.

BOBBIE: Well, I wish he'd go and be proud of it somewhere else. Look here, three distinct scratches.

MRS DERMOTT: Never mind dear. Griggs will get them out with sandpaper or something.

> BOBBIE *commences to play over the manuscript* JOYCE *has just copied. Occasionally he stops and alters something with a pencil. No one takes any notice. The dialogue goes on just the same.*

(*Coming down to* EVANGELINE.) If you've nearly finished, Vangy dear, do put the typewriter away. It looks so untidy.

EVANGELINE (*rather crossly, rising*): Of course I quite see that until my room's done, I shall never be able to do any work at all. (*Puts cover on typewriter, then pushes table up to back* L.)

MRS DERMOTT: Don't be cross, darling. You know how worried I am over everything this morning. It's one long rush.

EVANGELINE (*kissing her*): Sorry dear. I quite understand, only I must have this story sent to the *Clarion* by Tuesday. If not, it won't be out until the August number.

MRS DERMOTT: You're a dear darling, and you work terribly hard. I only hope you won't overdo it.

EVANGELINE: Oh no, these stories are only pot boilers. They just fill in the time until my next novel is ready.

BOBBIE (*suddenly*): Listen, don't you think this is a ripping change? (*He plays a few chords. He then sits back complacently.*)

MRS DERMOTT: Perfectly lovely, darling.

EVANGELINE: It sounds very much like everything else to me.

BOBBIE: Only because you haven't got any ear. As a matter of fact they're quite good chords. I shall put them into the new tombstone cycle.

EVANGELINE: Don't alter many of my words, will you?

BOBBIE: Not many, but the bit about 'worms gnawing the grave of my beloved' is a little too gloomy. Couldn't you make it butterflies.

JOYCE *giggles.*

EVANGELINE: Don't be silly, Bobbie! butterflies don't live in graves. Well, you can use the first two verses as they are.

BOBBIE: I will.

He starts to play again. MRS DERMOTT *is just going towards the stairs when there comes a ring and knock at the front door.*

JOYCE (*rising*): My goodness, the Crombies – I must go and wash. I'm covered in ink. (*Going to stairs.*)

EVANGELINE (*down L. of table*): I shouldn't worry, dear, they'll be so overdressed themselves they will amply make up for any deficiencies in our appearances.

JOYCE: I think I'd better go all the same. I must do my hair.

BOBBIE: Don't dazzle them too much, dear.

Exit JOYCE *upstairs.* GRIGGS *crosses in corridor to open front door.*

EVANGELINE (*going to corridor*): I'll be in presently, Mother. I've left my note-book in the summer house and I'm afraid of forgetting it.

BOBBIE (*still at piano*): You'll meet them on the doorstep.

EVANGELINE: No, I shan't. I'm going through the drawing-room window.

Exit EVANGELINE, R.

MRS DERMOTT (C.): Really it's most inconsiderate of her to leave me alone like this. Bobbie darling — (BOBBIE *crosses to her, kisses her.*)

23

Re-enter GRIGGS.

GRIGGS: Mrs Crombie, Miss Faith Crombie.

> *Enter* MRS CROMBIE, *and* FAITH. MRS CROMBIE *is a well-preserved, rather flashy woman.* FAITH *is a very pretty girl, perhaps a shade too self-assured. She is all right when by herself, but when compared with the* DERMOTT *girls, there is obviously a little something lacking.*

MRS DERMOTT (*going to her, drops quantity of papers*): I'm so glad you were able to come, dear Mrs Crombie. How are you, Faith dear? (FAITH *giggles, goes down to Chesterfield.*) I do hope you weren't too shaken up in the Ford, but Sylvia has taken the car up to Town to meet my brother.

> BOBBIE *kicks papers up stage, then moves to bottom of table.*

MRS CROMBIE (*up* R.C.): Not at all, we didn't expect to be met at all. It's such a little way. Well, Bobbie, have you been writing any more successes?

BOBBIE (*laughing*): I think I've done one or two bad enough to be good.

FAITH: Oh Mother, isn't he cynical?

MRS DERMOTT (C.): He always talks like that. Fancy, he says his Rose song is bad. Fancy that wonderful Rose song. I'm always humming it. (*Hums few notes of 'The Rosary',* BOBBIE *attempting to stop her.*) Well, I forget it now, but I love it.

FAITH (*down* R.): I love it too.

BOBBIE (*down* L.): Do you really?

FAITH: Of course. (*Moves to piano.*)

MRS DERMOTT: Now then, shall we all go out into the garden? Oliver and Vangy are somewhere about. We always sit under the big cedar in the afternoons. It's so beautifully shady.

MRS CROMBIE (*walking towards door with* MRS DERMOTT): I envy you your garden so much, Mrs Dermott. I have about two rose bushes and a tennis net. Faith insists on that.

MRS DERMOTT: You're lucky even to have a small garden in London.

MRS CROMBIE (*as they go off*): Yes, I suppose we are, you see ...

> *Exeunt to garden.*

FAITH: Come on, Bobbie. (*Coming* C.)

BOBBIE: No, stay here and talk to me. (*Goes to her and takes her hand.*)

FAITH: Mother will only come back and fetch me.

BOBBIE: No, she won't. They're both jawing quite happily. I have been so looking forward to today.

FAITH: So have I.

BOBBIE: I was terrified that you'd wire or something to say you couldn't come.

FAITH: Silly Bobbie.

BOBBIE: Do you realise it's a whole week since I've seen you. (*Dropping her hand.*) I've got something for you.

FAITH (*eagerly*): What is it?

BOBBIE: A song.

FAITH (*without enthusiasm*): Oh.

BOBBIE: Shall I play it?

FAITH (*moves to R. of table*): Yes, do.

> Enter JOYCE *downstairs.*

BOBBIE: Damn.

JOYCE: Hullo, Faith, how are you? (*They kiss.*) Come and play a single with me.

BOBBIE (*at piano*): Oh, do go away, Joyce. I'm just going to play her a song – her song.

FAITH: My song? (*Sits R. of table.*)

BOBBIE: I wrote it specially for her.

JOYCE: Aren't you lucky? Well, come out presently when you feel you're rhapsodised enough. (*Crosses to corridor.*)

BOBBIE: Oh, do shut up, Joy, and go away.

> BOBBIE *starts to play.*

JOYCE: All right, keep calm. (*Exits and re-enters.*) Have you seen my racquet?

BOBBIE: No.

JOYCE: Oh, thanks, dear, for your kind help. Sorry I came in at the wrong moment.

> Exit JOYCE *brightly.*

BOBBIE: Young sisters are a nuisance sometimes.

FAITH (*giggling*): They must be.

BOBBIE: Listen . . . (FAITH *reads magazine and takes no notice of song.*
He plays and sings a short love song.) There! Do you like it.

FAITH (*putting magazine down – ecstatically*): Oh, Bobbie, that's
simply too sweet for words. It has a something about it – did
you really write it for me?

BOBBIE (*ardently*): Every note.

BOBBIE *plays a well-known and hackneyed song.*

FAITH: Bobbie! that's wonderful! Wonderful! It's the best you've
ever done. Now I *know* you are clever.

BOBBIE (*coming* C.): Yes! but I didn't write that one.

FAITH (*goes to him*): Oh! didn't you. Well, I know you would if
you had thought of it – but never mind – Can you play the
Indian Love Lyrics – I never get tired of them?

BOBBIE: I don't want to play any more, I want to talk to you.

FAITH: What shall we talk about?

BOBBIE: I could tell you such wonderful things – but I don't
know whether you would understand.

FAITH (*pouting girlishly*): That's not very polite. (*Coming down
between armchair and Chesterfield.*)

BOBBIE: I mean that you wouldn't understand unless you felt like
I do. Oh, I don't know how to put it – but do you?

FAITH (*coyly*): Do I what? (*Sits* L. *of Chesterfield.*)

BOBBIE (*by armchair – desperately*): Feel as if you could ever care –
even a little bit – for me?

FAITH: I haven't tried yet.

BOBBIE: Well, will you try?

FAITH: I must ask mother.

BOBBIE (*in anguish – moving slightly* C.): Ask mother! But that's no
use. Why, my mother could never make me care for someone
I didn't want to, or not care for someone I did. Don't you see
what I mean. If you are ever going to care for me you will
have to do it on your own. Love isn't a thing to be ordered
about at will. Love is wonderful – glorious, but above all, it's
individual – you can't guide it. Why, you might fall in love
with a taxi-driver or a dope fiend —

FAITH: Mother would never allow me to *know* a dope fiend.

BOBBIE (L. *of Chesterfield – firmly*): But if you *did*, your mother's

26

opinion wouldn't have any effect at all – not if you had it in your heart – really and truly.

FAITH: Mother's disapproval might stop me falling in love.

BOBBIE: No, it mightn't – nothing could stop it. On the contrary it would probably strengthen it; opposition always does.

FAITH (*doubtfully*): Do you think so.

BOBBIE: I'm sure of it, but anyhow, I'm going to tell you something.

MRS DERMOTT *appears at window L.C. with telegram.*

MRS DERMOTT: Bobbie, darling —

BOBBIE (*irritably*): What is it, Mother? (*Goes up to window.*)

FAITH *powders her nose, etc.*

MRS DERMOTT: I've just received the oddest telegram. We met the boy in the drive. Do listen, I can't understand it. (*She reads.*) 'Come to lunch Monday and discuss Royalties – Claverton.' What *does* it all mean?

BOBBIE: It's not for you, it's for Vangy. Claverton's her publisher.

MRS DERMOTT: What on earth do they want to discuss Royalties for. It sounds *so* snobbish.

BOBBIE (*laughing*): Mother, at times you're inimitable. Royalties means money, so much per cent, you know. We've explained it heaps of times.

MRS DERMOTT: Of course, dear, how stupid of me; but still it is very muddling, when they call things by fancy names like that. Put it on the mantelpiece and give it to Vangy when she comes in.

She disappears.

BOBBIE: Mother never will grasp the smallest technicality.

Coming down to fireplace, he puts the telegram on the mantelpiece.

FAITH: You were going to tell me something.

BOBBIE: Yes, I know something that will banish your mother's disapproval altogether. . . .

FAITH: She hasn't disapproved yet. I only said she might.

BOBBIE: Well, she's pretty certain to want you to make a good match. I know what mothers are, they all do. I'm not a good match I know, but what she doesn't know is that I have wonderful prospects.

FAITH (*with interest*): Have you?

BOBBIE: I should never have proposed to you, otherwise.

FAITH: Well, you haven't proposed properly.

BOBBIE: I mean to when I've told you everything. Will you listen? (*Moves to R. of Chesterfield.*)

FAITH: Of course.

BOBBIE: Well, have you ever met my Uncle Daniel? (*Sits by her on Chesterfield.*)

FAITH: No.

BOBBIE: You will today, he's a wonderful chap. Eighteen months ago his doctor told him that he only had three years to live. (FAITH *giggles.*) And the day he came over from South America he gave us all a jolly good talking to – quite right too.

FAITH: Why?

BOBBIE: You see father had left mother badly off, and we were all drooping round doing nothing.

FAITH: Of course!

BOBBIE: Then Uncle Dan turned up and said he'd leave his whole fortune to the one of us who made good in some way or other. Of course that bucked us up no end, and look at us now – Vangy's raking in the dibs with her novel, Sylvia's on a fair way to be a big film star, Oliver has just been made assistant manager at the motor works, which is a good leg-up considering that he started as an ordinary mechanic. I'm doing jolly well out of my songs – specially 'The Rose of Passion Sweet'. Why they buy the beastly thing I don't know. It's the worst of the lot.

FAITH: Oh! Bobbie!

BOBBIE: Even Joyce has walked off with all the prizes at school and intends to be a great artist. You see we've all risen to the bait. Eighteen months ago it seemed providential that uncle should only have such a short time to live, now I rather hate it, in spite of the money. He's a dear, though of course we didn't see much of him. He went back to South America soon after he'd seen us, but still he left an impression. Here we are, all working like slaves, and helping mother to keep on the house. It would have broken her heart to have given it up. There are my prospects – a huge fortune, quite soon.

FAITH: Yes, but, Bobbie, one of the others might get it.

BOBBIE (*after looking round*): Ah, but there is just one more thing to tell you. Two days before he sailed Uncle Dan took me aside and told me – in the very strictest confidence of course – that I was the one out of us all that he had his eye on; he said he'd practically made out his will in my favour already. . . .

FAITH (*ecstatically*): Bobbie!

BOBBIE: Yes, but promise you won't breathe a word to the others; of course you understand he couldn't show favouritism openly.

FAITH: No – I see.

BOBBIE: Now that I have told you everything, Faith darling, will you – will you marry me?

FAITH: Yes, Bobbie —

BOBBIE: Oh! (*He kisses her.*)

FAITH: If mother says I may.

BOBBIE: Oh! (*Mastering slight irritation.*) But don't you think she will, now?

FAITH: Yes, I think so.

BOBBIE (*sadly*): I don't believe you love me a bit.

FAITH (*filled with reproach*): Oh, Bobbie, how *can* you.

BOBBIE: Well, do you?

MRS CROMBIE *sees them through window* L.C.

FAITH: Of course, silly! (*She kisses him.*)

BOBBIE (*joyfully – taking her hands*): Oh, Faith we'll have the most wonderful times in the world – just you and me together; say you're happy, say you're excited about it.

FAITH: I'm absolutely thrilled – I'm — (BOBBIE *sees* MRS CROMBIE. *Picks up papers on floor to hide his confusion.*)

Enter MRS CROMBIE. *They get up.*

MRS CROMBIE (*going L.C.*): You ought to be ashamed of yourselves, sitting indoors on a lovely day like this. (FAITH *giggles.*) Heaven knows we get little enough good air in town, without wasting it when we get into the country.

FAITH: Mother, something important has happened. (*By front of couch.*)

BOBBIE (*sincere*): Look here, Faith, you must let me tell her – it's my job, I won't shirk it.

29

FAITH: Don't be silly, Bobbie, go into the garden, there's a darling – I'll come out in a minute or two.

BOBBIE: But – but —

FAITH: Do be sensible.

BOBBIE: Oh, all right. . . . (*Goes up between Chesterfield and fireplace, and exits into garden.*)

MRS CROMBIE: You are a little fool, Faith. Fancy flirting with that – the elder one has much more in him.

FAITH: But I don't like Oliver so much, his chin's so scrubby.

MRS CROMBIE: Oliver is a steady man with an assured career in front of him – this one —

FAITH: Mother, we're engaged!

MRS CROMBIE: Of course you are. That has been perfectly obvious from the moment I passed the window. Now of course we have all the trouble of getting you disengaged again. Really you are very tiresome. (*Below table.*)

FAITH: Mother, how can you be so horrid, you will *not* understand? Bobbie has ever so much better prospects than Oliver.

MRS CROMBIE: Who said so? Bobbie?

FAITH: Yes, but it's true; his uncle is going to leave him a huge fortune in a year's time.

MRS CROMBIE: Which uncle? (*Takes out cigarette from case.*)

FAITH: He's only got one – Daniel Davis. He landed in England yesterday, and is coming here today. Eighteen months ago the doctor said he only had three years to live —

MRS CROMBIE: I've been caught like that before. (*Crosses to mantelpiece for matches.*)

FAITH: Why, how do you mean?

MRS CROMBIE: Experience has taught me one thing, and that is that in this world people *never* die when they're expected to. (*Sits on Chesterfield.*) The old man will probably live to a ripe old age, then where would you be?

FAITH: Well, anyhow Bobbie makes quite a lot out of his songs. (*Sits in armchair.*)

MRS CROMBIE: Don't be childish, Faith. You know perfectly well I should never allow you to marry a man without a settled income – prospects never kept anyone. Besides, if any of them get the uncle's money it will be Oliver – he's the eldest. (*Lights cigarette.*)

FAITH (*in chair* L.C.): That's where you are wrong, Mother. Just before he sailed back to America, he took Bobbie aside and told him in confidence that he was the one he meant to leave everything to. Of course the others mustn't know because it would be favouritism – don't you see?

MRS CROMBIE: How much is he going to leave?

FAITH: I don't know, but it's sure to be a lot.

MRS CROMBIE: Why?

FAITH: Well, he's a bachelor and – and he's been mining in South America.

MRS CROMBIE: There are hundreds of bachelors in South America who are absolutely penniless – whether they mine or not.

FAITH: You are horrid, Mother. (*Sniffs.*) I did feel so happy, and I wanted you to be happy too.

MRS CROMBIE (*with slight sarcasm*): It was sweet of you, dear. I really can't work myself up to a high pitch of enthusiasm over an uncle who though apparently in the last throes of a virulent disease is well able to gallop backwards and forwards across the Atlantic gaily arranging to leave an extremely problematic fortune to an extremely scatter-brained young man.

FAITH: Bobbie isn't *scatter*-brained.

MRS CROMBIE: The whole family is scatter-brained, and I expect the uncle's the worst of the lot – he wouldn't have been sent to South America otherwise.

FAITH: He wasn't *sent*, he went.

MRS CROMBIE: How do you know? He probably did something disgraceful in his youth and had to leave the country. Just like my brother, your Uncle Percy. I'm certain there's a skeleton of some kind in this family – anyhow he's sure not to die when we want him to.

FAITH: The doctor said three years.

MRS CROMBIE: Only to frighten him, that's what doctors are for. I believe they cured hundreds of cases in the army like that.

FAITH: Did they, Mother?

MRS CROMBIE: What's the matter with the man?

FAITH: I don't know.

MRS CROMBIE: It strikes me, dear, that you had better find out a bit more before you get engaged another time.

FAITH (*tearfully*): But I don't want to be engaged another time. I want to be engaged this time. Oh, Mother darling, won't you wait a little while? Just *see* the uncle. If you got him alone for a while you could find out anything – you're always so clever at that sort of thing. Oh, Mother, do.

MRS CROMBIE: I'll interview the man on one condition. That is that whatever decision I may make you promise to abide by it afterwards.

FAITH (*rises*): Yes, Mother, I promise. (*Kisses her, remains below fireplace.*)

MRS CROMBIE: Now I suppose we had better join the rest, they're being feverishly bright on the tennis lawn.

> *Enter* MRS DERMOTT *followed by* EVANGELINE. MRS DERMOTT *motions to* EVANGELINE *to pick up papers, who does so, placing them on table.*

MRS DERMOTT: Ah, there you are, Mrs Crombie; you were bored with watching tennis too. Of course Oliver and Joyce's efforts cannot really be called tennis, but still it's an amusement for them. (*Sits in armchair.*) Have you seen my knitting anywhere, Vangy darling? I'm certain I left it here.

> FAITH *sits on form* R.

EVANGELINE: You had it in the drawing-room before lunch. I'll go and look.

> *Exit* EVANGELINE R.

MRS DERMOTT: Thank you so much, dear. You know, Mrs Crombie, I imagined that all authors became terribly superior after a little time, but Vangy hasn't a bit – it *is* such a relief to me.

MRS CROMBIE: I haven't read her book yet; I must really order it from Boots.

MRS DERMOTT: Oh, you belong to Boots too, I did for years – there's something so fascinating in having those little ivory marker things with one's name on them; of course, I had to give it up when the crash came.

> *Re-enter* EVANGELINE *with knitting.*

EVANGELINE: Here you are, Mother. (*Crosses to below table.*)

MRS DERMOTT: Thank you so much, darling. Do you know, Mrs Crombie, I started this at the beginning of the war and I haven't finished it yet? I do hope you are not being terribly dull here, Mrs Crombie. (*Drops ball of wool.*) I'm afraid we're awfully bad at entertaining.

MRS CROMBIE: Not at all. You are one of those excellent hostesses who allow their guests to do as they like, it's so much more comfortable.

FAITH (*rising*): I think I'll go and talk to Bobbie in the garden.

> *Goes between Chesterfield and armchair.*

MRS DERMOTT: Do dear, I'm sure he'd love it. (*Kisses her.* FAITH *giggles.*)

> *Exit* FAITH.
>
> *During the following scene* MRS DERMOTT *gets into complications with knitting.* EVANGELINE *settles herself* L. *with illustrated paper.*

MRS DERMOTT: Your daughter is a dear girl, Mrs Crombie – we are all so fond of her.

MRS CROMBIE: It's charming of you – she simply loves being down here. Of course it is so good for her to get away from London for a little while.

MRS DERMOTT: I only wish we could have put you up as well, but really with all the children at home, there's no room at all. I was only saying to Tibbets – my solicitor, you know – that the one thing —

MRS CROMBIE: I understand perfectly. Anyhow, I can never leave my husband for long – men are so selfish, aren't they?

MRS DERMOTT: Sometimes I'm afraid, but still they're rather darlings when you know how to manage them. Vangy, dear, did I tell you how many stitches I set on this sleeve?

EVANGELINE: We have many confidences, Mother, but that is not one of them.

MRS DERMOTT: Dear me, how tiresome. I'm certain I told someone.

> *She gets up and rings bell above fireplace, and sits down again.*

MRS CROMBIE: I was saying, Miss Dermott, that I must make an effort to get your book from the library.

EVANGELINE: Oh, there are one or two copies in the house – I'll lend you one.

MRS CROMBIE: It's very kind of you.

MRS DERMOTT: I'm sure you'll like it, I did, though Vangy tells me I didn't understand half of it. Naturally being my daughter's work it thrilled me, though where she got all her ideas from I can't think – I've always been most careful with the children's upbringing —

Enter GRIGGS, R. *and moves to above Chesterfield. He coughs.*

What is it, Griggs?

GRIGGS: You rang, madam.

MRS DERMOTT: Did I? Now what on earth could it have been? Was it a flustered ring, Griggs, or just an ordinary calm one?

GRIGGS: Quite calm, madam.

MRS DERMOTT (*in anguish*): Oh, Vangy *dear*, what *did* I ring for?

EVANGELINE: You said something about your knitting just before.

MRS DERMOTT: Oh, of course, yes. Griggs, do you know how many stitches I cast on for this sleeve?

GRIGGS: Forty-seven, madam.

MRS DERMOTT: Oh, thank you so much – you're quite sure?

GRIGGS: Quite, madam, but if I might suggest it, next time an even number would be easier to remember.

MRS DERMOTT: Yes, Griggs – remind me, won't you? You're a great help.

GRIGGS: Yes, madam.

MRS DERMOTT: Thank you, Griggs. (*Exit* GRIGGS, R.) Really, I don't know what I should do without that man. I believe he's Scotch, but he's quite invaluable.

MRS CROMBIE: So it seems.

EVANGELINE: Will Sylvia and Uncle Daniel be here in time for dinner, Mother?

MRS DERMOTT: Yes, his train arrived at Euston at eleven-thirty. They ought to be here quite soon now, unless, of course, anything has happened to the car – but still, Sylvia drives very carefully. They taught her to do lots of things like that on the films, you know – they're awfully daring – I shall never forget

when they made her jump off Westminster Bridge on a horse
– my sister Amy was scandalised, and I said —

MRS CROMBIE: I can *quite* imagine it. It was very plucky of your
daughter to do it, though I'm glad Faith isn't on the films – I
should be worried to death.

MRS DERMOTT: Of course I felt like that at first – but one gets
hardened to anything – even my poor brother's approaching
death seems less terrible now – at the time when he told us it
was a fearful shock, but somehow —

MRS CROMBIE: It must be terribly sad for you. Faith told me
about it this morning. What is he suffering from?

MRS DERMOTT: Well, to tell you the truth, we don't quite know,
he will joke about it so – at first he said it was 'Sleeping
Sickness' and then 'Creeping quickness' or pneu-somnia or
something or other – one comfort, he doesn't seem to mind a
bit.

MRS CROMBIE: Perhaps the doctor diagnosed the case all wrong.

MRS DERMOTT: Oh, yes, they are careless – aren't they? Did you
say 'diagnosed', there now, that's the word you were trying to
think of the other day for your short story, Vangy. I knew it
was dia — something.

Enter OLIVER *and* JOYCE *from the garden – followed by* FAITH *and*
BOBBIE.

JOYCE: I won a set. (*Goes to chair L. of table past.*)

OLIVER: Only because I had the sun in my eyes.

OLIVER *puts racquet on piano.*

JOYCE: Well, I offered to change over, but you wouldn't.

MRS DERMOTT: What time will Sylvia and your uncle arrive?

OLIVER (*sitting on top of table*): They ought to be here any
moment now, unless Sylvia's bashed up the bus.

BOBBIE (*above Chesterfield to* MRS CROMBIE, *admiringly*): Isn't he
technical, the way he uses all the right expressions – it gives
one such a professional air to call cars 'buses'.

MRS DERMOTT: It's very muddling.

A motor horn is heard.

JOYCE (*rushing to window*): Here they are.

BOBBIE: I wonder how Uncle Daniel is.

MRS CROMBIE (*rising*): You must all be wondering that. (*Goes to table powdering.*) Faith, I shall go soon. I'm sure this man is going to be simply odious.

> *All except* MRS CROMBIE *and* FAITH *go out to meet* DANIEL. *All enter together talking about their various professions.* BOBBIE *to fireplace;* OLIVER *behind table;* SYLVIA *up stage;* JOYCE *to form;* EVANGELINE *above fireplace;* MRS CROMBIE *below table;* MRS DERMOTT C., DANIEL L.C.; FAITH R. *of table.*

MRS DERMOTT: Oh, Danny, darling – let me introduce you to Mrs Crombie – my brother. And this is Faith – such a dear girl.

MRS CROMBIE: How do you do. I've heard so much about you. Are you feeling better?

DANIEL (*L.C., jovially*): Better! Why, I never had a day's illness in my life (*look from all*) – at least – that is until I had the illness. Yes, it's very tiresome. (*He gulps.*) A short life and a gay one, you know. (*He laughs forcedly.*)

MRS DERMOTT: Danny, darling, I *do* hope ——

DANIEL: Nonsense, dear – there is no hope – but that's a comfort to me. I always imagine hope weary after a game of blind man's buff sitting on an orange – so uncomfortable.

> MRS CROMBIE *and* FAITH *sit below and* R. *of table respectively.*

MRS DERMOTT (*sits Chesterfield, dabbing her eyes*): Really, Danny, you are too absurd. . . . I'm so glad Sylvia brought you safely, I never really feel happy in my mind when she's out with the car. It's not really woman's work.

DANIEL (*sitting armchair*): As far as I can gather from what she has been telling me – filming seems to require a certain amount of unwomanly abandon!

SYLVIA (*at back of Chesterfield laughing*): I was only telling him about that day in the middle of the village street, when I had to do three 'close ups' on top of one another.

MRS DERMOTT: It all sounds vaguely immoral to me, but I hope it's all right.

DANIEL: Define the expression 'close up'. What does it mean?

SYLVIA: When they bring the camera right up to your face and you have to register various emotions – fear – suspicion – joy – yearning – sorrow – (*she does them*) that's a close up.

MRS DERMOTT: Isn't she wonderful?

MRS CROMBIE: It really is most entertaining.

DANIEL: I think they ought to film Evangeline's novel – it's chock full of incident.

EVANGELINE (*rising, poses by mantel*): Yes, Uncle, but only psychological incident – they want luridly exciting episodes for a real thriller. I mean to write a scenario one day though, it's a money-making game. (*Sits again.*)

MRS DERMOTT: Do, dear – but please don't make the heroine jump out of attic windows or anything – it *is* so trying for Sylvia – I shall never forget Westminster Bridge and that horse.

DANIEL: It appears to be a most dashing profession.

MRS DERMOTT (*with pride*): Oh, it is. Sylvia does the most thrilling things, I assure you. She had to rescue the Rajah from a burning house in Piccadilly only last Wednesday. It caused a great sensation.

DANIEL: So I should imagine, but why was the Rajah burning in Piccadilly?

MRS DERMOTT: Oh, it wasn't a real Rajah of course – but he was supposed to be in the clutch of Bolshevists – or was that another film, Sylvia? – I get so muddled —

SYLVIA: It *was* another film, Mother, but it doesn't matter. How's your illness, Uncle Dan? You look pretty bright.

DANIEL: Oh, I expect to be quite cheery right up to the last.

MRS DERMOTT: Oh, Danny dear, don't talk about it.

DANIEL (*with meaning*): I always think we attach too much importance to life and death.

MRS CROMBIE (*acidly*): It depends on circumstances, of course.

DANIEL (*dramatically*): Out there where I come from —

JOYCE: Go on, Uncle, do tell us.

DANIEL: I was just going to, only you interrupted me – out there on the limitless prairie, a man's life is not considered worth that much. (*He tries to snap his fingers without any success.*) There now, I can never do that properly – that much. (*He tries again.*) Damn!

BOBBIE: I can do it, Uncle. (*He does it.*)

JOYCE: So can I. (*She tries.*) Oh, no I can't – Sylvia, you can. You had to when you were playing in *Spanish Passion*.

37

SYLVIA: Never mind now, let Uncle get on with his story.

DANIEL: Out there Death waits round every corner —

BOBBIE: I didn't know there were any corners on the limitless prairie.

DANIEL (*testily*): I was millions of miles away from any prairie – and, anyhow, I was only speaking metaphorically.

SYLVIA: You are irritating, Bobbie, why can't you keep quiet.

MRS CROMBIE: There seems to be some doubt, Mr Davis, as to what part of America you were in.

DANIEL: South America – firmly South America – in the little tiny wee, bijou village of Santa Lyta – far away from the beaten track, this lonely place lies basking in the sun. Heavens, how it basked! it's natives carefree and irresponsible, dreaming idly through the long summer heat —

OLIVER: What did you do there, Uncle?

DANIEL: Eh?

OLIVER: What did you do there, Uncle?

DANIEL (*coming to earth*): Oh, er – lots of things – fishing – yachting.

BOBBIE: But I thought it was inland.

DANIEL: Eh?

BOBBIE: I thought it was inland.

DANIEL: So it is, but there's a lake, there's a lake! We used to sit round the camp fire in the evenings and cook the fish – yes, salmon and cucumber, and sing songs – sweet little homely ditties – your Rose song in particular, Bobbie, was a great success, I must say that —

BOBBIE: Don't perjure yourself, Uncle, I know perfectly well that it's the worst thing that has ever been written.

SYLVIA: It's your most successful.

BOBBIE: Of course – I've made literally hundreds out of it – the public wallow in it – roses and passion, and wine, and eyes of blue – it makes me absolutely sick every time I hear it, but still one must write down in this world if one wants to get up.

MRS DERMOTT: Speaking of roses, let's go out into the garden and talk – it's so stuffy in here – you can tell me some more of your adventures, Danny.

SYLVIA (*looking at him*): I'm sure he'd love to.

38

Everyone gets up and drifts out on to the lawn talking. BOBBIE *hangs behind for a moment with* FAITH.

BOBBIE (*anxiously*): What did she say? (*Catching her hand as she is going out.*)

FAITH: She said she'll see – wait until tonight. . . .

BOBBIE: Oh, Faith darling. . . .

FAITH: Come out now, quick, or they'll miss us.

BOBBIE (*grumbling*): It doesn't matter if they do.

FAITH: Oh, yes, it does – I don't want to be talked about.

They go out and bang into DANIEL, *who is coming in.*

BOBBIE: Hallo, aren't you going to tell us things?

DANIEL (*comes* C.): No, not now – I must unpack – I'm feeling rather tired – I have to change – I must send a wire. . . . The truth of the matter is, I just want a little peace.

BOBBIE: All right, we'll leave you to it.

Exit BOBBIE *and* FAITH. DANIEL *comes slowly down stage – lights a cigar and settles himself in Chesterfield.*

Re-enter SYLVIA, *quickly touches* DANIEL *on face – he jumps.*

SYLVIA: Uncle dear, why did you slip away?

DANIEL: I explained to your brother – because I felt a little tired and wanted a rest.

SYLVIA: You're not too tired to talk to me though, are you? (*Quite quietly.*)

DANIEL (*without conviction*): No. (*Lies full length.*)

SYLVIA: Well, I'll sit down then. (*To side of Chesterfield.*)

DANIEL: Do. (*Sees she wants to sit down. He takes his legs off Chesterfield.*)

SYLVIA: So you really are better? (*Sitting* L. *of Chesterfield.*)

DANIEL: Of course I'm better – I feel splendid.

SYLVIA: And you *still* believe what the doctor said?

DANIEL: I always believe what everyone says, I'm a most trusting person.

SYLVIA: Oh, is that how you made your money – by being trusting?

DANIEL: Certainly. I trusted other people to lose it and they did.

SYLVIA: How d'you mean – lose it?

39

DANIEL: Well, you see – look here, Sylvia, are you cross-examining me?

SYLVIA: Nothing could be further from my thoughts, Uncle dear, I only wondered, that's all.

DANIEL: Well, don't wonder any more – it's most embarrassing – what have you been doing with yourself lately? . . .

SYLVIA: You know perfectly well, Uncle, because you sat next to me in the car and I told you everything.

DANIEL: Well, tell me some more. Have you had any love affairs – girls always like to confide their love affairs.

SYLVIA: Only when they haven't got any – but I don't, anyhow. The only one of the family who has got it in the least badly is Bobbie; he's mad on Faith Crombie.

DANIEL: So I gathered – why, do you suppose?

SYLVIA: We can't think – she's the most irritating girl I've met for years – and her mother's hateful, too.

DANIEL: Why are they here?

SYLVIA: Oh, Bobbie wanted them asked, and mother's much too sweet to deny us anything in reason.

DANIEL: I shouldn't call Mrs Crombie in reason – she's trying to pump me.

SYLVIA: You are rather a mysterious person you know, Uncle, I should like to know lots more about you.

DANIEL: Everything about me is absolutely honourable and above board.

SYLVIA: I don't know that it is.

DANIEL: My dear Sylvia – you wound me, you grieve me – I feel deeply pained. I —

SYLVIA (*laughing*): It's no use trying to bluster out of it, Uncle, you know as well as I do that it wasn't honourable of you to single me out for your money without letting the others know anything about it.

DANIEL (*quickly*): You haven't told them, have you? (*Puts his feet down.*)

SYLVIA: No – I don't break *my* word.

DANIEL: And I don't break mine, so you needn't be so sniffy.

SYLVIA: It is breaking it in a way to show favouritism.

DANIEL: I only told you in the very strictest confidence because I had faith in you – trusted you. . . .

SYLVIA: It was very sweet of you, Uncle, but I don't think you should have.

DANIEL: Well, after all, I . . . it's my money and surely I —

SYLVIA: You see, it's so terribly unfair to the others – of course they don't know, and I shall never breathe a word, but, Uncle, I do wish you'd leave everything to one of them and not me – I shouldn't feel happy for a moment with the money – not for a single moment if I'd known all the time that I was going to get it. Rule me out of the list, there's a dear – I'm earning an awful lot now, you know, on the films and I really don't need any more – promise you'll do what I ask you?

DANIEL: I don't think you're quite in your right mind, but, still – (*smiling*) – I'll see.

SYLVIA: There, I knew you'd see what I meant and be a lamb. Now tell me some of your adventures and things, and how you made the money.

DANIEL (*uncomfortably*): Really, I don't think that . . .

SYLVIA: It must be so glorious out there – mining and prospecting and – by the way how does one prospect?

DANIEL: How does one prospect? When one prospects one scoops up water from rivers and finds nuggets in one's hands – if one's lucky, of course.

SYLVIA: You don't seem to know very much about it, Uncle.

DANIEL (*nettled*): On the contrary I know *all* about it – but you wouldn't understand if I went into technical details.

SYLVIA: I don't believe you would, either.

DANIEL (*rises and goes L.*): I think, Sylvia, that this lack of trust in your fellow-creatures is a very sinister trait in your character – you must remember that I am a much older man than you are and —

SYLVIA: I'm not a man at all.

DANIEL (*turns*): Sometimes I wish you were, then I could tell you what I really think of you.

SYLVIA (*rises and goes to him – laughing*): There, Uncle, I won't tease you any more, but still it must have been a wonderful moment when you discovered you had made a fortune out of your mine.

DANIEL: I didn't.

SYLVIA (*relentlessly*): But I thought —

DANIEL: That is – not exactly – you see it was like this. . . .

    Enter OLIVER *from garden.*

DANIEL (*under his breath*): Thank God! (*Sits chair below table.*)

OLIVER (*above armchair*): Hallo Sylvia. Mother's been looking for you – she wants you to help her pick strawberries for tea. Joyce is with her now, but she isn't much use because she eats them as fast as she picks them.

SYLVIA: I'll go now. Stay and keep Uncle Dan company, Oliver. Get him to tell you some of his South American experiences. They're awfully interesting. Bye-bye, for the present, Uncle.

DANIEL: Cheerio! (*Exit* SYLVIA, R.) I suppose you haven't such a thing as a whisky and soda about you, have you, Oliver?

OLIVER: Of course, I'll get you one.

DANIEL: I'm feeling rather exhausted.

    OLIVER *goes to side table, mixes drink, and gives it to him.*

(*Weakly.*) Thank you very much.

OLIVER (C., *fingering armchair*): I say, Uncle – can you – er – spare me a few minutes?

DANIEL (*apprehensively*): Yes – what is it?

OLIVER (*awkwardly*): Well, it's like this – I know it's rather bad form to talk about your will —

DANIEL: Yes, it is.

OLIVER: But I feel I must. I —

DANIEL (*hurriedly*): Wait until another time, don't you worry yourself about it now. You wait until I'm dead.

OLIVER (*firmly*): No, I must get it over – I want to ask you to leave your money to one of the others and not to me at all. It was awfully decent of you to single me out and it bucked me up a lot to feel that you thought well of me, but now – well, I'm earning steadily and I really don't need a lot, in fact, it might do me harm to feel that I needn't work – also it would seem frightfully caddish to the others for me to have known all along that I was going to get it. Don't you see what I'm driving at?

DANIEL: In a way, I do, yes. . . .

OLIVER: Well, you'll do what I ask, won't you? It's a ripping feeling, being independent (EVANGELINE *passes the window*) and earning money, and I want to go on at it. (*He glances out of the window.*) Here comes Vangy. Now leave it to her. Novel writing is a frightfully precarious show and she's a woman and – anyhow, will you?

DANIEL: I'll see.

    Enter EVANGELINE.

EVANGELINE: Ah, there you are, Uncle Daniel – I've been looking for you – I want to have a little talk with you. (*Above Chesterfield.*)

DANIEL: My God!

EVANGELINE: What did you say?

DANIEL (*feverishly*): I said, My God!

EVANGELINE: Wasn't that a little unnecessary – but still, I expect you get used to swearing over trifles out in the backwoods.

DANIEL: I wasn't anywhere near the backwoods.

EVANGELINE: Well, wherever you were then. Do go away, Oliver, I want to talk to Uncle Daniel privately.

OLIVER: Righto – you'll remember what I said, won't you, Uncle? Cheerio.

    Exit OLIVER, R.

DANIEL: Cheerio. What? Oh, yes, yes. (*After* OLIVER *has gone.*)

EVANGELINE (*goes to him*): Now, look here – about that will of yours – I don't feel that it's quite fair to the others to —

    Enter MRS CROMBIE *from garden.*

MRS CROMBIE: Oh, there you are, Mr Davis – I've been wanting to have a little talk to you about South America. I had a brother out there, you know. (*Behind chair* R.C.)

DANIEL (*rising, jovially*): Splendid – let's talk about him for hours.

EVANGELINE (*a little annoyed*): I'll come back later, Uncle. (*Moves to stairs.*)

MRS CROMBIE: I hope I'm not interrupting a heart-to-heart talk between uncle and niece.

DANIEL: Not at all, not at all – it's a pleasure, I assure you.

EVANGELINE (*on stairs*): It doesn't matter a bit. Uncle Daniel is going to stay with us a long time, I hope.

    Exit upstairs.

MRS CROMBIE (*settling herself in armchair*): Splendid – have you such a thing as a cigarette?

DANIEL: A cigarette, yes, certainly.

MRS CROMBIE: And a match.

DANIEL: And a match.

    He hands her a case, she takes one, goes to mantel for matches – then he strikes a match and lights it.

MRS CROMBIE (*girlishly*): Now we can be quite comfortable, can't we?

DANIEL: Quite. (*Sits on Chesterfield.*)

MRS CROMBIE: As I was saying just now, I had a brother out in South America.

DANIEL: What part?

MRS CROMBIE: I'm not quite sure – we don't hear from him much – he was sent out there for – for —

DANIEL: I quite understand.

MRS CROMBIE: For his health.

DANIEL: I know, they all are. It's a wonderful climate.

MRS CROMBIE: He hasn't written for ages and ages – we were wondering if he was making money or not – it seems so far away, anything may be happening to him.

DANIEL: In all probability everything is — (*laughs to himself.*)

MRS CROMBIE: Did you have any thrilling adventures when you were making your pile?

DANIEL: Oh yes, heaps and heaps.

MRS CROMBIE: I gather that you have a mine of some sort?

DANIEL: Yes – just near the Grand Stand.

MRS CROMBIE: The what?

DANIEL: The Grand Slam.

MRS CROMBIE: Slam!

DANIEL: It's the name of a mountain, you know.

MRS CROMBIE: What a strange name! Why do they call it that?

DANIEL: I can't imagine. It's often been a source of great perplexity to me.

MRS CROMBIE: I take it that yours is a gold mine.

44

DANIEL: Not so that you'd notice it.

MRS CROMBIE: I beg your pardon?

DANIEL: Well, I mean – it's not especially a gold mine – it's a mixed mine – a little bit of everything – there's tin and silver and salt and copper and brass, and God knows what – it's most exciting wondering what we are going to find next.

MRS CROMBIE: Yes, so I should imagine. . . .

DANIEL: Often on weary, dark nights – filled with the cries of the jackal and the boa-constrictor.

MRS CROMBIE: I didn't know boa-constrictors cried.

DANIEL: Only when they are upset about something. Then they can't help it. There are few animals as highly emotional as a boa-constrictor. Anyhow, as I was saying, we lay awake in the throbbing darkness – the darkness out there always throbs – it's a most peculiar phenomenon – and wondered – Heavens, how we wondered what we should find on the following day.

MRS CROMBIE: If you'll forgive my saying so, Mr Davis, I fear that you are a bit of a fraud.

DANIEL: I beg your pardon?

MRS CROMBIE: I said I thought you were a fraud.

DANIEL: Of course I am – all great men are. Look at George Washington.

MRS CROMBIE: He wasn't a fraud.

DANIEL: We only have his word for it. Besides he knew his father had seen him cut down the cherry tree. That's why he confessed. Anyhow, why should you think I am?

MRS CROMBIE: Because you obviously know nothing about mining, and I happen to know that there is no such thing as a mountain in South America called the Grand Slam. I was determined to find out as much as I could about you on account of my daughter.

DANIEL (rises): My dear madam, I assure you that there is nothing whatever between your daughter and me – my intentions are absolutely honourable. (Moves to fireplace.)

MRS CROMBIE (coldly): I was not alluding to you, but to your nephew – your youngest nephew.

DANIEL: Oh, I see.

MRS CROMBIE: He has been making love to her. This afternoon he proposed to her. . . .

DANIEL: Did he, by Jove!

MRS CROMBIE: He also spoke about a large sum of money that you intended to leave him – I'm sure you will understand my position – I naturally want my daughter to marry well – and —

DANIEL: And you mean to make quite sure of the money beforehand. I see.

MRS CROMBIE: You put it rather crudely.

DANIEL: I think matters of this kind are better discussed crudely. One thing I will promise you, Mrs Crombie. You shall know full particulars of my finances and everything else by the end of the day. Until then I fear that you must continue to regard me as a fraud.

MRS CROMBIE: I hope you are not offended at my inquisitiveness, but I really —

DANIEL: My dear Mrs Crombie, when you have knocked about the world as much as I have – one learns never to be either surprised or shocked.

MRS CROMBIE: It is very, very hard for mothers, nowadays.

DANIEL: Yes, isn't it?

MRS CROMBIE: The children are all so modern they become quite ungovernable. . . .

DANIEL (*coming forward slightly*): I can only say then that my nephews and nieces are exceptions to the rule.

MRS CROMBIE: I am so glad you are so satisfied with them.

DANIEL: I am! I never realised until today how absolutely splendid it was to be an uncle. How wonderfully proud I should be of the fact that they are related to me. I came home eighteen months ago expecting to find a family of irritating self-centred young people idling about – true they were idling, but I liked them in spite of it – I have returned this time to find them not only hard-workers, but successful hard-workers. There is not one of them who hasn't achieved something – even Joyce, the flapper, has set to and made good at school. I tell you I'm proud of them, so proud that I could shout it from the housetops, and may I say this, Mrs Crombie, that if your daughter has succeeded in making Bobbie fall in love with her, she is a very fortunate young woman.

> MRS CROMBIE *shows boredom during speech.*

MRS CROMBIE: Oh, is she?

DANIEL: Because he is a fine boy, so is Oliver, so are they all splendid – and she should be proud to know them.

MRS CROMBIE: It really is very lucky that you are so contented with your lot. Personally, I'm not so ecstatic. Admitting for a moment that your nephew has such a marvellously fine character – which I doubt – he should not have made love to my daughter without being certain of his prospects.

DANIEL: I will speak to him, Mrs Crombie.

MRS CROMBIE: I should be very grateful if you would. (*Rises and moves up to him.*) And please understand that nothing – nothing is to be settled without my consent.

DANIEL: I quite understand that.

MRS CROMBIE: Thank you so much – I think I'll rejoin the others in the garden now.

DANIEL: I'm sure they'd be charmed.

> *Exit* MRS CROMBIE *into garden.* DANIEL, *left alone, lights another cigarette.*

(*Feelingly.*) Whew! What a woman! (*Falls on Chesterfield.*)

> EVANGELINE *peeps downstairs.*

EVANGELINE: Has she gone?

DANIEL: Yes, thank Heaven. I say, Vangy, she is a very objectionable woman.

EVANGELINE (*coming down*): I know – we all loathe her. Now at last I can talk to you alone. (*Sits beside him.*)

DANIEL: Look here, Evangeline, I know exactly what you are going to say, and I'll settle it all on Griggs, if you like. He'll take it, he's a Scotsman.

EVANGELINE: How did you know?

DANIEL: Instinct, my dear, pure instinct.

EVANGELINE (*rises*): Let's talk it all over.

DANIEL (*rises and goes L.*): No, not now, I must go up to my room.

EVANGELINE: Oh, just a little talk!

DANIEL: I have some letters to write. Also I'm tired and I feel my illness coming on again. Also I must wash before tea. Also —

EVANGELINE (*laughing*): It's quite obvious that you don't want to, so I'll leave you alone. Cheerio for the present.

DANIEL: They all say that. Cheerio! I'm sure it portends something. . . .

> *He goes off upstairs.*
> *Enter* JOYCE *from garden dragging* FAITH *after her.*

JOYCE: Now you've just got to tell the others that.

FAITH (*flustered*): But I promised Bobbie I wouldn't say a word. . . .

JOYCE: Well, you've broken your word once, so you can do it again. Vangy! Vangy! (*She goes to window, still dragging* FAITH.) Sylvia! Oliver! Bobbie!

EVANGELINE: What on earth is the matter?

JOYCE: Faith will tell you when the others come. (*Dragging* FAITH *back to* C.)

FAITH: Look here, this isn't a bit fair of you. Bobbie will never forgive me. . . .

JOYCE: I can't help Bobbie's troubles – you should have thought of that before.

> *Enter* SYLVIA *and* OLIVER *from garden.*

OLIVER: What's up?

JOYCE: The moment Bobbie comes, you shall know – yell for him, Oliver. . . .

> FAITH *attempts to escape,* SYLVIA *stops her.*

OLIVER (*goes to window and yells*): Bobb-ie! Hurry up, we want you.

BOBBIE (*off*): All right – coming. . . .

> *They wait in silence –* JOYCE *still holds firmly on to* FAITH'S *arm. Enter* BOBBIE *from garden – rather breathless. The positions are as follows: –* EVANGELINE *down* R. SYLVIA R.C. *above Chesterfield.* BOBBIE *a little above* SYLVIA *slightly on her* L. FAITH C. JOYCE *on* FAITH'S L. OLIVER *up* L.

What's the bother?

JOYCE: Now, Faith, tell them.

FAITH: I won't.

JOYCE: Very well, I will – it's most important – listen, all of you –
Bobbie was flirting with Faith this afternoon, and he told her
that uncle had singled him out from us all to leave his money
to. . . .

BOBBIE: Oh, Faith, how could you. (FAITH *crosses to window* L.)

SYLVIA (*judiciously*): Is this true, Bobbie?

BOBBIE (*miserably*): Yes, but I couldn't help it. . . .

SYLVIA: Of course you couldn't. Don't be silly – now *I'll* tell you
something. Uncle said exactly the same thing to me.

EVERYONE: What!

OLIVER: So he did to me, the dirty dog.

JOYCE: Yes, I guessed as much when Faith told me – he
promised his whole fortune to me if I won prizes and things at
school.

EVANGELINE: Well, I needn't tell you that he said the same to
me.

BOBBIE: What's his game?

SYLVIA: Hadn't we better ask him?

OLIVER: Yes, where is he?

EVANGELINE: Upstairs writing letters, washing and being ill.

SYLVIA: Run up and fetch him, Bobbie.

BOBBIE: All right.

> *Exit upstairs two at a time.*

OLIVER: I'd love to know what he's up to.

JOYCE: You will in a minute.

EVANGELINE: I shouldn't be too sure, if he's deceived us once,
he'll probably try to do it again. I don't feel that I can trust him
at all now.

JOYCE: Look here, when he comes down, what are we to say to
him – Oliver'd better do it all, he's the eldest.

OLIVER (*comes down to table*): I'm hanged if I will.

SYLVIA: All right, dear, don't get crusty before the time; I expect
you'll have full opportunities for that later. I'll be spokesman.

EVANGELINE: All right.

> *Re-enter* DANIEL *followed by* BOBBIE, *wiping his hands on a towel.*
> BOBBIE *goes* R.

DANIEL (C.): I feel a little like Lady Macbeth, but Bobbie
wouldn't let me dry properly. What on earth's the matter?

EVERYONE { We want to know.
Look here, Uncle Daniel. . . .
We want an explanation, Uncle Daniel.

DANIEL: You all appear to be perturbed about something.

BOBBIE: We are.

SYLVIA: Shut up, Bobbie, I'm spokesman.

DANIEL (*weakly*): Couldn't it be someone else? Sylvia's so firm with me.

SYLVIA: I think, Uncle, that you occasionally need firmness. (*Coming down* R. *by Chesterfield.*)

DANIEL: We all do, it's a weakness of the human race – lack of stamina – I have it at the moment. Please may I sit down?

OLIVER: Yes.

DANIEL (*sinking into armchair*): Thank you so much. (*Weakly.*) I begin to feel sleepy. May I have perhaps – a small glass of water?

BOBBIE: All right – I'll get it. (*He goes to sideboard.*)

DANIEL: With perhaps the teeniest, weeniest little drop of whisky?

SYLVIA: This is all useless prevarication, you know – we have some very important questions to ask you.

DANIEL (*rising*): Perhaps I'd better stand up then, it's more imposing. (*He takes water from* BOBBIE.) Thank you a thousand times. Cheerio!!

They all make a movement of annoyance.

SYLVIA: Now then, Uncle, we've discovered that you have been deceiving us. . . .

DANIEL (*amazed*): I – deceive you? I'm pained! I'm hurt! You've wounded me to the quick.

BOBBIE: I don't believe you've got a quick.

SYLVIA: Shut up, Bobbie! (FAITH *is by window* L.) Yes, through the agency of Miss Crombie here.

DANIEL: Ah, Miss Crombie, I've just been chatting to your mother. (*Goes to table and puts glass on it.*)

SYLVIA (*ignoring his interruption*): Your dastardly trick has been exposed, is it or is it not true that you took each of us aside in turn a year and a half ago and filled us up with confidential lies about your will?

DANIEL (*bravely*): It's absolutely true.

> *Move from all.*

SYLVIA: Why did you do it?

DANIEL (*laughing with forced roguishness*): Ah. . . .

SYLVIA (*firmly – with emphasis on each word*): Why did you do it?

DANIEL: Do you really want to know?

EVANGELINE (*below form*): Of course we do.

DANIEL: Very well, then I'll tell you. The reason was this. You were a set of idle young bounders. (*A move from all.*) You'd never done a stroke of work in your lives – neither have I, but I didn't see why you shouldn't. There was your poor mother left comparatively hard up – you would have to have left this house which would have made her perfectly miserable, so I determined to spur you on to do something (*breaking into a smile*). I say, you must admit I've succeeded!

SYLVIA: Never mind that – go on.

DANIEL (*still smiling*): Well, not having a penny in the world with which to help you myself —

EVERYONE: What!!!!!

DANIEL: I repeat – not having a penny —

OLIVER (*below table*): Do you mean to say you haven't any money at all?

DANIEL (*cheerfully*): Not a bob! Except on the all too rare occasions when I win a bit. (*Laughing.*) If it were not for the darling little horses, I shouldn't be able to get across to England at all.

EVANGELINE: What about the mine you told us of?

> JOYCE *is* R. *of table.*

DANIEL: I never told you of a mine.

EVANGELINE: Oh, Uncle, you are a fibber!

DANIEL: You said I had a mine. As a matter of fact I am part owner in one. Unfortunately it was long ago proved to be absolutely worthless. But please don't worry yourselves over me. I shall be all right.

SYLVIA (R.C.): We weren't.

DANIEL (C.): I didn't say you were, I said don't. I also told you, now that I come to think of it, that I had only three years to live. That was put in as a bit of local colour. I hope to live to eighty-two or even eighty-three.

BOBBIE (*above Chesterfield*): Well, all I can say is – it's the rottenest trick I ever heard.

JOYCE: Uncle, how could you? (*She sniffs.*)

BOBBIE: How dare you come here and stuff us up with promises that you can never keep. I'm jolly well fed up. I thought you were such a sport and – oh, what's the use of talking. You don't give a damn. Come away, Faith.

FAITH (*tossing her head*): Very well.

> *Exit* BOBBIE *and* FAITH *into garden.*

EVANGELINE (*coming forward, moves between Chesterfield and armchair – contemptuously*): It strikes me as being a singularly pointless practical joke – I'm very disappointed in you, Uncle Daniel.

> *Exit* R.

OLIVER (*coming in front of* JOYCE): So am I – damned disappointed. I thought you were too decent to do a thing like that.

> *Exit* R.

JOYCE: I think you're horrid, it'll get all over the school now. (*She bursts into tears and exits* R.)

> SYLVIA *turns and looks at* UNCLE DANIEL.

DANIEL: They've all had a go at me. Haven't you anything to say too, Sylvia?

SYLVIA: No, I haven't anything to say at all.

DANIEL: Oh! (*Sits in armchair.*)

SYLVIA: You see I knew all the time. (*Goes to above him.*)

DANIEL (*incredulously*): You knew?

SYLVIA: Well, I guessed from the first and found out afterwards.

DANIEL: But how?

SYLVIA: Well, Uncle, darling, I knew that no one with a smile like yours could ever have a bob!

> *Kisses him, goes off laughing.* UNCLE DANIEL *settles himself in armchair, smiling.*

CURTAIN

ACT III

SCENE: *The scene is the same as the preceding acts. Alterations in the furniture are noted at the end of the play. It is seven-thirty on the morning following the events of Act II. When the curtain rises, the sun is streaming in through the open window L.C. BOBBIE can be seen standing just outside looking apparently at an upper window.*

BOBBIE (*calling softly*): Faith! Faith!

FAITH (*heard off*): What is it?

BOBBIE: Come down and talk to me.

FAITH: Don't be silly —

BOBBIE: Please do – I've got lots to tell you.

FAITH: Oh, all right – wait a minute. (BOBBIE *comes mooching into the hall through the window. Enter* FAITH *downstairs.*) Good morning, Mr Dermott. (*Offers hand coldly.*)

BOBBIE (L.C.): I say – you have been quick.

FAITH (C., *coldly*): I've been up for hours – what is it you want?

BOBBIE: I've had a perfectly miserable night – I couldn't sleep a wink. I want to know if you really meant what you said last night.

FAITH: Of course I really meant it, how silly you are.

BOBBIE: I'm not silly – I thought maybe it was only the heat of the moment that made you so utterly beastly.

FAITH: If you're going to be rude I shall go away. (*She sits down in chair by Chesterfield.*)

BOBBIE: Do you really care for me so little that you can give me up at a moment's notice like that?

FAITH: You will not understand, Bobbie – I had to.

BOBBIE: Why?

FAITH: Because mother made me promise.

BOBBIE (*up to her*): What did she make you promise?

FAITH: She made me promise that – that —

53

BOBBIE: Well?

FAITH: Well, you see I'm an only child, and mother wants me to be happy above all things and —

BOBBIE: I could make you happy – wonderfully happy.

FAITH: Mother doesn't think so. You see I've always been used to having money and comforts and things.

BOBBIE: Do you imagine that I shouldn't have been able to give you all the comforts you wanted whether I had uncle's money or not? Why, in a year or so I shall be making hundreds and hundreds. I mean to be successful – nothing will stop me.

FAITH: Well, Bobbie, if you come to me again then, perhaps mother would —

BOBBIE: You mean that I'm to go on working for my happiness on the off chance of your being free to accept me? Neither you nor your mother have enough trust in me to believe that I shall make a big name for myself. Good God, it was a pretty thought of your parents to call you 'Faith'. I suppose if you had a couple of sisters you'd call them Hope and Charity.

FAITH: It's no use being angry and beastly about it. One must use a little common sense.

BOBBIE: It isn't a question of common sense, but common decency.

FAITH: How dare you say that. (*She pulls him round by the leg of his trousers. He brushes her hand away. She repeats this business.*) Why can't we just be friends?

BOBBIE: You know I'm much too fond of you to be just friends. Men can't switch their feelings on and off like bath-taps. If they mean a thing they mean it, and there's an end of it.

FAITH: I wish I'd never come down at all if all you mean to do is grumble at me.

BOBBIE: It's more than grumbling – it's genuine unhappiness. (*Sits on form below table.*) I quite realise now that you never really cared for me a bit, in spite of what you said; but still I want to find out why – *why* you've changed so suddenly, *why* need you have hurt me so much. If you'd written breaking it off, it would have been different, but you've been so – so unnecessarily brutal.

FAITH: It was mother's fault.

BOBBIE: Is everything you do your mother's affair? Does she count every breath you take? Why, your life simply can't be worth living!

FAITH: I wish I could make you see. . . .

BOBBIE (*in a lower register*): I'm afraid you've made me see too much. I didn't know people could be so callous and cruel. . . .

FAITH (*quickly*): I'm not callous and cruel.

BOBBIE: Oh yes, you are, and you've made me determine one thing, and that is that henceforth I honestly mean to cut women out of my life for ever. (*A move from* FAITH.) I know it's a hackneyed thing to say, but I mean it. I ought to have taken a lesson from other fellows' experiences, but of course I didn't.

FAITH: I think you're very silly and childish to be so bitter.

BOBBIE: Bitter! (*Laughs satirically.*) What else could I be? The one girl whom I cared for and trusted has gaily thrown me over the first moment she hears that I am not going to have as much money as she thought. I'm losing my temper now, and I'm glad of it. I shall probably repent every word I say afterwards, but that won't stop me telling you exactly what I think of you. I don't suppose you've ever been in love at all – except to the extent of having signed photographs of Owen Nares and Henry Ainley stuck all over your bedroom, but when you do, I hope you get it really badly, you deserve to be absolutely utterly wretched, as wretched as you've made me, and I hope when you do marry that you get a rotten old Scotch marmalade maker who says 'Hoots!' and spills haggis all down his waistcoat.

FAITH (*bursting into tears*): Oh, Bobbie, how dare you. . . . (*Goes to her and goes down on his knees.*)

BOBBIE: Oh, Faith darling, forgive me, I didn't mean a word of it – I swear I didn't. . . .

FAITH (*they both rise*): Whether you meant it or not I hate you. (*Pushes him away.*) You're blatant and beastly, and I never wish to see you again. (*She walks upstairs and pauses.*) I shall have breakfast in my room. (*Exit.*)

> BOBBIE *stamps out and collides with* SYLVIA, *who is coming in with a bunch of freshly picked flowers.*

BOBBIE: Why can't you look where you're going. (*He stamps out of sight.*)

SYLVIA: Nice sweet-tempered little fellow. (*Moves to above table; puts roses in bowl. Takes 'Daily Mirror' from window-seat, goes down to Chesterfield and reads it.*)

> *Enter* DANIEL *downstairs with bag. He comes very quietly and doesn't see* SYLVIA. *He stumbles and* SYLVIA *watches him.*

SYLVIA (*suddenly*): Excuse me! Have you been stealing anything.

DANIEL (*putting down bag*): Damn! I didn't want anyone to see me.

SYLVIA: Where were you going?

DANIEL (*coming R.C.*): To the *Green Hart*. I couldn't face another meal like dinner last night.

SYLVIA: I know it was pretty awful, but you can't go out of the house like this. Mother'd be furious.

DANIEL: One more wouldn't matter – everybody else is. (*Coming L.C.*)

SYLVIA: I'm not a bit.

DANIEL: I know, I was just going to except you; you've been charming, but really it was terrible. I can't stay. Oliver has such a lowering expression, and if Joyce gives me one more 'dumb animal in pain' look, I shall scream.

SYLVIA: I can't understand why they're all being so silly – I gave them credit for more sense of humour.

DANIEL: And Bobbie – Bobbie was the worst of the lot.

SYLVIA: Well, one can forgive him a little more because of Faith.

DANIEL: Why? What about Faith?

SYLVIA (*rising, going to him*): Oh, the little beast chucked him last night, the moment she heard you weren't going to leave him a fortune.

DANIEL: Did she, by Jove!

SYLVIA (*returning R.C.*): Personally I'm delighted. I always distrusted her, and this proves what I've said all along. But that doesn't make Bobbie any better tempered about it.

DANIEL (*L.C.*): Poor old Bobbie, I bet he hates me.

SYLVIA: If he does he's a fool.

DANIEL: After all you can't blame him, it's only natural.

SYLVIA: He ought to be jolly grateful to you for being the means of showing her up.

DANIEL: Perhaps – but he won't be. I know what it feels like; we all go through it sometime or another. I'd love to wring that girl's neck though.

SYLVIA: You like Bobbie best of all, don't you?

DANIEL: With the exception of you – yes. I think it's because he's the most like me. He is, you know. If he'd lived my life he'd have done exactly the same things.

SYLVIA: I wonder. (*Sits L. of Chesterfield.*)

DANIEL (*smiling*): I know. (*He sits on chair, head of table.*) He's got just the same regard for the truth, the same sublime contempt of the world, and the same amount of bombast and good opinion of himself that I started with, I only hope he'll make better use of his chances, and carve out a better career for himself.

SYLVIA: If he does, he'll owe it all to you – first for rousing him up and making him work, and secondly for getting rid of Faith for him. Had he married her, she'd have been a millstone round his neck. He doesn't realise it now, but yesterday was one of the luckiest days of his life.

DANIEL: D'you really think so?

SYLVIA: I'm sure of it.

DANIEL: That's simply splendid. You've bucked me up tremendously. I shan't mind the *Green Hart* nearly so much now. (*Rising.*)

SYLVIA (*putting him back on seat*): Uncle, you're not to go to the *Green Hart* at all, I won't have it.

DANIEL: I must. When they all sit round looking reproachfully at me, it makes me feel as if I could sink under the table.

SYLVIA (*patting him and kneeling by him*): But they won't – they'll have got over it.

DANIEL: They're all much too young to get over being made fools of as quickly as that.

SYLVIA: But, Uncle —

DANIEL: It's no use – I'm firm. I won't come back until they want me. As a matter of fact I realise I've been very foolish. I shouldn't have let things go so far. Naturally they were terribly disappointed at my wanting to live till eighty-two or eighty-three, and not having any money to leave them.

SYLVIA: They're not really disappointed so much as outraged. They feel you've been laughing up your sleeve at them, as of course you have.

DANIEL: No, I haven't – you're wrong there – I haven't. I couldn't help you financially. I'd borrowed the money to come over and the cheque I'd sent before, I'd just won, so I thought that the only way to assist at all was to use mental persuasion on all of you. There's always something fascinating in the idea of having money left one. It seems such an easy way of getting it. Of course it answered better than I could have imagined in my wildest dreams.

SYLVIA: It was a little unnecessary to take each of us aside like you did and stuff us up with hope.

DANIEL: That and a bunch of keys was all I had. It was such a wonderful situation. I – never having had a penny in the wide world (*gaily*), arranging to leave you my entire fortune. (*He starts to laugh.*) You must confess it was very, very funny.

SYLVIA (*also laughing*): Yes, it was. . . . (*They both laugh heartily.*)

DANIEL (*still laughing*): And when I said I had sleeping sickness! . . .

SYLVIA (*weak with laughter*): Oh, Uncle, how *could* you.

DANIEL (*wiping his eyes*): Oh dear, oh dear!

SYLVIA: Poor mother getting more mystified every minute, and bothered poor Tibbets till he doesn't know if he is on his head or his heels.

DANIEL (*rising suddenly*): But look here, they'll all be down in a minute. (SYLVIA *stands up.*) They mustn't find me here, poised for flight. I must go at once. (*Going behind Chesterfield and picking up bag.*)

SYLVIA (L. *of him*): Yes, but will you promise on your word of honour to come back the moment I send for you?

DANIEL: If you give me *your* word of honour not to send for me until everything's quite all right and everyone is perfectly amiable towards me. I couldn't bear any more rebuffs. I should burst into tears if anybody even gave me a look!

SYLVIA: Yes, I'll promise.

DANIEL: I trust you because, after all, you spotted from the first.

SYLVIA: That wasn't very difficult. I've always had a good eye for hypocrites. (DANIEL *slaps her.*) Mind you don't go any further afield than the *Green Hart*!

DANIEL: You bet I shan't!

Exit DANIEL *through window.*

SYLVIA (*looking out of window after him*): Bye-bye! (*Coming down stage.*) Bless his heart!

Enter GRIGGS *from R. with breakfast dishes which he places on sideboard.*

GRIGGS: Will you do the coffee as usual, miss?

SYLVIA: Yes, Griggs. By the way, get me a bigger bowl for those roses when you have time.

GRIGGS: Yes, miss.

He bangs loudly on a big gong, and exits R. Enter MRS DERMOTT *downstairs.*

SYLVIA: Hello, Mother. (*Kiss across L. banisters.*)

MRS DERMOTT: Good morning, darling. Are there any letters?

SYLVIA: Only one for you, I think.

MRS DERMOTT (*taking letter from table*): From Tibbets, I expect. (*Sniffs at it.*) No! From Isobel Harris. (*Sits at the head of the table.*) I do hope she doesn't want to come and stay – I couldn't bear that. (*Opens it.*) Oh no, it's only to say that Fanny's engaged to an officer in the Coldstream Guards. How splendid of her.

SYLVIA: Poor Fanny – I'm glad. (*Sits in chair on her mother's left.*)

MRS DERMOTT: Why do you say poor Fanny, dear? I'm sure she's very fortunate. Nowadays when nice men are so scarce. I was only saying —

SYLVIA: She didn't say he was a nice man – only that he was in the Coldstream Guards. I said poor because I can just imagine all her awful relations as bridesmaids, and her father and mother shoving her up the altar steps in their efforts to get her safely married.

MRS DERMOTT: Isobel means well, although she's a little trying. But I've never liked Charlie – no man with such a long, droopy moustache could ever be really trusted. Besides, they're so insanitary. Sound the gong again, dear. I do wish they'd all learn to be a little more punctual.

SYLVIA does so, and returns to sideboard. Enter JOYCE downstairs followed by OLIVER; they are both obviously suffering from temper. They both kiss mother.

JOYCE (*disagreeably, as she comes downstairs*): All right! All right! – we're coming. What's the fuss? (*Sits on form.*)

OLIVER crosses to Chesterfield, picks up SYLVIA's paper and reads, pacing up and down.

MRS DERMOTT: There's no fuss, darling, but it's stupid to let the breakfast get cold. I've got mushrooms this morning, specially because Uncle Daniel likes them.

Enter BOBBIE from garden profoundly gloomy. Kisses mother.

BOBBIE: You could hear that beastly gong a mile off.

SYLVIA crosses to table with coffee and milk.

MRS DERMOTT: I'm so glad, dear. It shows it's a good gong. Ring the bell, will you, Oliver? (*OLIVER does so.*) Where's Evangeline? She's generally quite an early bird.

Enter EVANGELINE downstairs. She is distinctly depressed.

EVANGELINE (*on the stairs*): Here I am, Mother. (*Kisses MRS DERMOTT. With sarcasm.*) What a pity it is that the bath water isn't a *little* hotter. I hate tepidity in anything. (*Sits on SYLVIA's left.*)

BOBBIE serves bacon, sitting at the foot of the table, facing MRS DERMOTT.

OLIVER: If Joyce didn't bounce in and take it all it *would* be hotter.

JOYCE: I didn't have a bath at all this morning, so there.

OLIVER: Well, you're a dirty little pig then.

MRS DERMOTT: There's probably something wrong with the boiler. I'll see about it after breakfast. (*Enter GRIGGS, comes below MRS DERMOTT.*) Oh, Griggs, just tap on Miss Crombie's door, will you, and tell her that breakfast is ready.

GRIGGS: Miss Crombie wished me to say that she is taking breakfast in her bedroom, madam. I'm sending up a tray.

MRS DERMOTT: Quite right, Griggs. I wonder if she's feeling ill or anything. I'll go up presently. Oh, and will you find out if Mr Davis is coming down soon?

GRIGGS: Mr Davis is not in his room, madam.

MRS DERMOTT: Not? How very strange – he's probably in the garden somewhere. That'll do, Griggs. (*Exit* GRIGGS, R.) Perhaps you'd better sound the gong again, Bobbie, he might not have heard it. (BOBBIE *crossing in front of table goes to the gong and bangs savagely on it. Everyone stops up their ears.*) You seem to have taken a dislike to that gong, darling. We must start without him, that's all. Do sit down, Oliver, you're much too big to pace backwards and forwards like that. Pour out the coffee, Sylvia, dear, if it's ready.

> OLIVER *sits on* EVANGELINE'S *left.* BOBBIE *sits again at the foot of the table.* JOYCE *drops her fork with a loud clatter – everyone jumps.* SYLVIA *pours out coffee.*

EVANGELINE: If you'd endeavour to cultivate a little more repose, Joyce, dear, it would be an advantage.

JOYCE (*truculently*): I couldn't help it.

MRS DERMOTT (*brightly*): Fancy – Fanny Harris is engaged.

BOBBIE (*gloomily*): What fun.

MRS DERMOTT: It may not be fun to you, but it will be most amusing to Mrs Harris. I do wish Daniel would come in. Where can he be?

BOBBIE: No one cares, anyhow.

MRS DERMOTT: How can you be so horrid, Bobbie – I did think you'd have recovered from your silly temper before this. Fancy not being able to take a joke.

OLIVER: It wasn't a joke, it was true.

MRS DERMOTT: You really are utterly absurd. Pass me the toast. I wouldn't have believed you could all have been so silly. I expect Uncle Daniel is just laughing at you.

OLIVER: Yes, that's just what he *is* doing.

MRS DERMOTT: I really think, Oliver, that you, as the eldest, ought to set a little better example. And the marmalade – thank you. After all, considering how good he's been to us, we might allow him to have a little joke without becoming disagreeable – even if it doesn't amuse us very much. Why, I —

JOYCE: But, Mother, I tell you it isn't a joke – it's the gospel truth.

MRS DERMOTT: I've never known such a set of maddening children. Pass me the paper, will you, Sylvia? I wish to read it.

> SYLVIA *hands her newspaper from window-seat and she opens it out and reads it, ignoring the family altogether. 'Telegraph' – with extra pages inserted.*

OLIVER (*breaking the silence*): Has anyone seen my tennis racquet?

JOYCE: Bobbie had it yesterday.

BOBBIE: No, I didn't.

JOYCE: Yes, you did, you and Faith – I saw you.

OLIVER: Well, where is it now.

SYLVIA (*ruminatively*): I did see a racquet behind the summer house this morning. Would that be it?

OLIVER (*furiously*): Look here, Bobbie, if you go leaving my racquet out all night again I'll punch your head. . . .

BOBBIE (*rising, flaring up*): I tell you I never touched your damned racquet – I've got one of my own. (*Knocks his chair over.*)

JOYCE: A jolly rotten one, though.

BOBBIE: Shut up, Joyce, and mind your own business.

EVANGELINE: Don't speak to Joyce like that, Bobbie. You ought to be ashamed of yourself.

BOBBIE: I'll speak how I like.

OLIVER (*rising*): Not while I'm here, you won't.

BOBBIE (*jeeringly*): Come on, oh strong and silent elder brother, let's be manly and knock one another about.

OLIVER: A little more of that would do you a lot of good.

BOBBIE: Well, you'd better not try it. (OLIVER *knocks a plate on to the floor, breaking it.*) There, that's what happens when you let elephants loose in the house. (*Picks up his chair.*)

> *During this,* MRS DERMOTT *does comic business with newspaper, repeatedly dropping sheets and attempting to fold the paper.*

MRS DERMOTT: Oliver, if you and Bobbie can't stop quarrelling you'd better both leave the table. I can't think what's the matter with you all. Just because Uncle Daniel chose to have a little fun with you, you all behave like bears with sore heads.

> BOBBIE *and* OLIVER *re-sit and continue eating.*

EVANGELINE: Uncle Daniel meant every word he said, Mother. He hasn't got a penny in the world.

MRS DERMOTT: Nonsense, Evangeline. How do you suppose he could get backwards and forwards to America and send me large cheques and things?

JOYCE: He wins a little from time to time by horse-racing.

MRS DERMOTT: Rubbish. No one can ever win at horse-racing. I never did. The bookies and jockeys and people don't let you.

EVANGELINE: Mother dear, how *can* you be so obstinate. I tell you he told us all about it in here yesterday afternoon – gave us his solemn word —

MRS DERMOTT: But only in fun, darling, only in fun – he's obviously a very rich man.

OLIVER: Hah!

MRS DERMOTT: By the by, I wish one of you would just go into the garden and find him. The mushrooms will be ruined.

SYLVIA: He isn't in the garden at all, Mother, he's gone to the *Green Hart*.

All look surprised.

MRS DERMOTT: What do you mean, Sylvia? Why has he gone to the *Green Hart*?

SYLVIA: Because everyone here had been so beastly to him.

They all continue breakfast hurriedly.

MRS DERMOTT: You mean that he —? Oh, Sylvia! (*She burst into tears.*)

SYLVIA: Mother darling, don't cry. . . . (*Rises and kisses her.*)

MRS DERMOTT (*weeping bitterly*): Darling Danny. My only brother. And you've driven him away – after all his kindness and everything. Oh, how could you? How could you? He must be sent for at once. (*She rises and rings the bell, dropping bits of newspaper en route.*) You're wicked, wicked children, and you don't deserve anyone to be kind to you ever again. (*Enter* GRIGGS, R.) Oh, Griggs, send the car down to the *Green Hart* at once to fetch Mr Davis.

GRIGGS: Yes, madam.

Exit GRIGGS, R.

MRS DERMOTT (C.): How dare you behave like you have done. I shall never, never forgive you – you're cruel and horrid and —

OLIVER: It's all very fine, Mother, but he made fools of us.

MRS DERMOTT: He didn't do anything of the sort – he only meant it kindly – going to all that trouble, too (*she weeps again*), with one foot in the grave.

BOBBIE: And the other in the *Green Hart*.

JOYCE: He's not going to die. He said he meant to live to eighty-two.

MRS DERMOTT: Eighty-three, I think, was the age, dear, but that's just another instance of his dear unselfishness – so that you wouldn't worry over him. I knew! I'm going up to my room – you've upset me for the rest of the day. Call me the very moment he comes. Oh, how could you? How could you be so unkind? Oh, just look at my nose, it's all red and shiny.

> *Exit upstairs.* SYLVIA *follows, standing at the foot of the stairs, looking after her. There is silence for a moment.*

BOBBIE: That's torn it.

JOYCE: Now what are we to do?

SYLVIA (*moving down*): I know. (*At head of table.*)

OLIVER: What, then?

SYLVIA: Apologise to Uncle Dan, every one of you, for being such utter beasts.

OLIVER: Well, I'm hanged!

> *During the following speech, the others continue their breakfasts.*

SYLVIA: So you jolly well ought to be. Who do you owe your position in the motor works to, Oliver? Uncle Dan. Who do you owe your song successes to, Bobbie? Uncle Dan. And you, Joyce, d'you think you'd have won a single thing if it hadn't been for him? Do you imagine Evangeline would have had the vim to have stuck to her novel if it hadn't been for Uncle Dan's faith in her? I know I should never have done a thing, either. And all we did it for apparently, was that he could die off conveniently and leave us his money – the moment he'd done that I suppose we should have stopped working. What charming characters! Waiting for a man to die, and then getting disagreeable because he says he doesn't want to. Do you think any one of you would stop work now for anything? Of course you wouldn't. I know *that*. Don't you see that Uncle Dan chose the one and only way of really helping us? He's worked wonders and we ought to be thankful to him until our dying day. . . .

BOBBIE (*marmalade on toast in hand*): It's all very fine for you – he hasn't come between you and the only person you've ever loved. . . .

SYLVIA: And that's one of the best things of all – he's been the means of showing Faith up in her true colours. Bobbie, you must realise now in your heart of hearts what a rotter she is?

BOBBIE: She wouldn't have been if it wasn't for her beastly mother. Just because you found him out before us, by a fluke, you think you can preach to us about being rude to him. Well, you'd have been just as bad under the same circumstances, if not worse. The fact of you having spotted his game doesn't make it any the less disgusting. He's behaved atrociously and you know it, making fools of us all. What do you think my friends will say? Joyce's school girls? Vangy's literary nuts?

SYLVIA (*coming down R. to below Chesterfield*): It's your own silly faults. You shouldn't have told them.

EVANGELINE (*rising*): Don't be so superior. Of course we only did in confidence. (*Going up R., followed by* JOYCE.)

SYLVIA: Well, that's not Uncle Dan's fault, he only did it for the best. . . .

BOBBIE: Best be damned!

SYLVIA: If you can't curb your language I should think you'd better go outside.

BOBBIE (*rising, knife in hand*): I shall do exactly as I like. I'm fed up with you, Sylvia, you're as bad as he is. (*Throws knife on table.*) And if you think you can get round us by making excuses for him you're jolly well mistaken. I suppose all this is a put-up job! (*Moves to L.C.*)

SYLVIA (R.C.): How dare you, Bobbie! It's nothing of the sort. Only luckily I have a little discrimination, I can see the difference between good and bad, and Uncle Dan's good, good all through. He wouldn't do harm to anyone or anything in the world. He did all this out of genuine kindness. He couldn't help us in any other way, so he made us work, hoping it would improve us. And I should think he'd go back to America sick and wretched inside with disappointment having discovered that we, his only relatives, have only liked him and been nice to him because of his money – waiting for him to die like beastly treacherous ghouls. (EVANGELINE *attempts to speak.*) That's what you are, ghouls! (*Turning on* EVANGELINE.) And selfish pigs, and if you don't apologise to him I shall never speak to any of you again.

OLIVER: Hah! (*Throws down serviette and exits* R.)

SYLVIA: Oh, you're very dignified walking out like that without saying anything. I hate you! I hate you all! Poor Uncle Daniel – it's rotten. (*She bursts out crying, and subsides on Chesterfield.*)

> *Towards the end of her speech, the rest have risen and walked out with their heads in the air,* R. BOBBIE *kicks violently at paper on floor and goes upstairs. There is a moment's pause, then enter* DANIEL *from garden.*

DANIEL (*coming* C.): I left the car down the drive, hoping to make a sweet lovable entrance with perhaps a few rose leaves on my coat. Where is everybody?

SYLVIA (*sniffing on Chesterfield*): It's no use, they're still being beastly. Mother sent for you. She's frightfully upset at your going to the *Green Hart*.

DANIEL: If they're keeping it up, I think I'd better go back. (*Moving towards entrance.*)

SYLVIA (*rising*): No, you're not to do anything of the sort, you're to stay here. (*Firmly.*) They can be as disagreeable as they like, we'll go about together; you can come to the studio with me tomorrow morning.

DANIEL (*up to her*): You, Sylvia, are what is described as a sympathetic character. You've been very nice to me all along. Can I leave you anything?

SYLVIA: Don't joke about it, Uncle, it's all so horrid.

DANIEL: If I don't joke I shall burst into storms of passionate sobbing. (*Moves down* C.)

SYLVIA: That would be rather awful. Here comes mother....

> *Enter* MRS DERMOTT *downstairs.*

MRS DERMOTT: Danny darling, why were you so silly as to take any notice of the children? They're unkind and heartless, and I ordered the mushrooms specially for you this morning. Sit down and have them now. They'll be quite hot still. (*She pushes him into chair.*) Sylvia, get them, if you please. I can't think why they're all behaving like this, I shall never forgive them, Danny dear. You won't let them upset you, will you?

She kisses him. MRS DERMOTT *sits in* SYLVIA'S *chair,* DANIEL *in* MRS DERMOTT'S.

DANIEL: Well, they seem to have upset everything else.

Enter GRIGGS, R.

MRS DERMOTT: Bring some more toast and coffee, Griggs. Or would you rather have tea?

DANIEL: Tea, please.

MRS DERMOTT: Tea then, Griggs.

GRIGGS: Very good, madam. (*Picks up remains of paper above Chesterfield and exit R.*)

SYLVIA (*handing him plate of mushrooms and bacon*): Here you are, Uncle dear – I'm going upstairs. Call me if you want anything.

Exit SYLVIA *upstairs.*

DANIEL: I will.

MRS DERMOTT: I'm sure he won't.

DANIEL: Now look here, Anne, you're not to include Sylvia in your fury against the family. She has been perfectly sweet.

MRS DERMOTT: So she ought to be – and the others as well. Such nonsense, I never heard of such a thing. Not being able to take a joke better than that. I don't know what's happened to them, they were such dear good-natured children. They used to make booby traps and apple-pie beds for one another and not mind a bit.

MRS DERMOTT *keeps buttering toast for him, arranging it round his plate.*

DANIEL: But you see, Anne, this perhaps has irritated them more than an apple-pie bed.

MRS DERMOTT: I don't see why, it's just as harmless, and much less trouble.

DANIEL: If I had known they were going to take it so badly I should have thought of something else. I have lots of ideas.

But even now, when I come to look back over everything, I don't see what else I could have done.

MRS DERMOTT: You're just the kindest old darling in the world and everything, every single thing you have done for us, has been perfect.

DANIEL: Dear Anne, don't be absurd. It was nothing, worse than nothing, but I'd given it a lot of thought, and after all it has bucked them up and made them work. They're looking much better in health, too.

MRS DERMOTT: Oh, Danny, I only wish you were better in health. The shadow of your illness just hangs over me like a nightmare. I can't pass a flower shop without thinking of you.

DANIEL (*puts down knife and fork*): But I'm not ill at all. I've no intention of dying until I'm eighty-three or even eighty-four.

MRS DERMOTT: Dear old boy, you're only saying that so that I shan't worry. (*She dabs her eyes.*) But it's no use, you can't deceive me, you know.

DANIEL: But, Anne, I swear —

MRS DERMOTT: There, there, we'll say no more about it. It only upsets me and here's your tea. (*She takes tea from* GRIGGS, *who has entered with tea and toast. He goes off again.*) Have you seen your doctor, lately?

DANIEL (*resignedly*): Yes, I saw him the other day.

MRS DERMOTT (*pouring out tea*): And what did he say?

DANIEL (*confused*): Well – er – I don't know – he sounded me.

MRS DERMOTT: Yes, they always do that. I wonder why. Your illness has nothing to do with your heart, has it?

DANIEL (*firmly*): My dear Anne, I haven't got an illness.

MRS DERMOTT: I'm sure I hope not, dear, but if he said that, I should really get another more expert opinion if I were you. A man like that can't be really reliable. I don't believe in doctors ever since poor Millicent Jenkins died.

DANIEL: Look here, Anne, I really do want to make you understand that what I told the children is perfectly true. I haven't any money.

MRS DERMOTT: Nonsense, dear, you can't pull my leg as easily as that. How were you able to send that cheque when I most needed it, and those lovely Christmas presents, and the fares backwards and forwards to America – I believe you've got some big surprise for us all later on and you're afraid that we'll guess it.

DANIEL: Yes, I have.

MRS DERMOTT (*rising*): Now look here, dear, I must leave you for a little while. Saturday is the busiest morning in the whole week. Finish off your breakfast and smoke a pipe – or a cigar or something; if any of the children come near you, just ignore them or pretend to be frightfully angry with them. That will bring them round.

Enter GRIGGS *hurriedly,* R.

GRIGGS: If you please, madam, the boiler is making the most peculiar noises. Shall I send for Brown to come and look at it?

MRS DERMOTT: I don't think that will do it any good, but still perhaps you'd better. I'll come myself in a minute. (*Exit* GRIGGS, R. MRS DERMOTT C.) Really, everything is going wrong this morning, first you, Danny, then the boiler; sometimes life isn't worth living – I do hope it won't burst.

Exit MRS DERMOTT, R. DANIEL *sits thoughtful for a moment and then resumes his breakfast. Enter* JOYCE *from garden. She sees* UNCLE DANIEL *and comes rather sheepishly up to him.*

JOYCE: Uncle, I —

DANIEL (*gruffly*): Good morning.

JOYCE (*feebly*): Good morning. (*There is a long pause.*) Uncle Daniel – we've – er – we've all been talking —

DANIEL: That's quite a natural and healthy occupation.

JOYCE: We – we were talking about you.

DANIEL: That makes it none the less natural or healthy.

JOYCE: Of course it didn't. You see – I mean to say – we – well, they sent me in to tell you that —

DANIEL: Perhaps you'd better tell me another time when you are more in the mood. Have you seen the papers anywhere?

JOYCE: They ought to be over there. (*She points to window seat* R., *and goes down to* BOBBIE'S *chair.*)

DANIEL (*rising and moving quickly to* R.): Thanks. Don't you bother

– I can get my own paper. (*Gets newspaper and returns to his seat at the head of the table.*)

> *There is a long silence,* DANIEL *reads the paper.* JOYCE *shakes her head as* OLIVER *strolls in from the garden and looks at* JOYCE *for news.*

OLIVER: Have you had your breakfast, Uncle?

DANIEL: Yes, thank you, and I slept beautifully.

OLIVER: It's a jolly nice morning.

DANIEL: That remark makes up in truth for what it lacks in originality.

OLIVER: Oh. (*Moves to window, L.C., turns, catches* DANIEL'S *eye and turns quickly back.*)

> JOYCE *continues to fidget at the foot of the table. Enter* BOBBIE *downstairs and* EVANGELINE R. *They look meaningly at* JOYCE, *who shakes her head vigorously.*

DANIEL: Have you a headache, Joyce, you keep wagging it about.

JOYCE (*very politely*): No, thank you, Uncle, I —

DANIEL: Splendid, then I shan't have to offer you an aspirin.

EVANGELINE and BOBBIE (*together, coming forward hand-in-hand down* R.C.): Uncle, we've all been — (*They stop.*)

DANIEL: Yes? (*There is business of each of them wishing the other to speak to* DANIEL.) Tell me one thing, if any of you are capable of uttering a word, is this a game? Have I got to guess whether something's a vegetable or a mineral or something?

EVANGELINE: No, Uncle, it's a much harder game than that – for us, anyhow. We've come to apologise.

DANIEL (*lowering the paper*): Oh, have you? (*Turns to them.*)

EVANGELINE: Oh, won't you please be nice and make it easier for us?

DANIEL: You none of you made things in the least easy for me.

EVANGELINE: I know we didn't, but we're all sorry – frightfully sorry – we've talked it all over. Sylvia said we were beasts and ghouls and we wouldn't admit it then, but we do now. We are terribly ashamed of the way we've behaved. Please, please say you forgive us. (*Kneels to him.*)

BOBBIE (*placing chair behind Chesterfield*): And it doesn't matter about Faith, Uncle, I'm glad you were the means of showing her up. I don't love her a bit now. I hate her, and we all want you to understand that we'd rather have you alive and with us than all the beastly money in the world.

JOYCE (*leaning forward over table*): And we'll do anything you like to atone for it. We'll abase ourselves like they used to in the olden days to show they repented.

OLIVER: Will you let it go at that, Uncle? (*He comes forward to L. of* DANIEL.)

DANIEL (*softly*): I should just think I will. (*Kisses* EVANGELINE.)

JOYCE *comes round and kisses him.* OLIVER *moves down* L. EVANGELINE *moves behind table.*

JOYCE (*running to R.*): Sylvia! Sylvia! Mother, come here! It's all right!

Enter MRS DERMOTT *from* R.

MRS DERMOTT: I've just come out of the boiler. What on earth is all this noise?

JOYCE: We've all made it up with Uncle Daniel and he's forgiven us.

MRS DERMOTT: I'm sure I'm very glad, darlings, and I hope you're none of you too old to take a lesson from it. (*Comes to* DANIEL'S R.)

Enter SYLVIA *downstairs.*

SYLVIA: Is everything forgiven and forgotten?

DANIEL: Everything. (*Rising.*)

Enter GRIGGS, R., *with cablegram.*

GRIGGS (*handing it to* UNCLE DANIEL): For you, sir.

DANIEL: Excuse me. (*Takes it, opens it in silence and reads it.*) My God!

MRS DERMOTT: What is it, dear, what is it?

DANIEL: It's not true! After all these years, I can't believe it!

SYLVIA: What is it, Uncle, tell us, tell us, quick.

DANIEL: It's from my agent. Listen! (*Reads.*) 'Struck big vein, Santa Lyta mine – come at once!' I'm worth thousands, thousands. (*Going down R. gives* MRS DERMOTT *telegram as he passes her. The others, except* SYLVIA, *crowd round her C., excited at the news.*)

71

MRS DERMOTT: There now.... I told you so.

SYLVIA (*coming L. of him*): Uncle! Did you send that telegram to yourself?

DANIEL: Yes!!!

CURTAIN

THE YOUNG IDEA

The *Young Idea* received its first London production on 1st February 1923 at the Savoy Theatre, with the following cast:

GEORGE BRENT	MR HERBERT MARSHALL
GERDA ⎫ *his children*	⎰ MISS ANN TREVOR
SHOLTO ⎭	⎱ MR NOËL COWARD
JENNIFER, *his first wife, divorced*	MISS KATE CUTLER
CICELY, *his second wife*	MISS MURIEL POPE
PRISCILLA HARTLEBERRY	MISS PHYLLIS BLACK
CLAUD ECCLES	MR RONALD WARD
JULIA CRAGWORTHY	MISS NAOMI JACOB
EUSTACE DABBIT	MR CLIVE CURRIE
SIBYL BLAITH	MISS MOLLIE MAITLAND
RODNEY MASTERS	MR LESLIE J. BANKS
HUDDLE, *butler*	MR WALTER THOMPSON
HIRAM J. WALKIN	MR AMBROSE MANNING
MARIA, *servant at the Villa*	MISS IRENE RATHBONE

ACT I
Hall of George Brent's house in England.

ACT II
The same. A week later.

ACT III
Jennifer Brent's Villa in Italy. Three weeks later.

ACT I

SCENE: *The scene is the hall of* GEORGE BRENT'S *house in the hunting country. It is well furnished and comfortable. There is a door on the right leading to the drawing-room, a staircase at the back with a turn in it; a little to the left of this there is an opening into a smaller hall and the front door. Farther down left is a curtained window, and on the extreme left a door leading to dining-room.*

When the curtain rises, the stage is empty.

HUDDLE *enters through the hall door, and stands aside to admit* RODDY MASTERS.

HUDDLE: Will you come into the drawing-room, sir?

RODDY: No; I'll wait here. (*Crosses to table R.*)

HUDDLE: Very good, sir. (*He turns.*)

RODDY (*carelessly*): Mrs Brent is in? (R.C.)

HUDDLE: Yes, sir. I will tell her you're here.

Exit HUDDLE. RODDY *crosses down to window and looks out. Enter* CICELY.

CICELY: Hallo, Roddy! (*Crosses to C.*)

RODDY (R.C., *turning quickly; in eager tones*): Cicely!

CICELY: Well?

RODDY: Haven't you forgiven me – for last night?

CICELY: Oh, don't be silly.

RODDY: You were awfully cross.

CICELY: Well, it was the sort of 'obviousness' that I particularly dislike.

RODDY (*aggrieved*): I don't see why. We were all playing the beastly game – the whole house-party. Claud Eccles hid with Priscilla heaps of times.

CICELY (R.C.): That's not the point – anyhow, she's a silly little fool to let him. (*Moves to L.*)

75

RODDY (*crosses* L.C.; *sullenly*): I'm sure you exaggerate – no one really notices that sort of thing.

CICELY (*by fender, suddenly going close to him*): Roddy – I'm a little frightened – uncomfortable. I don't know why. It may be because I've stayed in all day. I wish I'd hunted, after all.

RODDY: What are you frightened of?

CICELY (*looking away*): I don't know —

RODDY (L.C., *suddenly taking her in his arms*): Silly old thing.

CICELY (L., *breaking away*): Roddy, you mustn't – George is in the house. Don't you understand he's in the house?

RODDY (*up to* C., *rather nonplussed*): I thought he was hunting.

CICELY: Well, he isn't; he's in the drawing-room, and he might come out at any minute.

RODDY: It doesn't matter if he does.

CICELY: It matters much more than you think. We've been together much too openly lately, and he's no fool — (RODDY *sits on settee.*) I wish I could make you understand.

RODDY: My dear old girl, you mustn't get nervy. George would never suspect anything in a thousand years.

CICELY (*with sarcasm*): It might afford slight food for suspicion if he came down and found me clasped tightly in your arms – you're never to do it again, not in the house. It's too dangerous.

RODDY: I hardly get you to myself at all.

CICELY: Now, that's not fair of you, Roddy – you know I do my best, but we must not be blatant. You will not understand. If George did by any chance discover – everything – well, he'd do something dreadful: shoot himself or divorce me, or – anyhow, there'd be a terrible scandal. (*Crosses* R.)

RODDY (*rises; down* C.): I think you're overrating George's character. He's not nearly strong-minded enough to do anything so dashing as divorce or shooting.

CICELY: I do wish you wouldn't despise my husband so, Roddy. It isn't good form.

RODDY (*crosses* R.C.): Damn good form, when it's a question of being in love —

CICELY: With someone else's wife – I see your point.

RODDY: Look here, Cicely, I – I— Why aren't you a little nicer to me?

CICELY (*drops back*): I'm perfectly nice, and the nicest part of me is not letting you run down George. I have some sense of duty left.

RODDY: You women are extraordinary creatures – I wonder if you realise what a grand passion means?

CICELY: Yes; it means wanting a thing very badly until you've got it.

RODDY: And after you've got it – always – for ever. You sneer at my love for you, and pretend it won't last; but you know in your heart that it's the truest thing that's ever been.

CICELY (*softly*): Is it, Roddy? Is it, really?

RODDY: My God! Just let me prove it.

> RODDY *takes her in his arms before she has time to resist, and kisses her passionately. As she breaks free from him* GEORGE BRENT *appears at drawing-room door.* CICELY *crosses to table R.*

GEORGE: Hallo, Roddy! Why aren't you hunting today? (*Crosses to L.C.*)

RODDY (*up to C., a little flustered*): Oh, I don't know – why aren't you?

GEORGE: I'm waiting in to welcome my two children. I suppose you're staying on to tea?

RODDY: Oh no, thanks. I just dropped in on my way to Dalsham. I'm going to see the new mare Rawlings has there.

GEORGE: Was that the one he was riding on Monday?

RODDY (*up R.C.*): I don't know. I wasn't out. Anyhow, he's willing to sell, and I'm going to have first refusal.

CICELY: Will you drive me over with you? – I want a little air. (*Slight movement up stage.*)

RODDY: Of course I will. Only —

CICELY (*to table; nervously*): I haven't been out all day; a drive would buck me up.

GEORGE: I rather wanted you to stay in this afternoon, Cicely.

CICELY (*crosses to* GEORGE, *L.C.*): I know – but I can't help it. You can make them both feel at home just as well without me.

> RODDY *drops R.*

GEORGE: They'll think it rather odd. (*Goes L.*) You ought to stay.

CICELY: Well, I can't – I simply can't. (*Crosses to* R., *up.*) I have a headache. Will you bring me back in time for tea, Roddy?

RODDY: Yes.

CICELY: There, George; I'll be back in time for tea.

RODDY: I'll go and start up the car.

    Exit, whistling.

GEORGE: If it's as necessary as all that, of course there is no more to be said. (CICELY *is about to follow* RODDY.) I want to speak to you for a moment before you go, Cicely.

CICELY (*stops*): What is it? (*Crosses down* L.C.)

GEORGE: I don't wish this affair of yours with Roddy to become public property – you'd better be careful.

CICELY (*astounded*): George! I — What do you mean?

GEORGE (*to* CICELY, *quite quietly*): This is what I mean. You think I'm a weak-minded ass, don't you? Sublimely unconscious of what goes on under my nose? You and Roddy both think that; you and Charlie Templeton thought it also, and Mark Hunter, and Douglas Green. You're awfully silly sometimes, Cicely.

CICELY (*horrified*): George! – what are you going to do?

GEORGE: I'm not going to do anything, providing you don't make a scandal. This is just a warning.

CICELY: But I —

GEORGE: Now don't be tiresome, Cicely; I don't feel in the mood for a scene.

CICELY: Look here, George (*movement to* GEORGE) – you see, we – we just care for each other, that's all. I'm sorry if I hurt you.

GEORGE: Rubbish! You haven't hurt me a bit.

CICELY (*starts back*): You mean because you don't love me any more?

GEORGE: Exactly.

CICELY: Then you don't?

GEORGE: Of course not. Why should I? You don't love me. Did you expect me to go on adoring you while you carried on various affairs with the whole county? I think it's simply maddening of you to underrate my intelligence like that – it's one thing Jennifer never did.

CICELY: How dare you talk to me of Jennifer!

GEORGE: Why not? You kiss young men in my hall.

CICELY (*furious*): To have her children here is bad enough, but for you to hold her up to me as an example! . . .

GEORGE (L.): I never held her up as an example. She was much too irritating to be good for anyone – dear Jennifer.

CICELY: Dear Jennifer, indeed! You didn't say 'Dear Jennifer' when you were married to her. (*Turns to* C.)

GEORGE: Yes, I did, quite a number of times; but it didn't have the slightest effect – dear Jennifer!

CICELY (*movement down to* GEORGE): I don't attempt to understand you, George. Are you trying to insult me? to drive me to my lover's arms?

GEORGE: I fail to see the point of my driving you, dear, when you trot there so nicely by yourself.

CICELY (L.C.): I'm going to tell you exactly what I think of you. You're not deceiving me a bit, you know. All this easy banter is only to cover your weakness, your lack of moral courage. You say you know of my affair with Roddy, and yet you won't take any decisive step. You're afraid – afraid, and I despise you for it. (*Turns away up to stairs.*)

GEORGE: It depends what you mean by decisive. If you expect me to hit Roddy over the head with a mallet, I certainly shan't – I like him too much. Of course, apart from women and horses, he's a half-wit, but still, he amuses me.

CICELY: That's right! Facetiousness and pretending not to care will eventually win me back to you – is that the idea? What have you been reading, George?

GEORGE: I am about to disillusion you, Cicely. (CICELY *sits on arm of settee.*) You think that I am too weak-minded to be firm about anything. True, I'm not firm over many stupid little things that other men would make a fuss about – merely because I don't consider that the end would altogether justify the means. You also feel that I love you still and desire to win you back to me by 'pretending not to care' – isn't that how you put it? Well, you're all wrong, absolutely wrong. I don't love you any more, and I should loathe to win you back to me. I can imagine nothing more uncomfortable. I'm quite content to jog along here with you, providing you behave yourself, but if you do anything blatant – and get talked about

– there will be trouble – bad trouble. Now go for your drive, and be back in time for tea.

Enter HUDDLE, C.

HUDDLE: Mr Masters is in the car, madam – waiting.

CICELY: Tell him that I have decided not to go, after all.

GEORGE: And that we shall expect him back to tea.

HUDDLE: Very good, sir.

Exit C.

CICELY (*after a pause, crosses to* C.): Thank you for being so frank with me, George. It's nice to know just where one stands. Your rudeness has only made me despise you a little more. Please don't expect me to be nice to your children when they arrive. I consider it an insult to me for you to have asked them here at all.

GEORGE (L.C.): I certainly expect you to be nice to them – I only hope they'll be nice to you. You're sure to be a novelty to them, at any rate. They've spent all their lives on the Continent, among a very haphazard set. It will be interesting for them to come to an English hunting county, where immorality is conducted by rules and regulations.

CICELY: Anyhow, I'm glad we shall have a full house for the next few weeks. There will be more opportunities for me to avoid them. (*Moves* R.)

GEORGE: If you continue in your present sunny mood, dear, I should think they'd be glad as well.

There is the noise of a motor outside, and then the loud pealing of the bell.

Here they are, here they are! (*Goes up* C.)

CICELY (*going upstairs*): I may come down before dinner, and I may not. (*Crosses towards stairs.*)

GEORGE (*jovially*): Well, it doesn't matter. Do exactly what you feel like.

CICELY: George, I think you're insufferable!

Exit, angrily.
There is a moment's pause. Enter HUDDLE.

HUDDLE (*announcing*): Miss Gerda and Mr Sholto, sir. (*Stands aside while they enter, and then withdraws.*)

Both GERDA *and* SHOLTO *are beautifully dressed. They come forward together,* C.

GERDA (C., *softly and, she hopes, appealingly*): Please, are you our daddy?

SHOLTO (C., *with a pronounced break in his voice*): Father!

SHOLTO *nudges* GERDA, *who runs forward and flings her arms round* GEORGE'S *neck.* SHOLTO *wrings his hand in a manly fashion.* GEORGE *is entirely dumbfounded.*

GERDA (*up* C.): Oh, Daddy, Daddy, we're so happy, happy – Mother sends you her love, Daddy. (*Moves* L.)

SHOLTO (*crosses* L.C.): Oh, Father. You can never guess how we have longed for this moment. We've —

GERDA: Don't break down, big brother.

GEORGE (L.C., *placing a hand on each of their heads*): Little girl – sonny – may I call you sonny?

GERDA (L., *ecstatically*): Sholto, he's *got* us! (*Laughing.*) I knew he would. You owe me twenty francs.

SHOLTO: Damn! I wanted to go on much longer. I've got that long speech we made up at Boulogne. (*Drops down* R.)

GEORGE: Never mind; say it now.

SHOLTO (*crosses to* C.): No, I'll wait until we meet our stepmother. Isn't it amusing having a stepmother and a real mother at the same time?

GERDA: Where is she?

GEORGE: Upstairs, having a headache.

SHOLTO: Was that photograph you sent like her? Mother *was* angry when it came. Wasn't she, Gerda?

GERDA: Absolutely livid.

They both shriek with laughter.

SHOLTO: She wanted to tear it up, but we stopped her. We made her keep it on her writing-desk.

GERDA: Now, tell us, were you glad to get Mother's letter? Were you looking forward to welcoming your long-lost darlings? I wanted to come in with a dog, like Peg o' my Heart, but we couldn't find one.

GEORGE: You know, you're both awfully like I thought you'd be.

GERDA: Are we?

SHOLTO: We weren't quite sure about you; we guessed you had a sense of humour, but we thought it would probably be submerged by now – that you'd be more hunty and sporty – you *do* hunt, don't you?

GEORGE: Sometimes four and five days a week.

GERDA: What do you hunt?

SHOLTO (C.): Don't be silly, Gerda. You know perfectly well they hunt foxes and stags and rabbits and things. Oh, by the way, we've got a letter for you from Mother. Give it to him, Gerda.

GERDA: I haven't got it. You have.

SHOLTO: No, I haven't.

GERDA: Yes, you have. I gave it back to you in the car.

SHOLTO: You didn't.

GERDA (*crosses to* SHOLTO): I *did*. (*Plunges her hand into his side pocket and produces letter.*) There!

GEORGE: I wonder if you'd both keep quiet for a moment. Take a look round. (*Sits in settee and commences to read letter.*)

> SHOLTO *and* GERDA *wander round the hall, examining things.* SHOLTO *nudges* GERDA, *who looks towards* GEORGE. *She comes to back of settee, L.C.*

GERDA (*conversationally*): Mother was looking awfully pretty when we left. She does her hair *so* nicely now.

GEORGE (*immersed in letter*): Humph.

SHOLTO (C.): And she's got rather sunburnt – you know, a nice berry colour. She does most of her writing out of doors.

> SHOLTO *looks questioningly at* GERDA, *who nods emphatically. Then he runs out into the smaller hall and returns in a moment with a large cardboard package. Goes to back of settee, L.C.*

GERDA: The climate is so lovely in Alassio – all balmy with orange-groves. Mother looks perfectly adorable in an orange-grove.

GEORGE: Does she, indeed?

SHOLTO (*back of settee, L.*): Yes, she does. Perhaps you'd like to see this? (*Takes large photograph from packet and gives it to* GEORGE.)

GEORGE: Thank you.

GERDA (*looking over his shoulder*): That's Mother – and that's us in the distance, and those are the oranges.

GEORGE (*drily*): How pretty.

SHOLTO: Yes, isn't it? I always think this is a better portrait. (*Takes another photograph and hands it to* GEORGE, *who winces slightly, as it is apparently a painfully good likeness.*)

GEORGE: By Jove! (*Stares at it.*)

> SHOLTO *and* GERDA *nudge one another, and smile.*

SHOLTO: That old seat there is where Mother wrote most of *Secret Lovers*. She used to wear a funny little scarlet overall thing, and Maria used to bring her lunch out to her.

GERDA: It's lovely and cool in the shade of those cypresses. (*Takes another photograph from packet.*) Personally, I always *like* this one best – it's so —

> GEORGE *rises hurriedly, dropping the two photographs on to the floor. He seems a little distrait.*

GEORGE: I don't want to see any more now, thanks. We must all go and wash for tea. (*Crosses up R.*)

SHOLTO (*picking up photographs*): Well, there's no need to trample Mother underfoot in your excitement. (*Round settee, picks up photos and puts them on settee.*)

GERDA (*crosses R.C.*): I don't want to go and wash yet – I want to stay here and talk. You know, you'll have to tell us lots of things if we are to be a success with everybody.

GEORGE: If you behave like the modest unassuming young things you are, you couldn't fail to be a success anywhere.

SHOLTO (*crosses to* GEORGE): It's all very fine for you to jeer at us, Father, but if you don't warn us about things, we're bound to make mistakes.

GEORGE: There's nothing very much to warn you about, except – except —

GERDA: Well? (*Movement to R.*)

GEORGE: Well, if you'll forgive me mentioning it – don't assert yourselves quite so much – be more retiring.

SHOLTO (R.): Of course. Violets won't be in it with us.

GEORGE: I'm afraid you won't have much in common with the others, so you mustn't mind feeling a bit out of it. You see, conversation in this part of the world is rather apt to run in grooves.

GERDA (R.C.): That will be good practice. We'll see how long we can talk in one groove.

GEORGE: I think the quieter you keep the better, anyhow, at first. Do you play any games?

SHOLTO: Only Poker.

GEORGE ⎫
GERDA ⎬ Hum, um!
SHOLTO ⎭

GEORGE (*apprehensively*): Do you play it well?

GERDA ⎫ (*together*): Very well!
SHOLTO ⎭

GEORGE: I might have known it!

> *All laugh.*

GERDA: We also play bridge – just a teeny bit.

GEORGE: Well, don't – while you're here.

SHOLTO: Very well, Father.

GEORGE: And for my sake, will you both try to refrain from doing anything utterly damnable?

GERDA (*wistfully*): Of course, Daddy – (*crosses to* GEORGE) – we'll do our best – we wouldn't wound our dear kind Daddy for anything in the world, would we, Sholto?

SHOLTO: No, little sister; we will work and slave for him.

GEORGE: All I ask is that you behave yourselves moderately well and try not to grate on everyone.

SHOLTO: I think we're going to be very happy here. (*Crosses L.*)

GERDA (R.C.): Did Stepmother Cicely like the idea of our coming?

GEORGE (R., *going down*): Well, you see —

SHOLTO: Or did she hate it?

GEORGE: Well, you see —

GERDA: She hated it. What did I tell you, Sholto?

SHOLTO: We shall have to be wistful with her, that's all, and make her love us. You can have a heart-to-heart talk with her, dear, and say how unhappy we are at home, and will she be a second mother to us.

GERDA: No, you'd better talk to her; being the opposite sex, it will probably appeal to her more.

GEORGE: Well, if you take my advice, you won't go on that line at all. Cicely would hate to be even a first mother to anyone, let alone a second.

SHOLTO: Do you think we shall like her?

GEORGE: I'm sure you will.

GERDA: He's lying.

GEORGE (*movement to* GERDA): Moments have cropped up during our comparatively short reunion, Gerda, when only the frailty of your sex has prevented me from striking you.

SHOLTO: Well, after all, it's only natural that she shouldn't want us. She probably thinks we're going to be odious. Won't she be surprised when she sees us?

GEORGE: That remains to be proved.

GERDA: Anyhow, you leave her to us. We'll make her yearn for our company every moment of the day. Is the house full of people?

GEORGE: Yes; they'll be back from hunting pretty soon.

There is the noise of a motor outside.

You'd better come and clean yourselves now. Here they are.

All turn up to C.

SHOLTO: Do you always hunt in motorcars in England?

All going towards stairs.

GEORGE (*as they go upstairs*): No, my uninitiated lunatic; they're out with the Cragmore today.

SHOLTO: Well, I only asked.

They are just at the top of the stairs when GERDA *stops.*

GERDA: Oh, I've left my bag! Get it for me, Sholto, there's a lamb. (*Winks heavily, unperceived by* GEORGE.)

SHOLTO: All right. (*Runs back downstairs.*)

GEORGE *and* GERDA *go off, talking.*
SHOLTO *quickly takes the two largest photographs from the packet, stands them up on the mantelpiece, shoves packet under chair, then takes* GERDA'S *bag and exits upstairs, two at a time.*

HUDDLE *throws open door C.*

Enter PRISCILLA HARTLEBERRY *and* SIBYL BLAITH, *followed by* CLAUD ECCLES. *All three are in hunting kit.*

HUDDLE *goes off L.*

SIBYL: Are you going to change now, or have tea first?

PRISCILLA: Oh, tea. I couldn't drag myself up those stairs without it. (*Lapsing into baby-talk.*) I'se dreffully tired. (*Sits settee, L.*)

CLAUD: Damned good day, though, taken all round. (*Crosses R.*)

SIBYL (*crosses top of stage towards stairs*): I should have liked it better if we hadn't been taken all round. I'm worn out. (*Looking at watch.*) It's late, too.

> HUDDLE *enters L. with tea-pot and milk-jug; puts them on table L. Exits.*

PRISCILLA: Do you want any, Sibyl?

SIBYL: Not now; I'm too muddy to enjoy it. I'll be down soon.

> *Exit upstairs.*

CLAUD (*crosses to table, up R.C.*): I shall have a whisky-and-soda. (*Helps himself; turns down.*)

PRISCILLA: I must drink tea all by my little self, then. (*Pours out a cup and helps herself to a sandwich.*)

CLAUD (*on his way down C. catches sight of photographs on mantelpiece*): Hallo! who's this? (*Goes L., to mantelpiece.*)

PRISCILLA (*vacantly*): Who's what?

CLAUD: These photos. Some friend of Cicely's, I suppose. (*Picks up photos, shows them to* PRISCILLA.)

PRISCILLA: Who can it be, now? It isn't Gracie Fancourt; I know her by sight. I've never noticed it before, have you?

CLAUD: No.

PRISCILLA: Oh, well, we'll ask Cicely when she comes down. (CLAUD *replaces photographs.*) Oh, dear! how I adore nice hot tea. I wonder if they drink it much in Poona.

CLAUD (*sits on club fender*): I wish you weren't going to Poona at all.

PRISCILLA: But think what poor Maurice would say if I didn't. He's waiting out there, counting the weeks until I come – poor lonely darling. Still, I shall hate leaving England and – and – everybody! (*Casts an arch look at* CLAUD, *who doesn't notice, as he is gazing gloomily into the fire.*)

CLAUD: I wonder if you will – really.

PRISCILLA (*reproachfully, taking another sandwich*): You *know* I will. . . . 'Ickle Prissy 'll often feel very homesick out there among nasty, creepy, crawly insects and snakes and things.

CLAUD (*with some bitterness*): You'll have Maurice.

PRISCILLA: Only in the evenings; he'll be out all day.

CLAUD: Perhaps you'll have time, then, to write to me occasionally?

PRISCILLA: Would you like me to very much?

CLAUD: Yes. (*Crosses to her.*) More than anything else in the world. (*Goes and sits by* PRISCILLA *on settee.*)

PRISCILLA (*overcome*): Oh, Claud! (*Takes another sandwich.*)

CLAUD: When you've gone, I don't quite know what I shall do. We've been together a lot lately, haven't we?

PRISCILLA: Do you think people have noticed?

CLAUD: Oh no. I shouldn't be such a cad as to get you talked about.

PRISCILLA (*with obvious relief*): I know you wouldn't, Claud. 'Ickle Prissy has a very soft corner in her heart for you.

CLAUD: You'll dance with me as much as you can at the Hunt Ball next week, won't you? It'll be your last night down here.

PRISCILLA: Of course I will. I love dancing with you; our steps go so well together.

CLAUD: If only you weren't tied down, our steps might have gone together through life.

PRISCILLA (*with gentle reproach*): You mustn't talk to me like that, else I'll be cross wiv you.

CLAUD: I simply must say what I really feel, for once. I can't keep it back; I —

PRISCILLA (*hurriedly*): Claud! – think of Maurice. (*Quickly takes another sandwich, presumably to calm herself.*)

> Enter JULIA CRAGWORTHY, *followed by* EUSTACE. JULIA *is in riding-habit;* EUSTACE *is not.*

JULIA: If you hadn't insisted on staying behind to jaw to Lady Churchington, Eustace, we should have been saved the hideous boredom of having to drive with the Crossleys. (*Moves to L.C.*)

EUSTACE (R.C.): I had to stop, because she was a great friend of my aunt's; also she is twice removed from the Cheshire Churchingtons.

JULIA: She'll be removed from Leicestershire soon if she rides her horse to death like that. Everyone was talking about it. Tea, for the love of heaven! (*Gets tea from table* L.)

EUSTACE: Have the young prodigals arrived yet?

CLAUD: Which young prodigals?

EUSTACE: George's children. They're due today.

JULIA: So they are. I'd forgotten about them. I expect Cicely's in a flaming temper. Poor Cicely! she has no repose in a crisis.

PRISCILLA: Why should it be a crisis?

JULIA: It must be a crisis to any second wife to have the first wife's offspring suddenly foisted upon her. No, thanks, Claud.

> CLAUD *has worked up and round to back of settee with cakes, which he offers to* JULIA.

Plain bread-and-butter.

EUSTACE (C.): I think it was in doubtful taste for Jennifer to send them.

PRISCILLA: You knew her, didn't you?

EUSTACE: Oh yes, years ago.

CLAUD: What was she like?

EUSTACE: Very tiresome, very tiresome indeed – she and George used to jar on one another terribly. I shall never forget — By jove! (*Suddenly catches sight of photographs; crosses to fireplace.*)

PRISCILLA: What is it?

> JULIA *moves back of settee,* L.

EUSTACE (*examining them closely*): This is Jennifer – very like she used to be – very like. A bit *passée*, of course, since I saw her – been knocking about too much. Damn fool ever to have left George.

PRISCILLA: Did she leave him? I thought it was the other way round.

EUSTACE: As a matter of fact, they arranged it between them; said they were too temperamental, or some such rubbish. (*Takes cup of tea and sits on club fender.*)

JULIA: I know the sort of thing. I only hope history won't repeat itself —

PRISCILLA: What do you mean, Mrs Cragworthy?

JULIA: Well, I'm a plain woman, and I generally have the moral courage to speak out —

EUSTACE: You mean Cicely and —

JULIA (*top of settee*, L.C.): Roddy. Precisely.

PRISCILLA: But that wouldn't be history repeating itself exactly, would it? I mean, Jennifer didn't care for anyone else – I mean —

Re-enter CICELY, *downstairs.*

CICELY: So sorry, all of you. I've had a beastly headache all the afternoon. Had a good day, Julia?

JULIA: Top-hole. Collins was out on that knock-kneed old chestnut. He told me all about the Hinto girls and Roger Gray. I've never laughed so much in my life.

PRISCILLA: Nora Brand was out too, and Nicky and Boy Fenton. I saw them all glaring at one another.

CICELY: Some people are amazing, aren't they? (*She sees photographs.*) Who put those there? (L.C.)

EUSTACE: I don't know. Didn't you?

CICELY (*looking at them hard*): But – but – why, it's Jennifer! Really, I — (*Crosses to mantelpiece and back to* C.)

EUSTACE: Yes, it is Jennifer. Hasn't changed much, considering. I remember her – let me see now —

CICELY (C.): Sometimes George goes a little too far. I must ask him to take them down; they crowd up the mantelpiece so.

EUSTACE: Where are the two children, Cicely? Do they fall below or come up to your expectations?

CICELY: I haven't seen them yet. My head was too bad for me to come down when they arrived. (*Sits at table* R.) George has carried them off somewhere. To be perfectly frank, I'm rather dreading them.

EUSTACE: One instinctively mistrusts the idea of young people bred on the Continent – instinctively. I don't wish to depress you, Cicely, but they're certain to be precocious.

PRISCILLA: How old are they?

CICELY: The boy's twenty-one, and the girl's eighteen.

JULIA: Where were they at school?

CICELY: I don't know. They've been mostly educated at home, I think.

JULIA: I thought as much. They'll know all the things they ought not to know.

CICELY: Perhaps you'd like to take them in hand, Julia dear. I feel sure you could be sufficiently firm.

JULIA: I can bear anything except artificiality. As long as they are natural, and don't try to push themselves forward and monopolise the conversation —

CLAUD: Here they are. (*Up behind settee* L.)

Re-enter GEORGE *downstairs, followed by* GERDA *and* SHOLTO.

GEORGE (*coming down* R. *to* CICELY): Cicely – this is Gerda and Sholto.

GERDA *and* SHOLTO *go to* C. *and walk down.*

CICELY (*rises*): How do you do.

GERDA (*crosses to* CICELY, *firmly kissing her on both cheeks*): Please, are you our new Mummie? (*Falls back.*)

SHOLTO (*crosses to* CICELY; *with simple manliness*): We have waited a long time for this moment. (*Takes her hand.*)

CICELY (*by table* R., *staggered*): Oh – er – have you?

SHOLTO (R.C.): Yes, indeed we have. Gerda said to me in the train – didn't you, Gerda?

GERDA (C.): I did.

SHOLTO: 'Sholto,' she said, 'aren't you simply pining to see our stepmother Cicely?' 'Yes, Gerda,' I said. Didn't I, Gerda?

GERDA: You did.

SHOLTO: 'Yes, Gerda; she looked so charming in the picture father sent.'

CICELY (*looking at* GEORGE): What picture?

GEORGE (R., *airily*): I just sent Jennifer one of your new ones. I thought you wouldn't mind.

CICELY: You sent Jennifer one of my new photographs?

GEORGE: Yes.

CICELY (*coldly*): Why?

GEORGE (*feebly*): Because I thought she'd like it.

GERDA (*conciliatively*): She did, too. Didn't she, Sholto?

SHOLTO (*with slightly overdone enthusiasm*): She adored it!

CICELY (*movement. Angrily to* GEORGE): I fail to see that there was the slightest necessity — Well, never mind now. Julia, these are George's children. Mrs Cragworthy, Mrs Hartleberry, Eustace Dabbit and Claud Eccles.

SHOLTO ⎱ How do you do?
GERDA   ⎰

EUSTACE: I'm an old friend of your mother's. (*Crosses to* L.C.; *shakes hands.*)

SHOLTO (*politely*): Are you?

GERDA (*moves* L.): Of course – yes! Don't you remember, Sholto, mother said, the very last thing before we started, 'Give my very best love to dear old Claud Eccles; he's certain to be there.'

EUSTACE: My name is Dabbit. (*Back to fender.*)

GERDA: Of course! How stupid of me – I mean Dabbit.

SHOLTO: It's no use, Gerda; you've floundered badly. (*To* EUSTACE.) I'm so sorry; my sister was only trying to be pleasant.

EUSTACE: I remember your mother – let me see, now – we were staying with Lady Dutton – or was it the Fenworths? – the Shropshire Fenworths, you know – not the Leicester ones.

SHOLTO (*relieved*): Oh, I *am* glad it wasn't the Leicester ones! I've heard such fearful things about them.

JULIA: Indeed! My aunt is a Leicester Fenworth.

GERDA: Forgive my brother; he was only trying to be funny.

SHOLTO (*holding* GERDA'S *hand; both cross to* CICELY): We're frightfully excited, you know. It's the first time we've been in England, anyhow since we were tiny. So don't be cross if we're stupid about things. You see, living on the Continent, as we have —

GERDA (*interrupting*): It's all, naturally, new and thrilling to us here. You can't imagine how funny it is, everything being grey instead of brightly coloured, and everyone talking English, and not waving their arms much and —

SHOLTO: Gerda, we're talking too much. Remember what Father said!

GERDA (*cheerfully*): Sorry, everybody!

GEORGE: Do you want any tea? (*Crosses to* L.C., *top of settee.*)

GERDA: Yes, please.

PRISCILLA: I'll do it, Cicely. You sit still and rest that poor tired head of yours.

GEORGE: Is it still bad, dear?

CICELY (*snappily*): Yes, it is.

GEORGE: It's a pity you didn't go for the drive with Roddy, after all; it might have done you good. (*He suddenly sees photographs.*) Hallo! Why? Oh, Lord! (*He bursts out laughing, and looks at* SHOLTO *and* GERDA, *who laugh too. Everyone else looks surprised, except* CICELY, *who is furious.*) You little beasts! Go and take them down at once.

SHOLTO (*going to mantelpiece* L.): Of course. I always think photographs look untidy without frames.

CICELY (*with a forced smile*): Give them to me. I'll tell Huddle to send them down to the village to be done. (*Sits by table* R.)

SHOLTO (*crosses to* CICELY; *sits at table, handing them to her*): I think black would be nicer than anything else, don't you? Just plain and narrow —

GERDA (R.C., *looking over* CICELY'S *shoulder*): Or perhaps brown wood —

CICELY (*scrutinising them with a smile*): So that's your mother? She's quite different from what I imagined. What a quaint dress! Is that typically Italian?

GERDA (R.C.): No; only an overall. She always wears them during the day – so cool and comfy – (*Crosses* C.)

CICELY (*still smiling*): Very pretty.

SHOLTO (*rises, goes to tea-table* L.): I think it's Mother that's pretty; not the overall.

CICELY: Remind me about those, somebody. (*Puts them on table.*)

CLAUD: Right-o!

CICELY: Was Bobby Armstrong out today?

PRISCILLA: Yes. I knew he would be. Beryl followed in a dog-cart.

EUSTACE: She's got no go in her, that girl. She borrowed the top of my Thermos, and never returned it. Shallow, very shallow.

JULIA: How she has the nerve to come to meets at all, after what happened at the Cragmore Ball, beats me.

CICELY: I knew she'd try to brazen it out.

JULIA: Bobbie behaved pretty well over the whole affair. Damn good value, Bobbie.

EUSTACE: Best stables in the Monday country.

JULIA: He sold Frank Forbes a ripping good filly last winter; never turned her head.

Enter RODDY *by front door.*

GEORGE: Hallo, Roddy. You *have* been quick.

RODDY: I didn't go to Dalsham after all; I've had some rather bad news. (*Moves down to* CICELY.)

CICELY (R.C.): Bad news? What is it?

RODDY (C.): My brother out in Jamaica is dead – I've had a cable – I've been more or less expecting it. It means I shall have to go out there at once, within the next fortnight.

CICELY (*gives a little cry*): Oh! (*Controls herself.*) How very tiresome for you, Roddy! I *am* so sorry.

GEORGE (L.C., *top of settee*): So am I, Roddy.

PRISCILLA: Will you have to stay out there?

RODDY (*to* L.C.): Yes. You see, I'm his only living relative. I shall have to take over control of his plantation – at least for a few months, until all his affairs are settled.

GEORGE: We shall miss you, Roddy – shan't we, Cicely?

CICELY: Yes – of course we shall.

PRISCILLA: Won't you be here for the Hunt Ball, after all?

RODDY: I don't know; it all depends – it's next Tuesday, isn't it? I shouldn't think I'd be able to get away before then.

GEORGE: By the way, Roddy, let me introduce my son and daughter.

SHOLTO *and* GERDA *get up and shake hands.*

SHOLTO (*crossing to* RODDY; *sympathetically*): How do you do? Jolly rotten for you. You say he was your only brother? (*Shakes his hand.*)

GERDA (*shakes his hand*): You'll have to cheer up and try not to think about it.

RODDY: It is such a beastly long journey.

GERDA: I meant about him dying. (*Sits down again.*)

SHOLTO: So did I. (*Crosses back of settee.*)

RODDY (*hurriedly*): Well, you see, I haven't set eyes on him for about eight years.

GEORGE: Look here, I must just go and write a note to your mother, to thank her for you. You'd better both wait here.

SHOLTO
GERDA } (*wistfully*): Very well, Father.

SHOLTO *chokes into his tea-cup.* GERDA *bangs him on the back. Everyone else goes on talking. Exit* GEORGE, R.

CICELY: Does anyone want to play bridge? – Julia?

JULIA: I will when I've changed. (*Crosses towards stairs.*)

CICELY: Eustace, I know you will – Roddy, do you feel like it?

RODDY (R.C.): Yes – all right.

JULIA (*going upstairs*): I shan't be five minutes.

    Exit.

CICELY (*crosses* L.C. *To* SHOLTO *and* GERDA): Do you want to play?

GERDA: I think we'd better not.

SHOLTO: You haven't such a thing as a ludo-board in the house?

CICELY: Priscilla?

PRISCILLA: No. I'm going to write a long long letter to Maurice before dinner. (*Rises and moves in front of settee towards stairs.*)

    CLAUD *follows. They pause up* C.

CICELY: Come on, Eustace; Claud, you can cut in later if you like. I shan't play for long.

CLAUD: Thanks awfully.

    Exeunt CICELY, EUSTACE *and* RODDY R.

GERDA (*conversationally*): Have you been hunting all day?

CLAUD: Yes.

SHOLTO: Did you find anything?

PRISCILLA (*giggling*): Oh dear, oh dear! – that's very funny! Oh dear!

SHOLTO: It wasn't meant to be. I was only taking an intelligent interest.

GERDA: Not intelligent, dear.

SHOLTO: Now, don't be superior, Gerda. You really know just as little about it as I do. (*To* CLAUD.) You see, we want to pick up all we can about hunting. So that we can get along all right in the groove.

CLAUD: The what?

GERDA: The groove, the hunting groove. You don't talk about much else down here, do you? You see, we're used to people who talk about everything – vice and art and food – and, of course, we don't want to be out of the swim —

SHOLTO: So will you tell us things?

94

PRISCILLA: I'm afraid I haven't time just now.

Enter HUDDLE, *to clear tea-things.*

CLAUD: You'll learn soon enough. Are you coming up now, Priscilla? (*Starts to go upstairs.*)

PRISCILLA (*following him*): Yes. If I don't catch this mail, poor Maurice will think his 'ickle Prissy dreffly neglectful – poor darling.

Exeunt PRISCILLA *and* CLAUD, *talking.*

GERDA: They don't seem to want to talk to us very much, do they?

SHOLTO: Silly asses.

GERDA (*to* HUDDLE, *still out to be pleasant*): What's your name?

HUDDLE: Huddle, miss.

SHOLTO: Have you been here long?

HUDDLE: Three years, sir.

GERDA: Do you like it?

HUDDLE: Yes, thank you, miss.

Exit with tray. There is a slight pause.

GERDA (*furiously*): Sholto – I hate them! I hate them all, except daddy. They're beasts – and that cat Cicely was trying to be horrible about mother. They're all against us just because we're not narrow and horsey, like them. I want to go back home now – I want Mother! (*She sniffs.*)

SHOLTO: Now don't give way and be absurd. Remember we have a mission in life. May the light of it guide you to a calmer state of mind – it's a very beautiful mission.

GERDA: I'm quite calm, really. But if you ever inherit this house, you can live in it by yourself – it's perfectly beastly.

SHOLTO: One thing cheers me up intensely.

GERDA: What is it?

SHOLTO (*complacently*): The look Cicely gave when Roddy What's-his-name said he had to go away.

GERDA: You mean that she's —?

SHOLTO (*smiling*): I think we're going to be very happy here!

CURTAIN

ACT II: Scene I

SCENE: *The same as Act I.*
TIME: *A week has elapsed.*

When curtain rises, CICELY, JULIA, SIBYL, PRISCILLA *and* GERDA *are seated about, having after-dinner coffee. They are all, with the exception of* GERDA, *shrieking with laughter. Their clothes are conventional, pinks and blues, not too well made.* GERDA *is in a chic and elaborately simple frock.*

SIBYL: Oh dear, oh dear! – it really was awfully funny, wasn't it?
PRISCILLA: I've never laughed so much in my life.

    Enter CLAUD, GEORGE, EUSTACE *and* SHOLTO *from dining-room.*

GEORGE: What are you all laughing at?
JULIA: Only the story of Bessie Clifton and Jack Mostyn.

    SHOLTO *sits on club fender.* PRISCILLA *crosses to* CLAUD, C.

EUSTACE (*comes* L.C.): Most amusing, most amusing. I always said to Bessie that the only thing more expensive than hunting was virtue! (*Goes up.*)
PRISCILLA (C): By the way, Cicely, is Roddy going away tomorrow for certain?
CICELY (*seated down* L.): Yes I think so.
JULIA: I've always liked Roddy, in spite of what people say about him and the Clifton girl. I'm sure it's not true.
CICELY: I *know* it isn't.
GERDA (*sweetly*): But still, he *has* rather the reputation of a Don Juan in the county, hasn't he, Stepmother Cicely?
GEORGE (*moving* L.C.): We all have reputations and traditions in the county, Gerda. Some of us try to live up to them, and others hope to live them down. Roddy is one of the latter.
SIBYL: Anyhow, we shall miss him.

    PRISCILLA *is* R.C. EUSTACE *goes to her and* CLAUD.

EUSTACE (C.): His uncle is one of the Monmouthshire Masters, I think. Very old family. (*Talks to* CLAUD.)

GERDA: I should love to be going to Jamaica. Wouldn't you, Stepmother Cicely?

CICELY: Not particularly.

SIBYL: I wonder if he'll get much good riding out there. He'll be wretched if he doesn't.

CLAUD (C.): Wonderful seat on a horse – old Roddy.

GERDA: That's the expression we were trying to think of, to tell mother. 'Wonderful seat on a horse'.

GEORGE: You're learning a lot, aren't you?

SHOLTO (*rises, crosses to settee*): Rather! A man in a red coat and a black velvet cap, with a lot of dogs, is called an M.F.H.

GERDA: Not dogs, dear – hounds!

SHOLTO: Sorry! Hounds.

CICELY: I really don't see the point of your trying to master hunting technicalities. You're surely not intending to take it up seriously?

SHOLTO: Why not? We're both young, and I'm sure we've got good seats.

CICELY (*contemptuously; looking across to* JULIA): You really are too absurd!

GERDA (*reminiscently*): I ride a frightfully fiery donkey at home. It's name is Muriel.

SHOLTO (*in hunting tones*): Damn good value, old Muriel – never turns her head.

GERDA: She can't, poor dear; she suffers from spavin.

PRISCILLA (C.): But that wouldn't have anything to do with it.

SHOLTO: Believe me, the slightest thing upsets Muriel; she is neurotic.

JULIA (*heavily*): If you two kids took things a bit more seriously, you might learn something.

    GEORGE *comes down.*

PRISCILLA: Let's push some of the things back and practise steps for tonight.

    CLAUD *comes down.*

97

CICELY: All right. Go and get the records will you, Claud? They're in the drawing-room.

GEORGE: Why not dance in there? The floor's ever so much better.

JULIA: Won't it be rather cold?

SIBYL (R.C.): Oh, no, we shall soon get warm. (*Goes up stage.*) Come on, everybody; you've got to dance, too, tonight, Mr Dabbit.

EUSTACE (*up* R.C.): Only a waltz. I can't stand these fox-trot things.

SIBYL: You'll have to hurry up and learn. (EUSTACE *moves towards drawing-room door.*) Is Roddy coming here first, before the ball, Cicely?

CICELY: Yes, I think he is – I really don't know.

> *Exit* SIBYL, GEORGE *following, into drawing-room.*

GEORGE (C.): I hope to goodness he brings his car. We shall never all squash into the Daimler. (*Exit.*)

SIBYL: Oh, he's sure to.

> *Exeunt* EUSTACE, JULIA *into drawing-room.*

SHOLTO (*back of settee*): What time does the ball start? (*Crosses to* C.)

PRISCILLA (L.C.): About ten, I think; but it won't be really jolly until after midnight.

GERDA: Will it be really jolly then?

CLAUD: Oh, yes, rather, rather. (C.) Last year Donald Hake slid down the stairs on a tray and broke ten empty champagne-bottles – damn good rag!

SHOLTO (*back of settee; laughing*): It sounds delightful. I love subtle humour.

GERDA: Don't be supercilious, dear. You know Stepmother Cicely doesn't like it.

CICELY: There's nothing in the least clever in deprecating people to whom you are not accustomed. Donald Hake is a normal, healthy and amusing boy.

SHOLTO: I'm sorry if I was supercilious, but it *does* sound silly to get drunk in public and make an abject fool of yourself.

CICELY: I'm sure I hope that your own lives have been spotless enough to allow you to criticise others.

GERDA (*hotly*): Sholto's never been drunk!

SHOLTO: Hush, darling! – that's not a crime; it's normal, healthy and amusing.

Fox-trot heard off.

PRISCILLA (*up with* CLAUD, *C.; intelligently*): Well, I suppose there are different ways of doing different things. Do come and dance, Claud; I want to learn that new cross-over step; it's so much better than the one, two, three, dip.

CLAUD: Righto. Are you three coming?

Exeunt CLAUD *and* PRISCILLA, *talking.* CICELY *follows. As she passes end of settee, stops C.*

SHOLTO (*to* CICELY): You *do* hate us being here, don't you?

CICELY (*C.*): I'm afraid I haven't given the matter enough thought. You amuse George, and, after all — (*Shrugs.*)

SHOLTO: After all, it is not easy at a moment's notice to become an adoring adopted mother. That is true.

CICELY: I have never had the slightest intention of being your adopted mother.

GERDA (*curiously*): Why do you loathe us so much? Is it because your husband's our father, or because we laugh at things, or because —

CICELY (*C.*): I don't see that there is any real necessity to discuss the subject any further, do you? (*Going.*)

GERDA: Of course we do. It may be unconventional to talk of anything really openly here, but —

CICELY: I'm afraid you frequently confuse lack of convention with lack of breeding.

SHOLTO: Oho! (*Pause.*) Oh! (*Exit* CICELY *to drawing-room. Moves down. After a slight pause.*) That's a nasty one. (*Sits on settee.*)

GERDA (*on settee*): We were asking for it, dear. Still, we had to give her a chance to be nice. Wouldn't it have been awful if she'd got all impulsive, and wept a little and said she wanted us all to be girls together? Thank heaven, she really is an unpleasant woman. Now we'd better start in and get busy.

SHOLTO (*on settee*): And the sooner the better. Do you think the crucial moment will occur tonight?

GERDA: It's certain to; it's Roddy's last night in England. How far have they gone already, I wonder?

SHOLTO: Which of the women here is most intimate with our gentle, loving stepmother? That's the first thing to find out.

GERDA: Well, not Sibyl, anyhow; she hasn't known her long enough.

SHOLTO: There's bounding Julia.

GERDA: No. Bounding Julia's too outspoken and straight-from-the-shoulderish to be really intimate with anyone.

SHOLTO: Priscilla, then; she's the only one left. We'd better try her. (*Rises, crosses to* C. *Pause.*) Shall I become amorous?

GERDA: No; you might go too far, and spoil everything.

SHOLTO (C.): I don't think one could go too far with Priscilla. She has no distance.

GERDA (*rises; crosses to* SHOLTO, C.): No; we'll do it together. We'll be rather wistful and say she is the only one here who really understands us.

SHOLTO: I doubt if she knows anything at all.

GERDA: We'll find out, or die. Go and call her.

SHOLTO: Now?

GERDA: Yes; we ought to discover as much as possible before the ball. You never know what crisis might happen at a ball. Think of Donald Hake!

SHOLTO (*going to drawing-room door*): Normal, healthy, amusing and drunk. (*Gramophone fox-trot heard off.*) Pretty dear! (*Crosses to drawing-room door; calls*) Priscilla! Priscilla! Do be a lamb and come and talk to us. (*Moves back to* C.)

GERDA (*who has followed and is now* R.C., *takes* SHOLTO'S *hand. In a hoarse whisper*): Don't look so cheerful! Remember, mother drinks like a fish, and our life's been hell! (SHOLTO *goes to top of settee, gloomy.*) We must get sympathy at all cost. (*Back to settee, sits.*)

PRISCILLA (*off*): All right – wait a minute. Claud, dance with Sibyl – and Sibyl dance with Claud. That's right. (*She enters.*) All alone! What is it?

GERDA (*hesitatingly*): Will you will you – close the door?

PRISCILLA (*closing it, crosses to* C.): What is it? You make me go all creepy-weepy. Do tell me!

GERDA: It's – it's — Oh, tell her, Sholto. I can't!

She bursts into tears. SHOLTO *looks rather flummoxed.*

SHOLTO (*lamely*): Well, you see, we —

PRISCILLA (*crosses to settee; sits*): Don't cry, Gerda. Tell Prissy all about it.

SHOLTO (L.C., *top of settee; pulling himself together*): It's this, Priscilla. We – we are both a little unhappy. Don't think me a silly ass and all that, but – but we've failed, failed miserably.

GERDA: And we've come to you because you are the only one who has been really kind, and can understand.

PRISCILLA: How do you mean, you've failed?

SHOLTO (C.): We wanted to make our stepmother Cicely – well, fond of us, and— Oh, I know you think I'm a sentimental fool, (*turns*) but we haven't had much real love in our lives, taken all round, and—

PRISCILLA: But your mother – your own mother? You're always talking about her!

GERDA (*dramatically rises, drops down*): Words, words, words! (*Blows nose.*) Oh, Priscilla – (*back to settee, sits*) – could you not see beyond? Listen; I'll tell you everything.

SHOLTO: So will I. (*Sits on settee.*)

GERDA: Our life up to now, has been a hell upon earth.

PRISCILLA: What?

GERDA: A bitter hell. Our mother —

SHOLTO (*sorrowfully*): God forgive her!

GERDA: Our mother has, among many others, one terrible trait in her character. She – she — Oh, how can I say it! – she drinks like a fish.

SHOLTO: Exactly like a fish. If you only knew how utterly damnable existence has been for us, you'd sympathise.

PRISCILLA (*thrilled*): But I *do* sympathise! I never realised – I never guessed.

All rise and move down to front.

GERDA (L.C.): Of course not. How could you? But we felt we just couldn't keep it back any longer. Stepmother Cicely hates us. We've tried— Ah!

SHOLTO: Ah!

GERDA: How we've tried to make things different between us! But it's no use – she's bitterly prejudiced —

SHOLTO (R.C.): You see, our mother —

GERDA (L.C.): God forgive her!

SHOLTO (*chokes, and recovers himself*): Our mother, when she left poor father —

PRISCILLA (C.): Left him! But I thought —

SHOLTO: That they mutually agreed to separate? I know. (*He laughs hollowly.*) That's what everyone thinks. (*Down R. and back.*) She ran away with an Italian count —

GERDA (*descriptively*): With a long black beard —

SHOLTO: Damn him!

GERDA (*hurriedly*): And it ruined her life and his life and Daddy's life and our lives and —

PRISCILLA: Oh, you poor darlings! (*Embraces* GERDA.)

SHOLTO (*warming to his work*): Daily we watched our mother sinking — Ah, Madonna mia! . . . che disastro!

　　　Gramophone fox-trot heard off.

PRISCILLA (*anxiously*): What does that mean?

GERDA: Oh, it's nothing. Sholto always lapses into Italian when he's worked up. But don't you see what we're aiming at? Cicely, our stepmother, is about to do the same fatal thing with Roddy Masters – *you* know, *we* know – and yet we're impotent, impotent!

PRISCILLA: How did you know?

SHOLTO: Oh, that doesn't matter. But you must help us — Oh! *please* — (*Both shake her hands.*) Please say you'll help us!

PRISCILLA: Oh, I will.

SHOLTO: It must be stopped at all costs. It —

PRISCILLA (*ruminatively*): Of course, people *are* beginning to talk.

　　　All cross L. Both pull her round.

GERDA: But you're intimate with her; she tells you everything. Is she – does she love Roddy as much as our poor mother loved —?

SHOLTO (*with vigour*): Dio perdoni la!

PRISCILLA: Was that his name?

SHOLTO: Yes. Count Dio Perdoni la – curse him!

PRISCILLA: Well, I know Roddy loves Cicely terribly – I've seen some of his letters – frightfully passionate they were. But whether she really loves him —

GERDA: Ah! that's the whole point.

PRISCILLA: Do you think George ought to be told?

SHOLTO (C.): No, no, no! (*Start apart.*) Not until it's absolutely necessary. All you want to do is to understand and watch with us. For instance, tell us tonight if you see them leaving the ballroom together.

GERDA: Do you think she loves him enough to – to —?

PRISCILLA: I know she's very fond of him.

GERDA: How fond?

SHOLTO: Sshh! Look out!

Enter CLAUD; *crosses to* C. *All break away.* GERDA *to* L.

CLAUD: I say, Priscilla, do come and dance.

SHOLTO (*with great display of presence of mind, crosses* R.C.): Don't forget, now, Priscilla – third fox-trot after we get there.

PRISCILLA (*nodding mysteriously*): I won't forget. (*Crosses to* CLAUD.)

CLAUD (C., *suspiciously*): Are you three up to some rag, or something?

PRISCILLA (L.C.): No, Claud; Gerda and Sholto were rather worried, and wanted to ask my advice, that was all.

CLAUD: What about?

SHOLTO (R.): The political crisis in Bulgaria.

CLAUD: But there isn't one.

SHOLTO: Nonsense! There's always a political crisis in Bulgaria, the same as there's always haggis in Scotland. It's traditional.

CLAUD: I say, you know, you are talking rot —

PRISCILLA: Come along and dance again, Claud. (*Going.*) You're too curious. Come to my room tonight, before you go to bed, Gerda, dear – we'll talk about – you know what!

Exit, soused in mystery.

CLAUD: There seems to be a lot of secrecy going on about something.

GERDA ⎫
SHOLTO ⎭ Hush!

CLAUD *follows* PRISCILLA *into drawing-room.*

GERDA (*sits on settee*): I don't believe she knows very much more than we do.

SHOLTO (C.): Never mind; we've got her on our side. She'll tell us at once if she *does* hear anything.

GERDA: Anyhow, I think Cicely's affair with Roddy is a little more serious than we thought.

SHOLTO: I hope to heaven it is. (*Crosses L.*)

GERDA: Yes, but the worst of it is, Cicely won't do anything decisive unless we force her hand.

SHOLTO: We're no use there. Father is the only one who would have the slightest effect. (*Sits on fender.*) If he could only be particularly irritating to her, tonight of all nights, everything would be all right.

GERDA: Couldn't we make him?

SHOLTO: Yes, but how?

GERDA (*thoughtfully*): Sweet memories that bless and burn are always useful. We must have a heart-to-heart talk with him. You see, it isn't a question of Cicely not caring for him any more; she frankly hates him.

SHOLTO: She's too silly to appreciate him.

GERDA: Exactly; but it makes things easier for us. Daddy loves Mother best, and always has, at heart – we know that. The question is —

SHOLTO: How to re-unite the two bleeding souls. Oh, for heaven's sake, let's concentrate! Think – think – think! (*Clutches his head.*)

Enter GEORGE *from drawing-room.*

GEORGE (*moving to L.C., head of settee*): What's the matter, Sholto? Got a headache?

GERDA: No; he's only feeling a bit homesick, that's all. We often get waves of it – don't we, dear?

SHOLTO: Rather. It's damnable being away from Mother for long. You see, we're so used to having her there always – to laugh with us.

GERDA: There's no one in the world with a sense of humour like Mother. No wonder you married her.

SHOLTO: What was she like then, Father?

GEORGE (*comes down* L.C.): Judging from your frequent descriptions, very like she is now.

GERDA: She told us all about the wedding and the honeymoon in the Channel Islands.

SHOLTO: And you took so much seasick cure that you were drugged into a state of coma for three days.

GERDA: So tiresome for any young bride.

GEORGE: Yes, but it didn't matter. Nothing mattered – we were gloriously happy. Jersey, Guernsey, Alderney, and Sark – they are magic names, aren't they?

SHOLTO: They're magic places, especially Sark.

GEORGE (C.): Have you been there?

SHOLTO: Of course. We go nearly every year – Mother always insists.

GEORGE (C.): Does she, by Jove!

GERDA: Yes; she's really a mass of sentiment, in spite of her literary cynicism. She likes old workboxes, and places where she lived when she was a girl; and, best of all – Sark.

SHOLTO: She makes us sit on the jetty of Creux harbour and watch the passengers land from the Guernsey boat, and when she sees a young man and woman together, she sniffs a little and says: 'That might be dear George and me. Aren't memories painful, darlings?'

GERDA: She always calls us darlings, even when she's lived with us. Habit, I suppose.

GEORGE (C., *far away*): Yes, she had lots of quaint habits.

GERDA: Why did you ever stop loving her?

GEORGE: Didn't she tell you about that, too?

SHOLTO: No; she only remembers pleasant things.

GEORGE: Well, so do I, so we won't discuss it. (*Crosses* R., *to table.*)

GERDA: You've never been very good at facing facts, have you, Daddy?

GEORGE: How do you mean?

SHOLTO: If only you and Mother hadn't shirked in the first place, we should all be together now, instead of being parted by the English Channel and the Divorce Courts.

GEORGE: In what way shirked?

GERDA: Well, you both thought yourselves too clever, and used

Temperament as an excuse for your rows. If only you'd faced the fact that it was pure selfishness and intolerance from beginning to end – all this trouble would have been saved.

GEORGE (*unexpectedly*): You mean the trouble you two are taking in order to reconcile your mother and myself – against our wills?

SHOLTO: He's got us again, dear. We must be more subtle.

The music stops.

GERDA (*rises, crosses to* GEORGE. *Gently*): If we really thought that it was against your wills, we should never attempt it.

SHOLTO (*rises, crosses to* C.): As it is, we mean to strain every nerve. (*Crosses* R., *behind* GERDA.)

GEORGE: Then you declare war on the peace of my country life – you intend to uproot me, regardless of any such trifling bonds as honour and good name!

GERDA (*firmly*): Yes, we do.

GEORGE: And you think it possible, supposing all obstacles were swept away and you accomplished this, that your mother and I should be happy together?

SHOLTO (*with equal firmness*): Yes, we do.

GEORGE (R.C., *defiantly*): Well, let me tell you you're wrong, thoroughly wrong. You're astute, precocious young devils, but you've made one grave mistake. You think that I'm still in love with your mother – well, I'm not. I don't love anyone. I'm content and peaceful here, my life is perfectly happy, I have a certain amount of responsibility, but not too much; I hunt and shoot and read and eat and sleep – and I'm getting too old to require anything more. (*Takes their hands.*) I agreed that you should come here, not because of any sentimental desire to see you, but because Sholto is to be my heir; it is right that he should get some idea of his future position in life. You and your mother mean nothing to me – nothing! And, apart from a certain amount of superficial amusement, I shouldn't mind if I never set eyes on you again. Your conceit is colossal to imagine that I should be willing to leave this life to which I have grown so accustomed, and join you in yours – even if it were possible. But, thank God, it isn't possible – it isn't possible. I'm entrenched here, and here I mean to stay.

Please never let me hear the subject mentioned again. (*Goes to chair at table* R., *and sits*.)

GERDA (*after a slight pause*): What a wonderful liar you are, Daddy!

SHOLTO: You don't suppose we believe a word of all that nonsense?

GEORGE: I allow you a certain amount of licence, but I will not stand rudeness.

GERDA (*following* GEORGE): It's no use blustering, Daddy; it won't have the slightest effect – you see, we know the truth. Why not give in – gracefully? You'll have to, in the end.

GEORGE (*suddenly serious*): I can't give in – you don't understand. I'm not like you, without any moral sense at all – I wish to God I were. I've blundered badly in life, and I've got to put up with the consequences. People don't get second chances of happiness in this world; they're lucky if they get even a first chance. Well, I've had that, and I chucked it away when I agreed to let your mother divorce me. Then, in order to tie me down still more, Fate ordained that I should be left this house and estate – I had to have someone to run it with me – I wrote to Jennifer, asking her to patch everything up and come back; but she wouldn't. She was always as obstinate as a mule.

GERDA (R.C., *going to* GEORGE): Yes, but a *nice* mule.

GEORGE: Then Cicely appeared. Cicely was quite adorable once, and radiantly pretty —

SHOLTO (R. *and now sitting on table* R.): Prettier than Mother?

GEORGE: Much. Then I married her and started the business of settling down. I religiously forgot Jennifer for almost two years, then Cicely began getting tiresome, and having affairs with stupid young men, and – Jennifer's memory came back and taunted me and laughed at me. It's been doing that for nearly fourteen years now.

The following scene to be played very quickly and excitedly worked up to a climax.

GERDA: And you're going to let it continue for fourteen years more? (*Moves* L.)

GEORGE: Oh, no; it will probably die a natural death before then.

SHOLTO (*on table, pensively*): It must be awful to have a conscience.

GEORGE: It is.

GERDA (L.C. *to* GEORGE, *softly*): It would be such fun – all going back together. (*Goes to and takes* GEORGE *by hands.*)

GEORGE (*holding up his hand*): Now then! (*Rises and moves to* C.)

GERDA: But it would. Think of the thrill of it!

SHOLTO (*rises, to* R.C.): We'd stop in Paris for a day or two —

GERDA: Just to do a little shopping, and go to some plays —

SHOLTO: Then the Orient Express!

> *One on either side of* GERGE.

GERDA (*excitedly*): The Orient Express! We get into it at about seven-thirty, and have dinner as we whizz through the suburbs —

SHOLTO: Then we come back and find our wagon-lits have been made up, so we sit in rather strained positions and play games —

GERDA: Clumps, and Being People in History! Lovely!

SHOLTO: You have to wake up for a minute in the middle of the night, because of the Swiss customs —

GERDA: Then in the morning – the very early morning – you peep out, and it's all mountains and valleys and rushing torrents and white, white snow as far as you can see —

GEORGE (*carried away*): Yes – yes – wonderful!

SHOLTO: Then the Simplon Tunnel, and Italy – Italy —

GERDA: We pass Lake Maggiore on the left-hand side – glorious clear blue water and mountains going straight out of it —

SHOLTO: And villas dotted over the hills like pink sweets in a green cake.

GEORGE: Shut up, both of you! I've seen it – I know it —

SHOLTO: Then Milan. We change at Milan.

GERDA: And there's two hours to wait, so we can drive about the town —

SHOLTO: In the gorgeous hot sun!

GERDA: We can send a wire to Mother from there to tell her what time to expect us —

SHOLTO: She'll be so excited —

GEORGE: Stop!! – Stop!! I tell you. (*Crosses down* L.)

Both follow GEORGE, L.

GERDA: Oh, Daddy darling, why not chuck all the honour and English gentleman stunts and come with us? It's worth trying.

SHOLTO (*crosses L.C. to behind* GERDA, *L.C.*): You've been divorced once; it's sure to be much easier a second time.

GEORGE (L.): It's no use — I shouldn't be happy — I've got to stick to my guns. I told Cicely on the day you came that, providing she behaved herself and didn't allow things to become blatant —

Enter PRISCILLA *and* SIBYL *from drawing-room.*

I would say nothing. I —

SIBYL: We're just going upstairs to tidy ourselves; Cicely says we'll have to be starting soon.

They go upstairs.

SHOLTO (L.C., *brightly*): Roddy isn't here yet — surely we shan't start without him?

PRISCILLA (*from landing*): Oh, he won't be long now. Anyhow, we must powder our noses.

Exeunt both, upstairs.

GEORGE *goes and sits on fender.*

GERDA (L.): Quick, Daddy! You've got to make up your mind. We'll help you in everything.

GEORGE (L., *quietly*): I have made up my mind. I'm going to stick to Cicely as long as she sticks to me — I must. It's not melodramatic self-sacrifice, it's just playing the game — though you may not see it in that light, it's true nevertheless.

SHOLTO (L.C.): Very well, then; if you intend to be as pig-headed as that, we shall have to be firm with you.

GERDA: And manage things in our own way.

Enter CICELY; *she comes to* C.

GEORGE (*alarmed*): Look here, what do you mean? I absolutely forbid you —

GERDA: It's no use trying to forbid us, Daddy darling; we're quite determined.

CICELY: George!

GERDA: Come, Sholto.

Both going up.

SHOLTO: All right.

Exeunt SHOLTO *and* GERDA *upstairs.*

CICELY (L.C.): I should be very much obliged, George, if you would ask your charming son and daughter to be a little more polite to me. They have been particularly rude this evening.

GEORGE (*by fender L., half laughing*): I notice that they both leave the room the moment you enter it.

CICELY: They're intolerable.

GEORGE (L.): Why are you always so prickly? – like a cactus-hedge.

CICELY (L.C.): I can see nothing amusing in calling your wife a cactus-hedge. Having placed me in an insufferable position, you —

GEORGE: If you're alluding to matrimony, dear, it's a trouble many better women have had to face.

CICELY: I don't think flippancy suits you.

GEORGE: Jennifer used to love me to be flippant.

CICELY: Need we talk about Jennifer? – is it quite good taste? (*Going up.*)

GEORGE: I only mentioned her in passing – she is now nothing but a memory.

CICELY (*turns down*): It's a pity you can't forget her.

GEORGE: The moment one forgets a memory it ceases to be a memory. I shall remember her always —

CICELY: I'm going upstairs. However charming Jennifer was in the flesh, as a topic of conversation she bores me (*She goes up towards stairs.*)

GEORGE (*follows* CICELY *up* R.C.): Don't go upstairs, Cicely. I'm sorry – honestly I am. I didn't mean to be irritating, but you were rather beastly about Sholto and Gerda, and that made me temporarily lose sight of my objective.

CICELY (*coming down to* GEORGE): What objective?

GEORGE: Oh, Cicely! (*Pause.*) Time was when we used to crouch together over the crackling logs and gaze on life in perfect unison. Let's try to get back.

CICELY: What on earth are you talking about?

GEORGE: I don't quite know. There are moments when I really

want to be sincere, and then all my facetiousness crops up and prevents me. I want to be sincere now; the crackling logs and gazing on life was all nonsense. What I really mean is this: let's stop being bitter and horrid to one another; it doesn't lead anywhere.

CICELY: Are you trying to apologise to me, George?

GEORGE: No, dear, but I will if you like. What shall I apologise for?

CICELY (*bitterly*): There are so many things. (*Crosses L. to settee.*)

GEORGE (*with a faint smile*): Oh, won't you meet me half-way, Cicely?

CICELY (*flaring up*): Why should I meet you half-way? You don't seem to realise that you've made me the laughing-stock of the county.

GEORGE: Nonsense! (*Drops down* R.)

CICELY: It isn't nonsense. What other woman would stand it? Those affected, artificial children of yours, always sniggering in corners and making inane remarks – they haven't attempted to learn anything about the life down here; they just laugh and giggle and talk about their mother. (*Sits on settee.*)

GEORGE (*hotly*): If you were nicer to them they wouldn't talk about their mother; you've ignored them and tried to snub them ever since they arrived. Isn't that rather asking for trouble?

CICELY: They ought never to have come at all.

GEORGE: Cicely – for the last time I ask you (*crosses to* L.C.) – let's stop dead now – and finish with all our bickering and beastliness. I mean it. We can't go on like this; we must pull ourselves together – make an effort.

CICELY: If you send Sholto and Gerda away, I'll think about it; but if you expect me to be nice and charming —

GEORGE (C., *losing control*): Well, I shall never expect you to be nice and charming – and I shall never ask them to go away. They shall come as often as they like, and stay as long as they like. I was preparing myself to do without them, but now I realise I couldn't. I couldn't ever, and I don't intend to try. (*Turns away up.*)

CICELY (*quietly*): I shall leave you, George.

GEORGE (C.): I shouldn't, if you don't like being the laughing-stock of the county.

CICELY (*bursting into tears of rage*): You've been horrible to me lately – all the time – you don't love me any more, and you let everyone see it.

GEORGE (C.): What steps have you taken lately towards making me love you? (*Laughs.*) Oh, this is all so stupid and useless! Tonight I made an effort to bury the hatchet, and you turned me down, as you always turn me down. We'd better go on as we are – cactus-hedges – so ornamental and so damned uncomfortable.

> *Exit* GEORGE, *to the dining-room.*
> CICELY *sits on sofa down stage, and twists her handkerchief into knots; she exudes fury at every pore.*
> *Enter* RODDY, *from front door C.; comes down.*

RODDY: Hallo, Cicely. What time are you all starting? Why, what's the matter?

CICELY: Nothing.

RODDY: Cicely, tell me.

CICELY: I tell you there's nothing.

RODDY: Why have you been crying, then?

CICELY: I have a headache and I'm generally depressed.

RODDY: Have you had a row with George?

CICELY: I wish you wouldn't say that. It – it sounds horrible.

RODDY (*doggedly*): Well, have you?

CICELY: Oh, Roddy, don't go on cross-examining me.

RODDY (*sits by her*): Now look here, Cicely; this is the last time I shall see you for months, and I won't have you unhappy without knowing the cause. I suppose you imagine that I'm not worthy of your confidence – that I haven't meant everything I've said —

CICELY: No, Roddy, no —

RODDY: Tell me – has George discovered about us?

CICELY: Yes.

RODDY: When? Tonight? – just now?

CICELY: No; a week ago.

RODDY: Why, in God's name, didn't you let me know?

CICELY: Oh, what was the use?

RODDY (*firmly*): This is the use – it means, you must come away
   with me – at once. You couldn't stay on here, with George
   knowing everything; it would be intolerable for you. I love
   you, Cicely; you know I do. I love you more than I've ever
   loved anyone before. (*She turns away.*) You've got to believe it.
   I want you – there's no sense in sticking to a man who no
   longer gives a damn for you – I love you, I love you, I love
   you! I feel I must go on saying it, over and over again, to try
   and convince you. I'll make you happy, gloriously happy.
   Don't turn me down, for God's sake! I can't go away without
   you now; I should go off my head longing for you, aching for
   you. Come with me, come with me. You must, you must . . .

CICELY (*suddenly*): Very well, I will come away with you. I hate
   George, I hate his children. I hate his house, I hate everything
   to do with him. How I've stood it for so long I can't imagine –
   his stupid jokes and what he thinks is a subtle sense of
   humour, the way he cringes – 'Don't let's be bitter and horrid
   any more' – what a manly choice of expressions! 'Bitter and
   horrid!' Oh, I tell you I hate him. If you want me, I'll go
   wherever you take me.

RODDY: Do you mean it? Do you honestly mean it?

CICELY (*rises, crosses to* C., *hysterically*): Yes, yes! can't you see I
   mean it? He can go back to his beastly Jennifer – Jennifer,
   Jennifer, Jennifer! I get nothing but Jennifer from morning till
   night. Well, I wish her joy of him, and dear Sholto and Gerda
   – 'such adorable young devils, with such adorable senses of
   humour!' Self-satisfied, odious little toads! I hate them and I
   hate George. Do you want me to come with you tomorrow?

RODDY: No – tonight, before you change your mind. (*Rises.*)

CICELY (*rather tremulous*): Do you really love me like that, Roddy?
   How wonderful of you!

RODDY: You know I do – now. (*Crosses to* CICELY.)

CICELY: What time does the boat sail tomorrow?

RODDY: Four-thirty from Liverpool. You'll have to see about a
   passport.

CICELY: Shall I have time?

RODDY: Yes, if you can get to London before tomorrow
   morning. We'll motor up tonight.

CICELY: How, without George finding out and trying to stop us?

RODDY: You'll have to pack a few things, won't you?

CICELY: Yes; it won't take a moment. Listen; meet me about two hours after we get to the ball, and motor me back here – I'll pick up my suitcase, leave a note for George, and we can go right away. Your stuff can be sent straight to Liverpool.

RODDY (*embracing her*): Oh, you're wonderful – wonderful!

CICELY (*struggling*): No, no, not now. Wait. George must know nothing until we've gone – oh, wait —

RODDY: Let them all come in – I don't care – I'm going to kiss you – now!

He kisses her passionately.

QUICK CURTAIN

Scene II

SCENE: *When the curtain rises, the stage is in darkness. The noise of a car is heard retreating.*

SHOLTO and GERDA enter and turn up lamp by staircase. There is still a certain amount of light from the fire. GERDA takes off her cloak and flings it over banisters; then sinks into armchair by table R., with a sigh.

GERDA (R.): What time is it?

SHOLTO (L.C., *looking at wrist-watch*): Half-past two. (*He takes off his coat.*) I expect that depressing orgy will go on until five or six. Thank heavens, the Brodies gave us a lift home.

GERDA: Yes, I couldn't have put up with another minute. (*Sits R.*) I suppose it was too much to hope that the county would be able to dance as well as ride.

SHOLTO (C.): I loved it all – the floral decorations and the nice jolly girls in pinks and blues and the heat and everyone treading on everyone else — Such a merry prank! (*Crosses L., to settee.*)

GERDA: I'm sorry you didn't have a rag, dear. I hoped you'd trip somebody up, or do something roguish like Donald Hake.

SHOLTO: Dear Donald Hake! Did you enjoy your dance with him?

GERDA: Awfully. His hands were like wet hot-water bottles.

SHOLTO: And your passionate waltz with Claud Eccles?

GERDA: That was sheer ecstasy, too. Have you ever danced with a threshing-machine?

SHOLTO: Not yet – but Bounding Julia's nearly as bad. Oh, I do wish we were in Alassio, at the Combattente.

GERDA (*rises, crosses to* C.): On a *festa* night —

SHOLTO (L.C.): With Tonio and Gianetta and Maria.

GERDA: And Giuseppe dressed as Pierrot, and all the confetti and everything— Sholto, let's go back.

SHOLTO: Not without Father.

GERDA (*dismally*): We could stop in Paris for a day or two —

SHOLTO (*equally dismal*): To do some shopping and go to some plays —

GERDA (*hopelessly*): Then – the Orient Express!

SHOLTO: Damn the Orient Express.

GERDA (R.C.): Oh, we've been fools. If only we'd never come at all, we shouldn't have wanted him – so much.

SHOLTO (L.C.): It will be absolutely miserable, that journey alone – after all we said this evening.

GERDA: I felt him trembling all the time – didn't you?

SHOLTO: Yes.

GERDA: And his face when he said about Mother's memory taunting him – I could have cried!

SHOLTO: Yes.

GERDA: You see, he wants to come back to us so desperately.

SHOLTO: If only it weren't for his beastly principles —

GERDA: He wouldn't be such a darling without them.

SHOLTO: No – I suppose not.

GERDA: But to think that his future happiness and Mother's and ours hangs on Cicely – it's miserable!

SHOLTO: I *did* hope she'd do something desperate tonight — After all, Roddy leaves England tomorrow!

GERDA (*crosses to* SHOLTO): Couldn't we force Cicely on board the boat as a cabin-boy, or something?

SHOLTO (C.): It's too late now. We've failed in our little mission. Let's go to bed before we burst into tears.

They take hands and go up the stairs.

GERDA (*taking up cloak*): All right. Turn out the light, dear — (*She yawns.*) Oh, I'm so tired!

SHOLTO (*switching off light*): Damn everything!

They go slowly upstairs in the firelight.

GERDA: I rather wish we hadn't put Priscilla up to Cicely and Roddy. She's sure to go and blurt it out to everyone; she's such an utter idiot.

SHOLTO: It doesn't make any odds – now. (*They just reach the top of the stairs when the noise of a car is heard. The headlamps shine right across the windows as it pulls up outside.*) Who can it be? Father?

GERDA: Go down and look through the window.

They both run down and look through the window.

SHOLTO (*excitedly*): It's Roddy!

GERDA: And Cicely – alone! Hide behind the curtains – quick!

SHOLTO goes up for coat, puts chair back. They conceal themselves behind curtains.

Enter CICELY and RODDY.

RODDY turns up lights.

CICELY: I've only got to get my motor-coat and hat – and the two bags —

RODDY (*following her upstairs*): What about the note?

CICELY: That's already written. I did it before I went out.

RODDY: You darling!

Exeunt both upstairs.

SHOLTO and GERDA come out of their hiding-place.

GERDA: What luck!

SHOLTO (*in a joyous whisper*): They're going to do it, after all. What luck! Oh, Gerda —

GERDA (*to* C.): Sshh! We mustn't let them hear us. I wouldn't disturb them for the world.

SHOLTO (*towards stairs*): This will clinch things finally – absolutely. He'll *have* to divorce her. . . .

GERDA (C.): And come back with us. . . . It's too, too wonderful Sholto darling – it's all going to be all right —

SHOLTO: They'll be down in a minute – we'd better get back. (*Crosses to window.*)

GERDA: Yes.

They are just about to re-conceal themselves when there is the noise of another car drawing up outside.

SHOLTO (*in anguish, looking through window*): My hat! It's Father!

GERDA: And Priscilla! What are we to do? Quick! they'll spoil everything —

SHOLTO (*grimly*): That's what they've come for. Priscilla's found out, and warned him – the stupid, blundering little fool!

GERDA (*frantically*): Oh, quick, quick! – what are we to do? (*Up.*) What are we to do? Cicely and Roddy – they're coming down —

SHOLTO: Hide – don't come out till it's absolutely necessary.

They hide behind curtains again. There is the noise of outer hall door opening.

Re-enter CICELY, *in travelling coat and hat, followed by* RODDY *with two bags. As they reach the bottom of the stairs* PRISCILLA *and* GEORGE *enter.*

RODDY *stops by stairs,* CICELY R.C. *up.*

PRISCILLA (*thoroughly in the picture, rushing forward*): Oh, Cicely, Cicely – thank God we came in time! (GEORGE *moves to top of settee.*) Stop, stop! You mustn't do this fearful thing – you'll break George's heart! He loves you, I love you, we all love you — Look before you leap – I mean, don't leap – I mean —

CICELY (R.C.): Priscilla – how dare you!

GEORGE (L.; *firmly*): Be quiet, Mrs Hartleberry. Cicely, what does this mean? (*Crosses to* CICELY, R.C.)

PRISCILLA (*turns to* GEORGE, *hysterically*): Don't you see? – It's what I told you – we came in the nick of time. Cicely, think of your honour, your good name — (*She bursts into tears; moves up* L.C.)

GEORGE: Please, Mrs Hartleberry, will you calm yourself. Cicely, I should like an explanation.

CICELY (*handing him a note*): Here's the explanation – there's nothing to say. I'm quite determined.

GEORGE (*taking it and tearing it neatly across*): The farewell note – thank you, Cicely. How dramatic! Roddy, will you please go. I wish to talk to my wife.

RODDY (R.C.): Not without Cicely. (*Looking at* CICELY.)

CICELY: There's nothing to talk about – my mind is quite made up.

GEORGE: On the contrary, there are several things to discuss. Roddy, I wish to talk to Cicely privately.

CICELY: Roddy, stay, please. You'd better say whatever you have to say quickly, George; we haven't very much time.

GEORGE: Very well. You wish to leave me for Roddy – openly?

CICELY (C., *defiantly*): Yes.

GEORGE (L.): I forbid it.

CICELY: You can't prevent it.

PRISCILLA (*by settee*): Oh, Cicely, how can you? It's wicked – it's — (*She sobs and comes round to front of settee.*)

GEORGE: Do you realise what you are doing? You're chucking home, position —

PRISCILLA: Your honour, your good name —

CICELY: I love Roddy, and I'm going away with him. I wish you'd put an end to this scene, George, and let us go.

GEORGE: You're going abroad to restricted Colonial society, with a man to whom you are not married. Can't you imagine what hell it will be? You'll be cut – universally – you won't like being cut, Cicely. Why don't you pause and think? You don't love Roddy really, you know.

CICELY: I do.

GEORGE: No, you don't love anyone. You're taking this step because you're rather tired of me, and in a general bad temper over everything. Those are not very good reasons for an elopement.

RODDY (R., *hotly*): You're wrong – we've loved each other for months – that is, at least, we've —

GEORGE: Will you please let me speak?

118

CICELY: This is all useless, anyhow – can't you see it is? Nothing you say will make any difference.

GEORGE: Cicely – once and for all, don't make this stupid blunder. Stay with me – have one more try to settle down contentedly. I'll help all I can, I promise – then, if it really is a failure, in spite of our united efforts, we'll arrange things quietly, without scandal. I'll let you divorce me, or —

CICELY (*rather shaken*): George, it's very magnanimous of you — I don't know that I —

RODDY (*anxiously*): Cicely!

CICELY (*putting her hand to her head*): Don't Roddy – let me think. I — (*Crosses down* R.C.)

> SHOLTO *and* GERDA *simultaneously burst from behind the curtains and more or less fling themselves upon* CICELY.

GERDA: Oh, Stepmother! Oh, Stepmother!

> GEORGE *goes up.*

SHOLTO (*dramatically*): Don't go, don't go, dear Stepmother Cicely! Don't go —

GERDA: We want you with us – we're going to stay here always —

SHOLTO: We can have such happy, happy times together —

> PRISCILLA *moves up to the back.*

GERDA: Just you and Daddy and us.

SHOLTO: Sometimes Mother can come and stay with us, too.

CICELY (*shaking with fury*): This is intolerable – intolerable! Don't speak to me, any of you – I hate you – I hate you all. (*Goes up* C.) I've finished with you, George, for ever – do you hear? – absolutely! I never want to see you again. Come, Roddy. (*Going.*)

> GEORGE *makes a last effort.*

PRISCILLA (*rushing after* CICELY *and clutching her*): Cicely, Cicely! For God's sake, stop! Their mother ran away with a Count and drinks like a fish! Oh dear, oh dear!

> CICELY *shakes her off, and goes out with* RODDY.
> PRISCILLA *staggers into* GEORGE'S *arms, sobbing. He tries vainly to rid himself of her.*

SHOLTO (*suddenly*): Great Scott! They've forgotten the bags! After them – quick —!

> SHOLTO *and* GERDA *each snatch up a bag and rush off the stage.*

CURTAIN

ACT III

SCENE: *The living-room of* MRS BRENT'S *villa in Alassio, Italy.*
When the curtain rises, the stage is in semi-darkness; the outline
of the room can be vaguely distinguished in the gloom. Two very
large arches at the back, with green shutters down over them.
  MARIA *enters quickly, and commences to pull up the shutters.*
As she does so, the room is flooded with hot sunlight. It becomes
obvious that the walls are painted salmon-colour and there are
various coloured cushions and rugs lying about. There is a grand
piano and a huge bureau writing-desk. On the writing-desk there
are two big frames containing photographs of CICELY *and*
GEORGE *respectively. The writing-desk is littered with papers; a*
typewriter stands on the floor beside it. The whole room has a
'lived-in' atmosphere; colours are jumbled together irrespective of
what goes with which, but the result is thoroughly pleasing and
comfortable. There is a straight line of terrace outside, also painted
salmon-pink; beyond this can be seen the tops of two or three
cypresses, and then deep-blue sky and sea.
  As MARIA *lets the sunlight into the room,* JENNIFER *sits up on*
the couch R., on which she had been resting. She is a chic, golden-
haired woman, dressed in a scarlet overall, with a belt. MARIA
comes down to settee.

JENNIFER: What time is it, Maria?
MARIA: Five minutes past three, Signora.
JENNIFER: I thought I told you not to disturb me until four?
MARIA: Si, Signora, but Signor Walkin has just arrived. (*She*
  sniggers.) He has with him a large bunch of flowers.
JENNIFER: How typical! Wait a moment, Maria; I suppose I must
  see him. Fancy clambering up that steep hill so soon after
  lunch! Americans have no repose. Give me my bag. It's on my
  desk.
MARIA (*crosses to desk L.*): Si, Signora.

MARIA, *in taking bag from desk, knocks the photograph of* CICELY *on to the floor.*

JENNIFER: That is the third time within the last week that you have knocked down my late husband's second wife's photograph.

MARIA *picks it up and scrutinises it.*

MARIA (*disgustedly*): It is not broken. (*She bangs it down on desk.*)

JENNIFER: You did it on purpose!

MARIA (*hotly*): She is a cow. I know it.

JENNIFER (*sharply*): Maria! – that is not the way to speak – anyhow, in English. If you must be disrespectful, keep to Italian.

MARIA (*in Italian*): Vacca! Figlia di molte Vacce!

JENNIFER: Maria that's enough. Give me my bag at once.

MARIA *gives her her bag, and then returns to desk and gazes at* GEORGE'S *photograph.*

MARIA: He very beautiful man!

JENNIFER (*powdering her nose*): No, Maria; boundless charm, but *not* beautiful.

MARIA (*shaking her head sorrowfully*): Dio mio, it is sad!

JENNIFER: Go away, Maria; you are getting on my nerves.

MARIA: Si, Signora.

JENNIFER (*rising and patting her hair into place before glass*): Show Mr Walkin in.

MARIA: Si, Signora. (*Crosses R.*)

JENNIFER (*crosses to fireplace L.*): You speak English very well now, Maria, but I do wish you'd remember to say 'Very good' when I ask you to do anything. English butlers always say it; it gives one a nice feeling of security.

MARIA: Ver' good, Signora.

JENNIFER: That's right.

MARIA *goes out, and in a moment returns.*

MARIA (*announcing*): Mister Walkin.

Enter HIRAM J. WALKIN. *He is a prosperous, stout man of about fifty. He goes C.*

HIRAM (*to C.*): Mrs Brent, please forgive me for coming up so early, but I had to bring you these. (*He offers her a large bunch of orchids.*)

JENNIFER (*to* C.): How perfectly delightful of you. Sit down and talk to me. (*To* MARIA.) Maria, fetch me that tall blue vase from my bedroom – no; take these and put them into it – carefully, with a nice lot of water. (R.C.)

HIRAM *goes up, puts down hat at the back.*

MARIA (*taking them*): Ver' good, Signora.

JENNIFER (*smiling at* HIRAM): Wait – I think I'd rather like to wear one. (*She detaches one from the bunch.*)

HIRAM *beams with delight.*

HIRAM: I knew that your youngsters are coming back today.

JENNIFER: Yes, isn't it splendid? I've missed them terribly.

HIRAM: I'm looking forward to making their acquaintance. I just love children.

JENNIFER (*raising her eyebrows*): Children? – Well – er – you won't be disappointed if they don't cluster round your knee, will you? (*Crosses* L.C.) I haven't brought them up to cluster.

HIRAM: You bet I shan't! I like kids to be independent.

JENNIFER: That's right. You'll be pleased.

HIRAM: Plucky little devils, going all that way by themselves.

JENNIFER: I feel I ought to tell you, Mr Walkin, that ... (*She smiles.*) Well, perhaps after all, it isn't necessary – you'll see for yourself. Would you like anything cool to drink? Maria is so good at mixing things up. (*Crosses, sits at desk.*)

HIRAM: No, thanks. I – er – knew your children were returning today.

JENNIFER (*brightly*): Yes – I know you knew.

HIRAM: And I came up here specially – because —

JENNIFER: Now don't tell me it's the same old purpose in a different disguise. My last answer was quite final.

HIRAM: Mrs Brent – by the way, you let me call you Jennifer last time.

JENNIFER: Yes, I was wondering why you were being so formal with me today. Call me anything you like – that is, I mean, anything in reason.

HIRAM: And you said you'd call me – Hiram.

JENNIFER (*firmly*): Never – never! If I were married to you eighteen times, I should never call you Hiram. As a name I dislike it intensely. But this is mere trifling —

HIRAM: I guess I've got to propose to you again, Jennifer.

JENNIFER (*wearily*): Go on, then.

HIRAM (*sits*): Will you marry me?

JENNIFER (*calmly*): Yes.

HIRAM (*flabbergasted*): What! You will? You say yes?

JENNIFER (*with a sigh*): Yes.

HIRAM: But you said your last answer was quite final.

JENNIFER: So it was at the time, but I've been thinking things over since then . . .

HIRAM: You are tantalising! (*Rises.*) I —

JENNIFER (*warding him off*): Now wait a moment. This ought by rights to be a great moment in both our lives; let's endeavour to keep calm in it. Sit down again.

HIRAM: But – but – you've bowled me over – you've —

JENNIFER: All the more reason for you to sit down. (*He sits.*) I have a lot to say to you. You have been a very persistent wooer, Mr – Walkin.

HIRAM (*appealingly*): Hiram!

JENNIFER (*firmly*): Never. We'll think of a name for you afterwards. I said you have been a very persistent wooer, and though you haven't exactly swept me off my feet, you certainly have worn me down. I have said yes, but before we come to any definite arrangement, there are several facts that will have to be faced.

HIRAM (*eagerly*): Look here, I don't care how many facts there are, I —

JENNIFER: If you don't listen to me quietly, I shall go and have a bath.

HIRAM: Proceed.

JENNIFER: Well, to begin with, I don't love you – any more than you love me —

HIRAM (*protesting*): Here – I guess I've —

JENNIFER (*holding up her hand*): Please let me go on. You were going to protest undying affection and heart-felt passion — Well, that's all rubbish. We are both getting too old for either of those things. Don't think I'm unable to see your point in wanting to marry me. I can see it perfectly. I'm quite nice to look at, something of a celebrity, very amusing as a companion, and you *think* you're in love with me —

HIRAM: I *am* in love with you.

JENNIFER: Well, we'll let that pass for a moment. The fact remains – that I'm not in the least in love with you. (*He rises.*) I know it's a dreadful habit being perfectly frank, but occasionally it becomes necessary. I like you – enormously — (*He sits again.*) You're altogether a charming person, and I'm willing to marry you, for many reasons.

HIRAM: It will be springing a grand surprise on the youngsters.

JENNIFER: They're one of the reasons. I've often felt that there should be a man in the background to help and advise them – that's why I sent them over to England to see their father; not that he would be much use – he gets so dreadfully muddled – but still . . . You would be good for Sholto; having been wildly ambitious all your life, you might be able to inspire him with some of it. And it would be so nice for them to live in your house; it's so much nearer the sea, and they'd be able to run straight out, with mackintoshes over their bathing-dresses – that's another of the reasons.

HIRAM: You're a wonderful woman! —

JENNIFER (*ignoring his interruption*): Also, they'll probably want to marry, or emigrate, or something tiresome, and I should be left alone – I hate being alone at any time; growing old is a dreary enough performance even when one is surrounded by grandchildren, and kindly relatives, and pattering feet —

HIRAM: I was thinking of that, too.

JENNIFER: Oh well! you need never want for pattering feet. I'm sure that there are lots of people who'd be charmed to marry you, apart from me altogether. You're a very rich man, you know —

HIRAM: I had noticed it.

JENNIFER: I feel more comfortable now that I have told you some of my reasons. There are lots of others, but I shall probably remember them later. – Now, let's think of an attractive name for you.

HIRAM: You know, I don't quite get you. You're sometimes very
    difficult to understand. – Are you laughing at me?

JENNIFER: My dear man, of course not. Why should I?

HIRAM: Oh, I don't know – but you were so very determined
    not to marry me last week, and now you say you will because
    your children will be able to run out of my house with
    mackintoshes over their bathing-dresses!

JENNIFER: If you're regretting your proposal, I'll release you
    without the slightest bitterness – I do see your point of
    view —

HIRAM: See here! cut that, now! I'm not backing out — (*Rises.*)

JENNIFER (*rises*): No, but I do – really. I ought either to have
    become terribly dignified when you asked me, and said, 'No; I
    live only for my work and my little ones!' or else I should have
    yielded blushingly to your embraces, and said, 'I'm so, so tired
    of living alone, with only Sholto and Gerda and Maria and the
    cook and my secretary and the dog. Take me; I am yours.'

HIRAM: Now you're laughing again! (*Sits.*)

JENNIFER (*sits*): I know it's dreadfully tiresome of me, but you'll
    soon get used to it. I have never been able to take anything
    seriously after eleven o'clock in the morning.

HIRAM: Are you going to tell Sholto and Gerda directly they
    arrive?

JENNIFER: Of course. They *will* be so surprised, the darlings!

>   *Enter* MARIA, *hurriedly.*

MARIA: Signora, the carriage is coming up the hill – you told me
    to let you know at once —

JENNIFER: It can't be! It's hours too early.

MARIA: But si, Signora; I see them from the terrace.

JENNIFER (*goes to window* L.): It is, it is! They'll probably get out
    at the bottom gate and walk up. You'd better go and help with
    the luggage.

MARIA: Si, Signora.

JENNIFER (*whispering*): Very good.

MARIA (*obediently*): Ver' good.

>   *Exit* MARIA.

JENNIFER: Isn't Maria attractive? She has no morals and many
    more children than are usual for a single woman. You'd better

be waiting in another room, like the lovers in tales of the *Decameron*, and I'll call you out. You can hide in the hall cupboard, if you like.

HIRAM: Why should I hide?

JENNIFER: Oh, of course there's no real necessity, but it's so much more amusing to be a little furtive. – They'll probably insist on interviewing you – alone – but don't let them see you're frightened, and all will be well.

HIRAM: I guess they won't scare me.

JENNIFER: Don't be too sure. They once upset the English parson so much when he came to call that he fell into the goldfish-pond from sheer nervousness. A lot of the goldfish died, too; it was most vexing. Now you go into the dining-room while I break the news and get the first joys of reunion over – then I'll call you.

HIRAM: Would you rather I went away, and came back later?

JENNIFER: Of course not. It will be much more dramatic if I can suddenly produce you. Go along, now —

HIRAM: All right. (*He advances towards her.*) You've made me a darned happy man.

JENNIFER: I *am* so glad. (*She proffers her cheek, which he kisses.*) You'll find some biscuits in a tin box on the sideboard.

> *She pushes him out of the room. She goes out on to the terrace and waves her handkerchief.*

JENNIFER (*calling*): Don't run so fast, darlings; you won't have any breath left. (*Comes back into the room.*)

> *Enter* SHOLTO *and* GERDA, *a little breathlessly, window R. They stand transfixed for a moment.*

SHOLTO (*dramatically*): Mother, Mother! – little Mother!

GERDA (*ecstatically*): Weep no more, tiny Mother – we have come home!

JENNIFER (C., *with arms outstretched*): Children, children! Thank God – my babes, at last!

> *They rush into her arms.*

SHOLTO (*disentangling himself*): That's all right. How are you, darling?

JENNIFER: Frightfully well, but I've missed you *dreadfully!* (*They *all sit on settee* R.) Would you like something to drink? Maria's been awfully clever lately with lemons and oranges and cloves and soda-water all mixed up. It sounds filthy, I know, but it isn't really.

GERDA: We'll have some in a minute – she's dragging our luggage up the hill, at the moment, with Giuseppe.

SHOLTO (*sinking back*): Whew! It's hot!

JENNIFER: Tell me at once – how was George? and did you like him?

GERDA: Of course we did. He's a darling.

JENNIFER: And did he wear a pink coat when he was hunting? – I should love to see George in a pink coat!

SHOLTO: He looked rather like a musical comedy in it.

JENNIFER: He wasn't born for the hunting world; he had it thrust upon him. Did you go to the meets and things?

SHOLTO: I should just think we did! We used to sit in a dog-cart on very cold mornings, with pinched, blue faces, and watch hearty women leaping about on horses – it was awful!

GERDA: And we'd drink lukewarm soup out of a Thermos flask, wrap the rug more tightly round our legs and think of the terrace here, in the hot sunlight, with the cypresses and flowers —

SHOLTO: And you reading bits of things out loud to us — By the way, we must hear what you've done with your new book.

JENNIFER: Yes, I've been wanting your help badly – I'm not a bit satisfied with it.

GERDA: Read it now!

JENNIFER: No, I simply couldn't, on your first day back, – there are so many springs of news bubbling up inside all three of us – you'd be sure to stop me in the middle by suddenly remembering something really thrilling that couldn't wait to be told!

GERDA: Yes, we probably should. (*She puts her arms round* JENNIFER's *neck.*) You are a darling lamb, Mother! – What a fool Daddy was.

SHOLTO: Shut up, Gerda! That was most tactless.

GERDA (*wistfully*): No, but it would have been so lovely if Daddy's second marriage had turned out a failure, and he'd come back to you, and we were all together again. (*She sighs.*) We did try so hard to pull it off.

JENNIFER: Yes, I thought you would. But you see the fact of his being so happy and contented proves that he was right after all.

GERDA: Yes, I suppose so.

SHOLTO: If only Stepmother Cicely hadn't been so nice!

JENNIFER (*without enthusiasm*): I'm glad you liked her so much.

GERDA: We adored her. We used to go for long picnics together.

JENNIFER: From what you said just now, I should have thought it was rather cold for picnicking.

SHOLTO (*with a warning glance at* GERDA): Not at all. We used to wear fur coats, and when we got back we played hide-and-seek all over the house.

GERDA (*reminiscently*): Sholto and I used to hide behind the curtains, and she and Roddy Masters —

SHOLTO: Such a dear!

JENNIFER (*rather irritably, releasing herself from* GERDA'*s clutch*): Don't, Gerda – you're tickling the back of my neck.

SHOLTO (*with a look of triumph at* GERDA): Now we've annoyed her – on our first day back, too! We're beasts.

GERDA: Utter beasts!

JENNIFER (*patting their backs*): No, no; you're nothing of the sort. But – somehow – it's rather a shock – Cicely being so pleasant.

SHOLTO (*with gentle reproof*): It's a little dog-in-the-manger of you not to want her to be pleasant.

JENNIFER: Oh, but I do – I'm awfully glad, really, for George's sake. I've wondered so often during the years you've been growing up – whether our parting like that wasn't a very stupid and bitter mistake – but now, you see, I needn't have wondered at all. He's happy, and I've got you – so everything was for the best, wasn't it?

SHOLTO: Yes, Mother – everything.

JENNIFER (*brightly, brushing away her memories*): And everything's going to be still more for the best.

GERDA: How do you mean, Mummie?

JENNIFER: I've got a surprise for you.

SHOLTO: We've got a *lovely* surprise for you!

JENNIFER: Not such a big one as mine!

SHOLTO: I bet you it is!

JENNIFER: Oh, but, my dears —

SHOLTO: Well, we'll tell you ours first.

JENNIFER: You don't do anything of the sort – I'll tell you mine first. You *will* laugh!

SHOLTO: Look here, we'd better toss for it. (*Takes a coin from his pocket.*) Come on, Mother; you call. (*He tosses it.*)

JENNIFER (*eagerly*): Heads!

SHOLTO: Damn! Heads it is.

GERDA: Go on, darling.

JENNIFER: Well, I give you one guess.

SHOLTO: No, there's no time for guessing – you must tell us.

JENNIFER: Well, it's this – I was a little doubtful as to whether it was a wise step or not, but you've both convinced me that I'm right. Prepare yourselves – I'm going to marry again!

SHOLTO
GERDA } (*aghast*): You're what!!

JENNIFER: I knew it would be a bit of a shock – but he's really quite a dear, and so rich. He made his money out of putting soft roes in tins, or something – so resourceful.

SHOLTO: But, Mother, it's – it's impossible – you simply can't!

GERDA (*kicking him furtively*): Nonsense! Why not? *I* think it's thrilling. And *what* a surprise! Where is he, Mother?

JENNIFER: In the dining-room, having biscuits – you know, those nice crackly ones you like so much.

> GERDA *and* SHOLTO *rise.*

GERDA: We must see him at once.

JENNIFER (*relieved*): Of course you shall. I am so glad you've taken it so well. I was a little frightened of telling you – but, you see, he has that lovely villa just beyond the Convent garden – practically on the beach. Think how convenient it will be —

SHOLTO (*dolefully*): It will be lovely.

JENNIFER: He honestly is quite devoted to me, and I'm sure, if only you're both a little tolerant, you'll grow very fond of him. He's not unlike your Uncle Bob in appearance, but of course with a much stronger face.

SHOLTO: Uncle Bob was a complete dolt!

JENNIFER: Sshh, Sholto! Your Uncle Bob may have been a little stupid, but God knows he paid for it when he married your Auntie Clara.

GERDA: All this is beside the point, Mother.

JENNIFER: Nothing of the sort. I want to convince you, before you see him, that I really am doing a sensible thing in agreeing to marry him. It will mean lots and lots of money to do exactly what we like with – we shall be able to travel all over the place – and you know how we've always longed to go to China and Tibet and see all the monasteries and things. We shall be able to indulge all our wildest dreams; and he's got quite a sense of humour, too – I think – anyhow, it will be fun digging for it – and above everything else he really *is* rather nice. I expect it's because he's so emphatically *not* one of the best American families!

SHOLTO: Yes, but, Mother —

JENNIFER: And he told me the most divine things about Chicago. I never dreamt it was such a sweet place – what with the skyscrapers and soda-fountains – like the Palace of Versailles —

GERDA: Those were wine fountains, Mother —

JENNIFER: Well, you know you don't like wine very much – soda'll be ever so much nicer —

GERDA (*to* JENNIFER): You'll let us interview him alone, Mummie, won't you?

JENNIFER: Yes, if you like; but —

SHOLTO: You see, we feel a little responsible for you.

JENNIFER: Tell me your surprise first.

GERDA (*airily*): Oh no, ours will wait – it's not nearly so exciting as yours.

JENNIFER (*apprehensively*): You *will* be nice to him, won't you?

SHOLTO: We'll be charm personified. Send him in, Mother.

Both, on either side of her, take her hands.

JENNIFER: Now? But we've hardly talked about anything – I'm sure he won't mind waiting a little longer.

GERDA: No; we can talk our heads off afterwards – we must get this over first; see what his intentions are.

JENNIFER: Dear old darlings! (*Rises; kisses them both.*) I'll go and fetch him. Call me when you've finished cross-examining him. (*Crosses* R.)

SHOLTO: All right.

JENNIFER (*at door*): I think he imagines you're about twelve years old. Let him down lightly.

> JENNIFER *goes out.*
>> SHOLTO *and* GERDA *look at one another in horror.*

SHOLTO: What are we to do?

GERDA (L.C., *frantically*): This is frightful – frightful! Let me think . . . (*Crosses to* C.)

SHOLTO (L.C.): I suppose we couldn't make him drunk – like David Garrick —?

GERDA: We haven't time —

SHOLTO (*clutching his head; throws himself on couch*): This is appalling!

GERDA (*pacing up and down in anguish. At desk*): Oh dear, oh dear —!

SHOLTO: We must terrify him – (*to* C.) lie to him – somehow —

GERDA: I know! (*Both down.*) Dreadful story about Father – follow my lead, and try not to overdo it.

> *The door rattles.*

SHOLTO: All right – look out —

> *Enter* HIRAM, *very sure of himself. He sees the children, and gasps.*

HIRAM (R.): Good God!

SHOLTO (R.C.; *to* HIRAM): Good afternoon.

GERDA (C.; *to* HIRAM): How do you do?

HIRAM: But, see here, I – you're not — (*Looking round, goes across to between them.*)

SHOLTO: I'm afraid we are.

HIRAM (*recovering himself*): I guess you're much, much older than I expected.

GERDA (*politely*): Are we?

HIRAM: Your mother's a great little woman.

SHOLTO (R.): Isn't she?

HIRAM (*weakly*): Yes – she sure is. (*There is a pause.*) She told you that I – we – we're going to be married?

GERDA (C.): Yes. Ah! (*Sigh.*)

HIRAM *looks from one to the other.*

SHOLTO: Oh! (*Sighs.*)

HIRAM (R.C.): Well – what do you say to it?

GERDA (*firmly*): Close the door, Sholto.

SHOLTO *obeys in silence.* HIRAM *begins to fidget.*

HIRAM: See here, you know, I — (*Crosses R., after* SHOLTO.)

GERDA (*stops him*): It's all right, Mr — Mother never told us your name.

HIRAM: Walkin. Hiram J. Walkin.

GERDA: Thank you. I should like to tell you, Mr Walkin, how delighted we are that this has happened. (*She smiles sadly.*)

HIRAM: Delighted! I thought you seemed a bit depressed about it.

GERDA (*seriously*): We have almost prayed for this moment – haven't we, Sholto?

SHOLTO (R.): Yes – almost.

GERDA (C.): Our mother —

SHOLTO (*mechanically*): God help her?

GERDA: Our mother – we've got to tell you this, Mr Walkin.

HIRAM (R.C.): See here, are you two trying to put something over on me?

SHOLTO (*reprovingly*): We should never do that, even if we knew what it meant.

GERDA: You must listen attentively to what we have to say. It's very upsetting, but somehow I feel that you have strength of mind, and that I can trust you.

SHOLTO: We can both trust you.

GERDA: Sholto and I have felt it our duty always to tell the real truth to all the people who have wanted to marry our mother; but, thank heaven, something tells me that you won't be like the others, and – run away!

HIRAM: What are you getting at?

GERDA: Mother told you that she divorced Father?

HIRAM: She did.

GERDA (*impressively*): Well, it's not true!

HIRAM: Not true? But – why – what do you mean?

GERDA: Our father – (*her voice breaks*) – our father was put into a lunatic asylum eight years ago.

HIRAM (*astounded*): What!! (*Drops in settee, R.C.*)

SHOLTO: Mother pretends she divorced him – she carried her head high in spite of all the shame and horror she had had to endure – gallant, gallant little woman —

HIRAM (*incredulously*): Lunatic asylum! But I —

GERDA (*sits on settee. Gently*): Now, Mr Walkin, why should we try to tell lies to you? (SHOLTO *sits.*) You will be able to take care of Mother; you will be able to comfort her when she has these uncontrollable fits of depression, which we have endured, willingly, but for so long —

HIRAM (*still distrustful*): But it's incredible! I mean to say —

GERDA: Lots of frightful things that happen are incredible.

SHOLTO: Father used to be so gay, so merry – and now — (*He turns away.*)

GERDA: Now —! (*She turns away.*)

SHOLTO (*brokenly*): Now he eats the buttons off padded chairs!

　　　　HIRAM *looks at* SHOLTO.

GERDA (*sharply*): Sholto, pull yourself together! There's no need to harrow poor Mr Walkin with these depressing details. He will have enough to bear, God knows!

SHOLTO: The most fearful thing of all is that it has affected Mother.

HIRAM: How do you mean?

GERDA (*frowning at* SHOLTO): Not much, of course – just the teeniest little bit. She just says rather odd things now and then. You've probably noticed?

HIRAM: You mean she's a bit dippy?

GERDA (*pained*): Mr Walkin, you are a frank, outspoken man, I know – but not – not – dippy!

HIRAM: Well, then, mentally deranged. (*Rises, crosses L.C.*)

GERDA (*on settee*): No, no – not quite. (*Bursts into tears.*) We had to tell you this, we had to – don't you understand? We love our mother; we want her to have help and protection; we're so desperately tired! You could take her (*rises*), and we should have no more of this awful sense of responsibility. You're not the sort of man to be bound down by convention; and no one need ever know you were a – a – bigamist. (*Working to L. to* HIRAM.)

SHOLTO: It breaks our hearts sometimes to hear Mother talk of Father – quite happily and brightly, as though nothing were wrong with him. Occasionally, you know, I believe she almost succeeds in convincing herself. We went to England hoping against hope that he would be better – but no; he was just the same.

GERDA: There were some new chairs – that's all.

HIRAM *looks at her.*

HIRAM (*drops down*): Where is this – asylum?

SHOLTO (*glibly*): Just near Guildford – such pretty surroundings.

HIRAM: And your father's there now?

GERDA: Yes, Mr Walkin.

SHOLTO (*glancing at his wrist-watch*): He's probably just having his tea – unbreakable crockery, of course.

GERDA: He cried dreadfully when we left him, didn't he, Sholto?

SHOLTO: Dreadfully. He said, 'Don't go, don't go!' It was most harrowing.

GERDA: I can hardly bear to think of it.

HIRAM: And you say there's no chance of his getting well?

Enter GEORGE, window R., back.

GERDA: None! (*Dabs her eyes.*) Oh, Mr Walkin!

SHOLTO (*with the calmness of despair*): None. I doubt if we shall ever see him again.

GEORGE *starts on seeing HIRAM.*

GEORGE: Oh! Sholto, Gerda – have you —

SHOLTO (*crosses to GEORGE up R., with great presence of mind*): Why, it's Mr Peasemarsh!

GERDA (*crosses to GEORGE up R., shaking him warmly by the hand*): So it is! After all this long time!

SHOLTO: We *are* so glad to see you. How's Mrs Peasemarsh?

GERDA: Sholto, you forget! Mrs Peasemarsh was burnt to death last Tuesday week.

SHOLTO: Oh, I'm so frightfully sorry – you must try not to think about it. Let me introduce you to Mr Walkin. Mr Peasemarsh.

HIRAM (*advancing*): Pleased to meet you, Mr Peasemarsh.

GEORGE (*crosses to L., dazed*): How do you do? I'm afraid I don't quite understand – I —

GERDA (*nudging hm*): We'll explain later.

HIRAM (L., *suspiciously*): Explain what later?

GERDA (L.C., *hurriedly*): About you being here, Mr Walkin. Mr Peasemarsh is naturally surprised.

HIRAM (*irately*): In heaven's name, why?

GERDA (*desperately*): Because of Mother's vow. (*Gently.*) Didn't we tell you about Mother's vow?

HIRAM: You did *not*.

GERDA: Well, perhaps you'd better explain, Sholto, while I talk to Fath – Mr Peasemarsh.

HIRAM: I don't want any more explained to me. I —

SHOLTO (*crosses to L., quickly*): Oh, but you must. You see, it was like this – when Mr Peasemarsh was a little boy, he and Mother used to play together, and one day, when they were playing at – at — What were they playing at, Gerda?

GERDA (*crosses to L.C., promptly*): Dances of all nations. (HIRAM, L. GEORGE *crosses* R.) And Mother tripped over the Stars and Stripes and hurt herself very much; so she made a vow never to let an American cross her threshold —

GEORGE (R.C., *unexpectedly*): I should have thought she was too young to have a threshold.

SHOLTO: Please don't interrupt, Mr Peasemarsh. We're trying to make things clear to Mr Walkin.

HIRAM: Clear! Good God!!

GERDA: Sshh! Now, will you listen? —

HIRAM (*loudly*): No, I will not listen. (*Crosses to* C.) You've both been joshing me all along, and I've had about enough of it —

SHOLTO: But, Mr Walkin —

HIRAM: Don't lie to me any more. Do you think I'm half-witted? Do you imagine that I can't see you're trying to get rid of me? If you don't want me to marry your mother, why the hell couldn't you say so?

GEORGE (*sharply*): What!!

GERDA: There now! – you've upset Mr Peasemarsh.

GEORGE (*losing control*): My name is *not* Peasemarsh!!!

> GERDA *and* SHOLTO *go up to* GEORGE *and surround him.*
> *Enter* MARIA. *She pauses for a moment, looks from* GEORGE *to the photograph on desk, then back again. Then, with a shrill cry of*

recognition, she rushes at him and, clasping his hands, covers them with kisses.

HIRAM *moves to* L.

MARIA (*ecstatically*): Il Pedrone – Il Pedrone – Il Pedrone! Sia Tornato – l'ho sognato sta sera – Madonna mia adesso tutto stara benissimo! Porta la felicita alla Signora – Oh, signor, signor, che miracolo! Dio mio!

SHOLTO: Stai zita, Maria, stai zita!

Everybody proceeds to talk at the top of their voices – the noise is deafening.

GERDA: Please, Mr Walkin, don't be cross. Come back in about an hour, and we'll explain everything properly, and you'll understand perfectly why we've been behaving like this. It —

GEORGE: I should very much like to know what you meant just now, sir, when you said — I come here, and a perfect stranger suddenly announces that he is intending to marry my wife —

SHOLTO: It's all quite simple, if you'll only listen to reason. Our mother is a most peculiar woman, and she has always —

HIRAM: I guess you're all trying to put something over on me, and I should like you to know that I'm not the sort of man to be joshed up hill and down dale by a set of —

MARIA: Dio grazia – Dio grazia – Dio grazia!!!

Enter JENNIFER.

JENNIFER: I never heard such a noise! What are you all shouting about? *George!!!*

GEORGE: Jennifer!

SHOLTO: That's done it!

JENNIFER: This is infamous!

HIRAM (*ominously*): I'm beginning to see things a bit more clearly now.

GERDA
SHOLTO } (*to* HIRAM, *together*): If you'll only let us explain —

HIRAM: God forbid!

GEORGE (*oblivious of all but* JENNIFER): Jennifer – I've come back.

JENNIFER: That would be obvious to the meanest intelligence. Mr Walkin —

HIRAM (*crosses to* R.C.; *with biting sarcasm*): I guess it isn't necessary to try to explain anything more to me – I know all.

Sholto and Gerda have made it perfectly clear. I'm sorry that
your husband eats chairs in an asylum, and I'm sorry that you
played with Mr Peasemarsh when he was a boy and tripped
over the Stars and Stripes – it must have been most painful.
I'm also sorry that you hadn't the moral courage to tell me I
was unwelcome, and that you had to employ your dear
children to do it for you. (*Crosses up; gets hat.*)

JENNIFER (*startled*): My poor man, you're talking nonsense!

SHOLTO (*L., hoarsely*): Sshhh! Be gentle, Mother. Mr Walkin is
not quite as other men!

GERDA (*L.C., whispering*): He had a bad fall when he was a child,
and —

> HIRAM *comes down* C.

HIRAM (*struggling manfully to control his rage*): Mrs Brent, I release
you unconditionally from your engagement to me. On closer
acquaintance, I find I couldn't altogether cope with your –
your – (*he looks venomously at* SHOLTO *and* GERDA) your
atmosphere! I am going straight back to Chicago. (*Up to window*
L.)

JENNIFER (*following up to window; distressed*): Won't you have
some tea before you go?

HIRAM (*still fighting for politeness, but shouting*): No! Thank you very
much. No!!

> He stamps off on to the terrace.

JENNIFER: It's perfectly disgraceful of you to upset that poor
man like that. You've placed me in an appalling position, and I
refuse to speak a word to any of you.

> She makes a dive for the door, but GERDA and SHOLTO bar the way.
> The three sit on settee.

GERDA: Now, Mummie, do sit down and keep calm. Daddy's
awfully in love with you, and has been all the time, and he's
come over with us to make a formal proposal.

> GEORGE moves L.

SHOLTO: Don't go and spoil everything by being obstinate.

GERDA: Think how wonderful it will be – all together again! He
is such a darling!

> Enter MARIA.

MARIA (*comes down, excited*): Yes – yes – all together – that is good! (*In Italian.*)* The saints will preserve us and keep us rich to the end of our lives.

SHOLTO (*in Italian*): Go away now, Maria; we'll come and talk to you in the kitchen presently.

MARIA: Ver' good, signor.

   She goes out, laughing happily.

JENNIFER (*on settee; almost in tears*): I shall never forgive either of you for this —

GEORGE: Jennifer! (L.)

JENNIFER: How dare you spring on me without any warning – like – like a rattlesnake!!!

GEORGE: They made me come.

JENNIFER (*quickly*): Then you didn't want to?

GEORGE (C.): You *know* I did.

JENNIFER (*crossly*): Well, all I can say is, it's very inconsiderate.

GEORGE (*irately*): It's nothing of the sort. It's a pleasant surprise.

JENNIFER (*rises*): Pleasant! Huh! You ought to be ashamed of yourself!

GERDA (*softly to* SHOLTO): It's all right; they're going to have a row. Come on.

   They commence to go up to back, quietly.

GEORGE (*quite cross*): Why should I be ashamed just because I love you still?

JENNIFER: Where's Cicely?

   GERDA *and* SHOLTO *go out, window* L.

GEORGE: Damn Cicely!

JENNIFER: I consider that remark in very bad taste. I suppose,

---

*Che felicita, che felicita, che romanzo, dopo tanti anni! L'amore c'e che l'amore!

SHOLTO: Lasci, lasci, Maria; vai al' cucino – soubito vai, vai —

MARIA: Che cosa e caduto?

SHOLTO: Ti contero dopo piu tardi.

MARIA: Si, signor.

   She goes out, laughing happily.

when you first married Cicely, you used to damn Jennifer all
day long!

GEORGE (L.C.): Cicely's left me for good and all. I shall never see
her again.

JENNIFER (R.C.): Have you any aspirin on you?

GEORGE: No; I'm so sorry.

JENNIFER: I'm sure I shall have a headache in a minute. To have
you suddenly reappearing like this is enough to unman any
woman.

GEORGE: Don't trifle with me – don't be flippant. This is our first
meeting after fifteen years. Let's treat it in the proper spirit.

JENNIFER: If only you'd given me a little warning, I could have
worked myself up into the right atmosphere without the least
trouble. I should have put a lamp in the window.

GEORGE (appealingly): Jennifer!

JENNIFER: As it is, I'm taken utterly by surprise.

GEORGE: Let's wait to discuss it until later, when the shock has
worn off a bit.

JENNIFER: Are you really so eager, then?

GEORGE (crosses to JENNIFER): I want to come back here to you
and the children more than anything in the world, Jennifer.
(He catches her hand.) Don't be tiresome.

JENNIFER: Really, you are amazing! After living fourteen years
with another woman, you drop out of a cloudless sky and call
me tiresome.

GEORGE: Well, you are – thoroughly!

JENNIFER: Perhaps I am – rather. (Sits on settee.)

GEORGE: Jennifer – in a few months all the divorce business will
be settled – and we're both getting on, you know – we shan't
be as Temperamental as we used to be.

JENNIFER: Nonsense! I shall always be Temperamental – that's
just it. You jump at conclusions so. As a matter of fact, I'm
ever so much worse than I was, having been left alone to do as
I like.

GEORGE (sits): I'm not afraid.

JENNIFER: If I agree to marry you again, I want you to
understand that it will be solely on account of Sholto and
Gerda.

GEORGE: Very well.

JENNIFER: And I should like to arrange things on a more or less business basis. We must make a list of the subjects that we cannot discuss calmly. (*Counting on her fingers.*) Religion, George Moore, Democracy, my novels —

GEORGE (*amiably*): I won't criticise a word of your novels, if you don't want me to.

JENNIFER: I don't mind your criticisms, George, as long as they're sensible and enthusiastic.

GEORGE: Anything more?

JENNIFER: Certainly. You mustn't dominate me – I hate being dominated.

GEORGE: I never did.

JENNIFER: And you must never try to make me eat things I don't like – you always used to.

GEORGE: I didn't.

JENNIFER: Yes, you did. One of our fiercest quarrels started with Apple Pudding.

GEORGE: You were so faddy.

JENNIFER: Never mind; I like being faddy. (*Rises, crosses to* C.)

GEORGE (*meekly*): All right.

JENNIFER: Promise me that you won't persuade me to live in England for good.

GEORGE: I promise. (*Rises, to* C.)

JENNIFER: And, above all things, you must never become reminiscent about Cicely.

GEORGE: You will want to talk about Cicely more than I shall.

JENNIFER: Oh no, I shan't!

GEORGE: Won't you say 'Yes' or 'No' now?

JENNIFER: There you go, dominating me! (*Sits.*)

GEORGE: Will you answer one question?

JENNIFER: That depends. What is it?

GEORGE: Do you care for me at all – any more?

JENNIFER: I suppose I do, really, but still, that doesn't settle things by any means. I had to crush down so much unhappiness fifteen years ago that – do you know, I believe I crushed all my capacity for happiness with it also. The fact of our caring for one another didn't prevent our quarrelling before.

GEORGE: We're older now.

JENNIFER: I know. There's no need to keep harping on it.

GEORGE: You're much too sensible to mind growing old.

JENNIFER: Am I? I wonder!

GEORGE: I know. Once we're together again, it won't matter a bit. There's such a lot of happiness waiting for us just round the corner – if only we're careful.

JENNIFER: Perhaps!

GEORGE (*going towards her*): Jennifer – you are a darling.

JENNIFER (*rises, warding him off*): George, it's too late. That poor American – I've given my word.

GEORGE: He released you from it. (*To* C.)

JENNIFER: Only because he was cross. I can't let him go all the way back to Chicago by himself.

GEORGE: He'll have to. He doesn't love you as much as I do.

JENNIFER: More, I'm afraid. You see, not having been married to me before, he doesn't know of my disadvantages.

GEORGE (*firmly*): I'm sorry, but he'll have to do without you.

JENNIFER (*horrified*): George, how can you be so selfish?

GEORGE: I love you.

JENNIFER: So does he, and you're calmly suggesting that I should break his heart!

GEORGE (*unmoved*): Yes.

JENNIFER: No, George – on second thoughts, I'm afraid. (*Sits at desk.*)

GEORGE: Stop, stop! Don't go on any longer – I won't have it. I know you, and I can see through you. You determined in your own mind to have me back the very first moment you saw me, and you're prevaricating and arguing just to keep me on the rack. This is one of the most delightful moments in your life, and you're revelling in it at the cost of my peace of mind. You love me – it's no use pretending you don't, because every nerve and instinct I possess is screaming that you do – you do! You only tolerated the thought of that wretched American at all on account of the children. You love me! You love me! You've wanted me all these years, as much as I have wanted you. The sight of you has completely annihilated the time we've been parted. The only thing in the world that matters is Youth. And I've got it back again. I'm twenty-one, and I want to laugh and shout and tear the house down! Come and kiss me!

JENNIFER (*going to him*): George! You haven't altered a bit!

CURTAIN

'THIS WAS A MAN'

To

JOHN C. WILSON

Characters

(in order of their appearance)

EDWARD CHURT

CAROL CHURT

HARRY CHALLONER

MARGOT BUTLER

BERRY

BOBBIE ROMFORD

ZOE ST MERRYN

MAJOR EVELYN BATHURST

BLACKWELL

————————

ACT I: Scene I

EDWARD CHURT'S *studio in Knightsbridge is furnished with mingled opulence and good taste – he is a successful modern portrait-painter.*

When the curtain rises it is about 2.30 a.m. There is a faint glow from the fireplace on the left; a table stands more or less C., upon which is a reading lamp illumining a decanter of whisky, some siphons, a plate of biscuits and another of sandwiches, and two or three glasses; there are also a box of cigarettes and matches. The rest of the room is in comparative darkness. There is the sound of a taxi drawing up in the street, then after a suitable pause the noise of the front door being opened. CAROL CHURT *enters, followed by* HARRY CHALLONER. *They are both in evening dress.* CAROL *is lovely and exquisitely gowned; her vivid personality is composed of a minimum of intellect and a maximum of sex.* HARRY *possesses all the earmarks of a social success – he is an excellent ballroom dancer, compared with which his activities in the city are negligible.*

CAROL: Don't make a noise.

HARRY: I wasn't.

CAROL: I didn't say you were – I said don't.

HARRY: All right.

CAROL: Do you want a drink?

HARRY: Yes, please.

CAROL: Help yourself then – and give me one. (*She takes off her cloak and lights a cigarette.*)

HARRY: Say when.

CAROL: That's enough. (*He fills up the glass with soda and hands it to her.*)

HARRY: Here.

CAROL: Thanks.

HARRY: You are a marvel.

CAROL: Why?

HARRY: You're so steady.

CAROL: I don't see any reason for being anything else.

HARRY: You don't think he'll find out?

CAROL: Of course not.

HARRY: Where does he sleep?

CAROL (*pointing to door, R.*): In there.

> HARRY, *with big drink in his hand, tiptoes over and listens at the door.*

HARRY: I can't hear a sound.

CAROL: He doesn't snore unless he's taken to it lately.

HARRY (*returning*): Darling, do you love me?

CAROL: What a silly question!

HARRY: It's all been so wonderful.

CAROL (*smiling*): Has it?

HARRY: Well, hasn't it?

CAROL: Yes, it has rather. (*He puts down his drink and takes her in his arms.*) Look out — (*She is holding her glass out at arm's length to prevent it upsetting.*)

HARRY: Put it down, darling — (*There is a good deal of passion in his voice when he says 'darling'.*)

CAROL: Why?

HARRY: I want to kiss you.

CAROL: Again?

HARRY: Yes, again and again and again – for ever. (*He takes her glass and slams it down on the table.*)

CAROL: Shhh! Don't be a fool.

HARRY: I don't care — (*He kisses her lingeringly.*)

CAROL (*gently disentangling herself*): I do – it's silly to be reckless.

HARRY: I don't believe you love me as much as you did before.

CAROL: It isn't that at all – you know it isn't.

HARRY: Kiss me then.

CAROL: Very well. (*She goes up to him and quietly kisses him on the mouth. They stand there motionless for a moment.*)

HARRY: I want you – all over again – for the first time.

CAROL (*stroking his face*): Darling.

HARRY: I'm crazy about you.

CAROL: You must go home to bed now.

HARRY: Will you telephone me?
CAROL: Yes.
HARRY: First thing?
CAROL: Yes.
HARRY: Promise.
CAROL: Promise.

> *They go out of the door. There is a little whispering in the hall. Then a silence and the sound of the front door closing gently.* CAROL *comes back into the studio pensively. She finishes her whisky and soda, takes a biscuit, and flings her cloak over her arm; then she switches off the light and goes slowly off up R. Her door closes. After a slight pause* EDWARD CHURT *rises from the big armchair by the fire in which he has been sitting with his back to the audience, and goes over to the table. He switches on the lamp again and helps himself to a sandwich; he munches it thoughtfully for a moment, then with an air of determination picks up the whole plate, switches off the lamp and – retires to his room.*

CURTAIN

Scene II

> *The scene is the same. It is an afternoon a few weeks later about five o'clock.*
>
> *When the curtain rises,* LADY MARGOT BUTLER *is seated down stage in a slightly picturesque attitude. She is a good-looking woman of about thirty-five.* EDWARD *is working on a sketch of her and is hidden from view behind an easel.*

MARGOT: I'm much more comfortable now, Edward.
EDWARD: Yes, I see you are. Would you mind getting uncomfortable again?
MARGOT (*rearranging herself*): It is a shame. Why do you insist on drawing people in such agonising positions?
EDWARD: It makes them feel they're getting their money's worth. You can rest in a moment and have a cigarette.

MARGOT: Was Violet Netherson pleased with your malicious portrayal of all her worst points?

EDWARD: Delighted. As a matter of fact, it *is* one of the best things I've done.

MARGOT: Yes, but hardly from her point of view. I should never forgive you if you did that to me.

EDWARD: I shall do something much worse if you don't keep still.

MARGOT: What about that cigarette?

EDWARD: Shut up.

MARGOT: All right. (*There is silence for a moment.*) Is that one by the door new?

EDWARD: Yes, it's the Fenwick girl – her mother's convinced that she's a wild woodland type.

MARGOT: St John's Woodland.

EDWARD: I had a bit of a tussle with her.

MARGOT: I like it.

EDWARD: There now, you can relax. I shan't do any more today. (MARGOT *rises quickly and strides about.*)

MARGOT: I should loathe to be a professional model.

EDWARD: There are worse fates I believe. Would you like tea or cocktails or anything?

MARGOT: I should like some tea now and a cocktail later on.

EDWARD: Are you going to stay a long time?

MARGOT: I told Bobbie to pick me up.

EDWARD (*ringing bell*): How is Bobbie?

MARGOT: Splendid. I'm still mad about him.

EDWARD: That's right.

MARGOT: You don't like him, do you?

EDWARD: I hardly know him.

MARGOT: He's such a darling, and a great comfort to me.

EDWARD (*standing back and regarding his sketch*): I shall only need one more sitting.

MARGOT: I believe you disapprove of me and Bobbie.

EDWARD: Don't be ridiculous. Why should I?

MARGOT: You must *never* disapprove of things, Edward. It's so second rate.

EDWARD: You don't mean that a bit.

MARGOT: Yes, I do.

EDWARD: You secretly disapprove of the whole affair, yourself, really. That's why you always talk about it so much – to sort of brazen it out and put yourself straight with yourself.

MARGOT: Edward, how *can* you! Anyhow, why shouldn't I talk about it. You all know. Everybody knows.

EDWARD: Reticence as a national quality seems to be on the wane.

MARGOT: What a pompous remark!

EDWARD: Perhaps – but true. (*Enter* BERRY.) Tea please, Berry.

BERRY: Very good, sir.

MARGOT: Lemon with mine, please, Berry.

BERRY: Yes, my lady.

    He goes out.

MARGOT: You're an awfully difficult person to know properly.

EDWARD: Am I?

MARGOT: You don't give an inch, do you?

EDWARD: Why should I?

MARGOT: Oh, I don't know. Confidences and discussions of everything make life so much more amusing.

EDWARD: Modern society seems to demand intimacy all in a minute. You all lay bare your private affairs to comparative strangers without a qualm.

MARGOT: Oh, Edward, dear, *we're* not strangers.

EDWARD: We met for the first time six months ago.

MARGOT: It seems *ever* so much more.

EDWARD: You'd told me all about Jim and Bobbie and your exact feelings towards each of them before we'd known each other a month.

MARGOT: It's because you're so sympathetic; you invite confidence.

EDWARD: Nonsense.

MARGOT: You're being perfectly horrid today. Has anything happened to upset you?

EDWARD: No, I don't think so.

MARGOT: Well I shan't sit for you again unless you're in a better temper.

EDWARD: Don't be cross.

MARGOT: I'm not cross. I'm hurt.

EDWARD: I think perhaps I do feel a little nervy.

MARGOT: There now, I knew it.

> BERRY *enters with tea.*

EDWARD: Here's tea, anyhow. When Lord Romford calls, Berry, show him straight in, will you?

BERRY: Yes, sir.

EDWARD: You'd better make some cocktails.

BERRY: Very well, sir.

> *He goes out.*

MARGOT: Do you want lemon or milk?

EDWARD: Neither, thanks. Just plain unvarnished tea.

MARGOT: Is that Katherine Loring? (*Looking at picture.*)

EDWARD: Yes, unfinished.

MARGOT: She always is unfinished. She has a negligible personality, I'm afraid. Here you are. (*She hands him his tea.*)

EDWARD: Thank you.

MARGOT: I hear Zoe's back.

EDWARD: Yes, she rang me up this morning.

MARGOT: Where's she been, exactly?

EDWARD: All over the place.

MARGOT: Who with?

EDWARD: By herself, I believe.

MARGOT: My dear, she must have been with *somebody*. She couldn't have been all alone after all that awful business. She'd have gone mad.

EDWARD: She'll be here soon. You'll be able to ask her about it.

MARGOT: You were engaged to her once, weren't you?

EDWARD: Now then, Margot.

MARGOT: You were. I *know* you were. Carol told me.

EDWARD: Well, as a matter of fact, we weren't actually. We've been friends since we were children and we did discuss marriage at one time, but without great conviction.

MARGOT: I can't understand why she let Kenneth divorce her. Everybody knows —

EDWARD: Zoe wished for her freedom and just went about getting it as quickly as possible.

MARGOT: Well I don't know how she could have faced it. I shouldn't have dared —

EDWARD: You're less independent than she is.

MARGOT: I believe you're going to be horrid again.

    BERRY *enters.*

BERRY (*announcing*): Lord Romford.

    BOBBIE ROMFORD *enters. He is a nice-looking, meaningless young man.*

BOBBIE: Excuse me butting in like this, Churt. (*He and* EDWARD *shake hands.*)

EDWARD: We were expecting you. The cocktails will be here in a moment.

BOBBIE: Hallo, Margot! How's the picture going?

MARGOT: It's nearly finished, but Edward won't let me see it. He's been thoroughly soured up all afternoon.

EDWARD: Margot has been trying to persuade me to brush my hair with her.

BOBBIE (*puzzled*): Brush your hair?

EDWARD: Yes, metaphorically speaking.

BOBBIE (*relieved*): Oh, I see.

EDWARD: Hair-brushing is a symbol of girlish confidences. Even the nicest people do it.

MARGOT: Edward shuts up like a clam the moment I try to discuss anything in the least interesting. Where have you been, Bobbie?

BOBBIE: Playing squash with Evie at the Bath Club.

EDWARD: Why didn't you bring him along?

BOBBIE: He said he was coming on later.

MARGOT: I suppose he won.

BOBBIE: Yes; he always does.

    Enter BERRY *with a tray of cocktails.*

EDWARD: Put them down here, Berry. (*He clears a space on the table.*) Do you want any more tea, Margot?

MARGOT: No thanks.

EDWARD: Take away the remains, then, Berry.

BERRY: Yes, sir. (*He piles the tea things up and takes them out.*)

BOBBIE: I saw your wife in St James's Street, Churt.

MARGOT (*eagerly*): Who was she with?

BOBBIE: Harry Challoner.

MARGOT: I love Harry. Don't you, Edward?

EDWARD: Passionately.

MARGOT: I expect they were going to Fanny's. She's got a mah-jong party. She seems to imagine it's a novelty. I ought to be there, really, but I just felt I couldn't bear it – all those hot scented women squabbling over the scores.

BOBBIE: Do you mind if I take a cigarette, Churt?

EDWARD: Of course not. I'm so sorry. (*He hands the box.*) Margot?

MARGOT: Thanks, Edward dear.

> BERRY *enters.*

BERRY (*announcing*): Mrs St Merryn.

> ZOE ST MERRYN *enters. She is beautifully dressed and pleasantly unexaggerated.*

ZOE: Edward! (*She takes both his hands.*) I'm terribly excited at seeing you again.

EDWARD: It's grand, isn't it, after a whole year.

ZOE: I've got so much to say I don't know where to start. (*She sees* MARGOT.) Margot, this is lovely. How are you? (*They kiss.*)

MARGOT: You look divine, darling. Do you know Bobbie?

ZOE (*shaking hands with him*): Bobbie who?

MARGOT: Romford, dear.

ZOE (*with a soft glance at* MARGOT): Oh, yes, of course. I've heard of you.

MARGOT: *What* have you heard? You must tell me.

ZOE: I can't remember at the moment. Edward, give me a cigarette and a cocktail and tell me all about everything.

EDWARD (*ministering to her*): Cigarette – cocktail – there.

ZOE: Thank you. Now then —

EDWARD: I don't know where to start any better than you do.

ZOE: How's Carol?

EDWARD: Awfully well.

ZOE: Where is she?

EDWARD: Out. She leads rather a hectic life I'm afraid – matinées, bridge, mah-jong, dancing —

ZOE: You reel off those four harmless occupations as though they were the most ignoble of human frailties.

EDWARD: I didn't mean to, really.

ZOE: They're wonderful *pis allers* for people who don't do things.

EDWARD: I don't believe in *pis allers*.

ZOE: That's not a virtue; it's just part of your creative equipment.

MARGOT: I want to hear all about your travels, Zoe – where you've been and who with.

ZOE (*laughing*): It's difficult to remember accurately who I was with all the time. You may rest assured that I had an endless succession of lovers, beginning with an elderly mulatto in Honolulu and finishing with a retired matador in Seville.

EDWARD: I hope you're satisfied, Margot.

MARGOT: Don't be so annoying, Zoe. I really am frightfully interested.

ZOE: You always are, darling, in other people's affairs.

MARGOT: Naturally – they all sound so much more entertaining than my own. Did you see Jim anywhere about in Spain?

ZOE: Yes, in Barcelona. He'd just come in from a yachting cruise.

MARGOT (*eagerly*): *Who* was with him? *Do* tell me!

ZOE: Nobody. I met him coming out of a bathroom at the Ritz.

MARGOT: Did he look more or less unattached?

ZOE: Yes. He seemed quite happy.

EDWARD: Margot's interest in her husband is so maternal, it always makes me feel as though I were in the presence of something sacred!

MARGOT: I'm awfully fond of Jim, really – particularly when he's on a yachting cruise.

ZOE: Are you definitely living apart now?

MARGOT: Oh yes – except for religious festivals like Easter and Christmas; then we forgather and go down to Draycott with the children.

EDWARD (*smiling*): It seems a comfortable arrangement, doesn't it?

ZOE: Frightfully.

MARGOT (*reflectively*): We *could* get a divorce, I suppose, but it would make such dreary complications. And then when you're free there's the awful danger of starting the whole thing over again with someone else.

ZOE: I haven't noticed it.

MARGOT: You will, I expect, dear – later on. (*She rises.*) I've enjoyed my nice cocktail very much, thank you, Edward. I must go now. Come and lunch on Thursday, Zoe darling. I've only got Rebecca coming. She'll adore seeing you again.

ZOE: All right. One-thirty?

MARGOT: Yes. Come along, Bobbie. Goodbye, Edward. Give my love to Carol.

EDWARD: I will. Goodbye.

BOBBIE: Goodbye.

MARGOT (*at door*): You've come back from abroad a changed woman, Zoe, if *that's* any comfort to you.

> *She and* BOBBIE *go out.*

ZOE: What a sham Margot is, isn't she?

EDWARD: Not really. Just a type.

ZOE: Yes, but she's a type that couldn't exist unless surrounded by false values.

EDWARD: She's making the best of a bad job.

ZOE: She's letting everything slide – morals, dignity, and discretion. Thank heaven, I broke away. I might have got like that.

EDWARD: I wonder if breaking away *is* such a very good plan.

ZOE: Of course it is. It's the most regenerating thing in the world.

EDWARD: You're so dashing, Zoe. Have another cigarette?

ZOE (*taking one*): Thanks. I feel almost panic-stricken, you know.

EDWARD: Why?

ZOE: Coming back anywhere is always such a dreadful anti-climax.

EDWARD: Not such an anti-climax as staying still.

ZOE: To think that all this used to be my life before I let Kenneth divorce me.

EDWARD: It's pretty futile, isn't it?

ZOE: Futile! I return after a year's oblivion, thrilled and excited, longing to see all my old friends, and what do I find? Clacking shallow nonentities doing the same things, saying the same things, thinking the same things. They're stale. They seem to have lost all wit and charm, and restraint – or perhaps they never had any. Oh dear! I've never felt so depressed in my life.

EDWARD: I hope I haven't let you down, too.

ZOE: No, Edward. You're unchanged; a little dim, perhaps.

EDWARD: Dim?

ZOE: Yes. All your vitality seems to have been snuffed out by something. I expect it's success. That's always frightfully undermining.

EDWARD: Yes, I suppose it is.

ZOE: Are you pleased with everything?

EDWARD: Naturally.

ZOE: I'm sorry.

EDWARD: Why? Oughtn't I to be?

ZOE: You oughtn't to pretend.

EDWARD: Pretend?

ZOE: Yes. You never used to – with me, anyhow.

EDWARD: One gets into the habit of accepting things at their surface value and not looking any deeper.

ZOE: It's a bad habit.

EDWARD: I must pretend. Don't you see?

ZOE: No.

EDWARD: I'm successful – prosperous. I've got everything I wanted.

ZOE: You haven't. You've merely got what other people think you wanted.

EDWARD (smiling): You're wonderfully stimulating, Zoe – like a breath of Brighton air.

ZOE: You look as if you need stimulating, badly.

EDWARD: I do.

ZOE: I'm glad I came back now.

EDWARD: So am I. Devoutly glad.

ZOE: What's wrong?

EDWARD: Lots of things.

ZOE: Carol?

EDWARD: Yes.

ZOE: I thought so.

EDWARD: You were right from the first. It's been a dreary failure.

ZOE: I apologise. It's so irritating being right.

EDWARD: It doesn't irritate me in the least. With anyone else it would, perhaps. But you're different; you always have been.

ZOE: I know you better than most people.

EDWARD: I know you do.

ZOE: What has she been doing?

EDWARD: The obvious thing.

ZOE: I must say I consider marriage an overrated amusement.

EDWARD: I feel rather lost.

ZOE: Yes, I did, too – over Kenneth. It's a nasty feeling.

EDWARD: It's so difficult to know exactly the right attitude to adopt.

ZOE: Are you in love with her still?

EDWARD: I don't know, really. Not violently like at first – that's died down, naturally – but somehow – things get an awful hold on you, don't they?

ZOE: Yes, fortunately for the sanctity of home life.

EDWARD: But the hold ought to be mutual.

ZOE: Quite.

EDWARD: I have moments of fierce rage, you know; then it evaporates, leaving a dead sort of a calm.

ZOE: How long have you known?

EDWARD: Ages, subconsciously; definitely, only a few weeks.

ZOE: Does she know you know?

EDWARD: She hasn't the faintest suspicion. She's always been marvellously self-assured.

ZOE: She's a lovely creature – governed entirely by sex. That's why she's self-assured.

EDWARD: Will she always go on like this?

ZOE: I expect so. Anyhow, as long as she remains attractive – probably after. That's the penalty of her type.

EDWARD: It's beastly, isn't it?

ZOE: Yes, but quite inevitable, I'm afraid. You see she's got no intellect to provide ballast.

EDWARD: Poor Carol.

ZOE: I think you're the one to be considered most at the present moment.

EDWARD: Do you think I ought to have a scene with her about it? I shrink from that. It seems to double the humiliation.

ZOE: I honestly don't know what to say. She's been actually unfaithful to you?

EDWARD: Yes.

ZOE: Often?

EDWARD (*wearily*): I suppose so. Harry Challoner is in possession at present.

ZOE: Oh dear! How typical.

EDWARD: Everything of that sort is made so much easier for people nowadays. I suppose it's an aftermath of the war.

ZOE: It's the obvious result of this 'barriers down' phase through which we seem to be passing. Everyone is at close quarters with everyone else. There's no more glamour. Everything's indefinite and blurred except sex, so people are instinctively turning to that with a rather jaded vigour. It's pathetic when you begin to analyse it.

EDWARD: What fools they all are!

ZOE (*half smiling*): Has being a success made you realise that?

EDWARD: Yes. There wasn't time before.

ZOE: Why don't you do what I did – go away?

EDWARD: It means sacrificing a good deal of work here in London. I've only just got my foot in, really.

ZOE: Divorce?

EDWARD: I don't feel equal to it at the moment – all the vile publicity, and the lascivious curiosity levelled at Carol and me. It makes me shudder to think of it.

ZOE: For a society portrait-painter you seem unduly sensitive.

EDWARD: If I felt vindictive towards Carol it would be so much easier. But I don't – I merely feel nauseated and frightfully, frightfully bored.

ZOE: The longer you allow it to drift, the worse it will become.

EDWARD: You think I ought to clinch it finally.

ZOE: Yes, I do. Once you've embarked you'll feel better.

EDWARD: No, I shan't.

ZOE: I believe you are still in love with her.

EDWARD: No; but I could be again if everything were all right. Oh, Zoe, I loathe this age and everything to do with it. Men of my sort are the products of over-civilisation. All the red-blooded honest-to-God emotions have been squeezed out of us. We're incapable of hating enough or loving enough. When any big moment comes along, good or bad, we hedge round it, arguing, weighing it in the balance of reason and psychology, trying to readjust the values until there's nothing left and nothing achieved. I wish I were primitive enough to thrash Carol and drive her out of my life for ever – or strong enough to hold her – but I'm not; I'm just an ass – an intelligent spineless ass! (*He flings himself into a chair and takes a cigarette.*)

ZOE: All the same, being the product of an Age equips you for grappling with it. You've got more chance as you are than, say, Evie Bathurst, for instance.

EDWARD: Evie goes straight for what he wants and gets it.

ZOE: He doesn't demand as much as you.

EDWARD: He's a damned sight happier.

ZOE: I should imagine he misses a good deal.

EDWARD: What does that matter? This situation could never happen to him. He wouldn't let it.

ZOE: You mustn't place too much faith in the strong and silent, Edward. They crumple up quicker than any of us when confronted with something outside their very limited range.

EDWARD: You don't like Evie, do you?

ZOE: You forget I've been married to one of his species.

EDWARD: Evie's not a cad.

ZOE: How do you know?

EDWARD: He could never behave as foully as Kenneth.

ZOE: Kenneth was never anything but an honourable, clean-living Englishman.

EDWARD: He divorced you.

ZOE: Only because I made him.

EDWARD: Why didn't he let you divorce him?

ZOE: It would have been bad for his military career.

EDWARD: You deliberately put yourself in the wrong.

ZOE: Yes.

EDWARD: And you really think it was worth while?

ZOE: Certainly I do. Our natural boredom was verging on hatred – there was no hope of getting back, ever. What's the use of going on with a thing that's dead and done for? I decided to break free.

EDWARD: Is one really happier free?

ZOE: Don't be fatuous, Edward darling.

EDWARD: I don't think I have enough initiative to do anything definite like that.

ZOE: You don't need much initiative. All you've got to do is wait for your opportunity, and grab it!

Enter BERRY.

BERRY (*announcing*): Major Bathurst.

Enter EVELYN BATHURST. *He is tall, handsome, soldierly, and essentially masculine. His gaze is frank and correct.* BERRY *exits.*

EVELYN: Hullo, Edward! Zoe, I haven't seen you for years. (*They shake hands.*)

ZOE: How are you, Evie?

EVELYN: Splendid! I feel awfully guilty, though. I meant to have written and sympathised over all your beastly divorce business. Will you forgive me?

ZOE: There's nothing to forgive. It was all a howling success, anyway.

EVELYN: Success! Whew! You must have had the hell of a time!

ZOE: It was unpleasant but illuminating.

EDWARD: Want a cocktail, Evie?

EVELYN: No, thanks.

EDWARD: Cigarette?

EVELYN: Rather – yes. (*He takes one.*)

ZOE: How was India?

EVELYN: I don't know. I haven't been there.

ZOE: I'm so sorry. I thought you had.

EVELYN: No. Morocco was quite warm enough for me.

ZOE: You arrived at an opportune moment. We were just discussing you.

EVELYN: Good God! What for?

ZOE: Edward was wishing he were more like you.

EVELYN: That's uncommonly nice and right of him. Why this sudden burst of inferiority, Edward?

EDWARD: It's been brewing up for a long time.

EVELYN (*laughing*): Oh, well, we all come to our senses sooner or later.

ZOE: Not always, Evie.

EVELYN: My only quarrel with Edward is he doesn't take enough exercise.

EDWARD: I'm not very good at exercise.

EVELYN: You never make any effort. Why don't you come and play squash with me sometimes?

EDWARD: That's not exercise, it's flagellation.

EVELYN: He's looking a bit off colour, don't you think, Zoe?

ZOE: Only comparatively.

EVELYN: Been over-working, I suppose?

EDWARD: No, not really.

ZOE (*rising*): I must go now, Edward.

EVELYN: I shall take it as a personal affront if you leave the moment I arrive.

ZOE: No, you won't, Evie. Goodbye.

EVELYN (*shaking hands*): Come and have a bit of food sometime.

ZOE: I should love to.

EVELYN: Where are you staying?

ZOE: Claridge's.

EVELYN: Right. I'll call you up.

ZOE: Goodbye, Edward.

EDWARD: Come again soon, please.

ZOE: Of course. Telephone me tomorrow morning.

EDWARD: I will.

ZOE: Give my love to Carol.

> EVELYN *opens the door for her and she goes out.* EDWARD *stands looking after her thoughtfully.*

EVELYN (*sitting down again*): Extraordinary woman Zoe.

EDWARD: Why extraordinary?

EVELYN: I don't know. She's so self-assured.

EDWARD (*absently*): Yes. I think she has every reason to be.

EVELYN: She faced all that divorce business very pluckily. Kenneth seems to have behaved like a pretty average swine.

EDWARD: Yes.

EVELYN: Why on earth did she ever marry him?

EDWARD (*wearily*): Why does anyone ever marry anyone?

EVELYN: I've never felt the urge very strongly. I suppose I've seen too much of it.

EDWARD: That doesn't make any difference, really.

EVELYN: Women are so damned complicated to live with – specially Zoe's sort.

EDWARD: I don't think Zoe is particularly complicated. She's always appeared to me to be pretty clear-headed and direct.

EVELYN: Oh well, you know her better than I do.

EDWARD: You're wonderfully single-minded, aren't you?

EVELYN: Single-minded?

EDWARD: Yes. You live according to formulated codes, and you never try to look either under or over them. I do envy you.

EVELYN: You needn't. I have my ups and downs.

EDWARD: Do you, really? Ever since we were at school I've always regarded you as being quite invulnerable.

EVELYN (*complacently*): Don't be a fool, old man.

EDWARD: I suppose it's a remnant of hero worship.

EVELYN: Rot! I'm a bit more balanced than you, that's all.

EDWARD: That wouldn't be very difficult.

EVELYN: I came here today with a purpose. I'm a bit worried. I want to talk to you seriously.

EDWARD: What about?

EVELYN: Lots of things.

EDWARD: All right. Go on.

EVELYN: I don't know how to start, quite; it's difficult.

EDWARD: Why difficult?

EVELYN: Well, you're a bit touchy at times, aren't you?

EDWARD: What's the matter, Evie?

EVELYN: Nothing actually yet – at least, I hope not.

EDWARD: I know what you're driving at.

EVELYN: Do you?

EDWARD: Yes.

EVELYN: Are you sure you do?

EDWARD: People have been talking about Carol, I suppose.

EVELYN: Exactly.

EDWARD: Well, you needn't worry.

EVELYN: I shouldn't, ordinarily, but somehow in this case it's different.

EDWARD: No, it isn't; it's exactly the same; it's a situation that occurs over and over again with everybody. That's why it's such a bore.

EVELYN: That's a silly sort of attitude to take up.

EDWARD: No sillier than any other.

EVELYN: Aren't you going to do anything?

EDWARD: O God! (*He turns away.*)

EVELYN: Well, you'll have to sooner or later.

EDWARD: What is there to do?

EVELYN: Read the riot act.

EDWARD: Do you seriously imagine that that's in any way a final solution?

EVELYN: It ought to bring her to her senses a bit, if you did it with conviction.

EDWARD: That's the trouble. I haven't got a conviction.

EVELYN: Hang it all man, she is your wife!

EDWARD: I'm not a man of property.

EVELYN: How do you mean?

EDWARD: I mean I can't look on Carol as a sort of American trunk.

EVELYN (*exasperated*): What *are* you talking about?

EDWARD: She's a human being, not an inanimate object over which I can assert legal rights.

EVELYN: If all husbands adopted that tone, England would be in a nice state.

EDWARD: It *is* in a nice state.

EVELYN: You make me tired sometimes, Edward.

EDWARD: I expect I do, but it can't be helped.

EVELYN: Yes, it can.

EDWARD: How?

EVELYN: Pull yourself together; show a little spirit.

EDWARD: I suppose you think that if I grabbed Carol by the hair of the head and banged her about and hurled abuse at her, she'd fall at my feet in ecstasies of adoration?

EVELYN: I shouldn't be surprised. Anyhow, it probably would do her good.

EDWARD: For an upstanding British soldier you have an astounding sense of the theatre.

EVELYN: Oh, you can think me a red-blooded savage if you like, but I'm damned if I'd sit down quietly and let my wife make a fool of me.

EDWARD (*gently*): You haven't got a wife, Evie. If you had you'd probably be utterly vanquished quicker than anyone.

EVELYN: Not me. I know the game too well.

EDWARD: Only from looking on, though. That makes an enormous difference.

EVELYN: Look here, Edward. Why not be sensible about all this?

EDWARD: I am, really.

EVELYN: Nonsense!

EDWARD: It's no use, Evie. Things will have to take their course.

EVELYN (*contemptuously*): Line of least resistance, eh?

EDWARD: Yes.

EVELYN: To hell with the line of least resistance.

EDWARD: She can't help herself; she's made like that.

EVELYN: Rubbish!

EDWARD: It isn't rubbish. She's the sort of woman who must attract people all the time. One conquest isn't enough; she must go on and on.

EVELYN: You talk as though she were only just flirting about for the fun of the thing.

EDWARD: Perhaps she is.

EVELYN: What's the use of blinding yourself?

EDWARD: Oh, shut up, Evie!

EVELYN: This is more serious than you think.

EDWARD: No, it isn't.

EVELYN: What do you feel – honestly?

EDWARD: I've told you – bored.

EVELYN: That's not true.

EDWARD: All right.

EVELYN: I know it isn't. We haven't been pals all these years for nothing. You can't deceive me as easily as that.

EDWARD: What do you want me to feel, exactly?

EVELYN: You've got to *do* something.

EDWARD: What?

EVELYN: If you don't, I shall.

EDWARD: Evie, if you mention one word of all this to Carol or anyone in the world, I'll never forgive you.

EVELYN: You needn't worry. I've got a better plan than talking.

EDWARD: What is it?

EVELYN: Leave it to me.

EDWARD: Evie —

EVELYN: She ought to be taught a lesson.

EDWARD: What sort of lesson?

EVELYN: She wants some of the self-assurance knocked out of her.

EDWARD (*smiling*): Really, Evie!

EVELYN: She needs humiliating.

EDWARD: You're positively vindictive.

EVELYN: Perhaps I am, but it's for your sake.

EDWARD: I'd no idea you disliked Carol so heartily.

EVELYN: It isn't that at all. I don't like or dislike her. She never pays attention to me, anyhow.

EDWARD: To think that there's even a streak of feminine in you!

EVELYN: What do you mean?

EDWARD: Never mind.

EVELYN: I won't stand by and see you let down all along the line.

EDWARD: It's awfully sweet of you, Evie, to be so cross, but you really mustn't be. I'm the one to get cross if necessary.

EVELYN: It is necessary.

EDWARD: You must allow me to be the best judge of that.

EVELYN: Now look here, Edward —

EDWARD: Remember, what I said – you're not to interfere. It's my affair, and mine alone.

EVELYN: I know a good deal more about women, than you.

EDWARD: Do you, Evie?

EVELYN: I've handled too many of them not to.

EDWARD: How mechanical that sounds. (*He laughs.*)

EVELYN: Oh, you're hopeless.

> The door opens and CAROL comes in. She is, as usual, looking delightful.

CAROL: Hallo, Evie! (*She shakes hands with him.*) Are there any telephone messages for me, Edward?

EDWARD: No.

CAROL (*taking off her gloves*): I'm quite exhausted.

EDWARD: Where have you been?

CAROL: Playing mah-jong with Fanny. I won a good deal.

EVELYN: Splendid.

CAROL: How's Margot's picture going?

EDWARD: It's nearly finished.

CAROL: Give me a cigarette, Evie.

EVELYN (*handing her a cigarette*): You look remarkably fit, Carol.

CAROL (*smiling*): I am fit, but I'm a tiny bit worried over Edward.

EVELYN: Why, he looks all right to me.

CAROL: You don't know him like I do. I can always tell when he's tired and overworked, can't I, darling?

EDWARD: Yes, I'm sure you can.

CAROL: It's all these people buzzing round him all day. Let's go away, Edward, and have a real holiday – somewhere quiet!

EVELYN: That's a damned good idea.

EDWARD (*smiling*): I can't – for the next six weeks, anyhow.

CAROL (*with a slight shrug*): There you see? It's quite impossible to do anything with him.

EVELYN: Why don't you chuck everything, and just go?

EDWARD: Funnily enough, Zoe suggested that this afternoon.

CAROL: Zoe? I didn't know she was back.

EDWARD: She arrived yesterday.

CAROL: Why didn't you tell me?

EDWARD: I didn't know until this morning. She rang me up.

CAROL: Well, she didn't lose much time anyhow.

EDWARD: I don't see why she should.

CAROL: I suppose she talked and talked and talked as usual.

EDWARD: Yes, we both talked a good bit.

CAROL: What about?

EDWARD: Everything.

CAROL: No wonder you look tired.

EVELYN: She looked awfully well.

CAROL: She always does. She's wonderfully healthy.

EDWARD (*with a faint malice*): She sent you her love.

CAROL (*bored*): Oh – give her mine when she rings up again.

EDWARD: You'll see her tonight at the Harringtons'.

CAROL: No, I shan't. I'm not going. They're going to have that awful string quartet again. I suffered so acutely last time.

EDWARD: I shall go by myself, then.

CAROL: Never mind. You'll be able to talk to Zoe.

EDWARD: Where are you dining?

CAROL: With the Challoners at the Embassy; then we're going on somewhere.

EDWARD: Do you want the car?

CAROL: No. They're picking me up.

EDWARD: Right. I'll go and dress. Don't go, Evie. We might have a slight aperitif at one of your disreputable clubs before dinner.

CAROL: Are you dining together?

EDWARD: No. I'm going to the Russian Ballet with Richard and Sheila. They've got a box or something.

> EDWARD *goes off into his bedroom.*

EVELYN: You're looking charming, Carol.

CAROL (*raising her eyebrows*): Thank you.

EVELYN: That's a splendid hat. Is it new?

CAROL: No – incredibly old.

EVELYN: Well, it doesn't look it.

CAROL: I'm glad. (*She goes towards the door.*)

EVELYN: Carol —

CAROL (*turning*): Yes?

EVELYN: Nothing.

CAROL (*surprised*): Is there anything the matter?

EVELYN: No – honestly it's nothing.

CAROL: Oh well, I must go and dress, too. See you later on.

EVELYN: I shall be gone when you come down.

CAROL: Really, Evie, you're behaving very strangely.

EVELYN: Why?

CAROL: I don't know. You seem different, somehow.

EVELYN: Won't you stay and talk for a moment. I haven't seen you to speak to for ages.

CAROL: That's your fault.

EVELYN: You're always so engaged.

CAROL: I never seem to have a minute for anything. I *do* wish life wasn't so hectic.

EVELYN: Why do you let it be?

CAROL: I don't. It just happens like that.

EVELYN: I'd resent it a good deal if you were my wife.

CAROL (*smiling*): Aren't you glad I'm not, Evie?

EVELYN: I don't know.

CAROL (*surprised*): Well, now! I thought you disliked me thoroughly.

EVELYN: Disliked you?

CAROL: Yes. You always have such a polite preoccupied air with me. It makes me feel terribly frivolous and shallow.

EVELYN: How can you, Carol?

CAROL (*gaily*): It's true. You're the kind of man who despises women dreadfully – I know you are.

EVELYN: You're quite wrong. I adore them.

CAROL: Well, that's a lovely surprise, isn't it?

EVELYN: I can't get over you imagining that I disliked you.

CAROL: I expect it's because you're so tremendously fond of Edward. One always feels that with one's husband's friends.

EVELYN: I don't see any reason, just because I like Edward, that —

CAROL: Don't you, Evie?

EVELYN: Of course not.

CAROL: Well, I'm very, very glad.

EVELYN: That's settled, then, isn't it?

CAROL: Quite. I shan't be frightened of you any more.

EVELYN: Frightened of me. How ridiculous!

CAROL: It isn't ridiculous; it's quite natural.

EVELYN: I don't see why. I'm perfectly harmless.

CAROL: Are you?

EVELYN: Mild as a kitten.

CAROL: I wonder.

EVELYN: To think you've been building up the most frightful image of me in your mind all this time and I never knew.

CAROL: You can't blame me, really.

EVELYN: Yes, I can. It's awfully suspicious and distrustful of you.

CAROL: It's your own fault, for holding so aloof.

EVELYN: I don't hold aloof a bit.

CAROL: You've never talked anything but commonplaces to me ever since I've known you.

EVELYN: You never gave me the chance.

CAROL: What did you expect me to do?

EVELYN: I don't know. Just be nice.

CAROL: Haven't I been nice? I'm so sorry.

EVELYN: Yes, I suppose you have, really, but I've always felt you thought me rather dull.

CAROL: You have been – up to now.

EVELYN (*despondently*): There you are, then!

CAROL (*quietly*): I said 'up to now'.

EVELYN: Men of my sort are all wrong in society. We don't seem to fit in, somehow.

CAROL: Are you glad or sorry?

EVELYN: Well, to be frank, I'm glad, until moments like this crop up.

CAROL: You're awfully funny, you know.

EVELYN: Funny?

CAROL: Yes. You do despise women, after all.

EVELYN: How do you mean?

CAROL: You think we only like men who play up and talk well and dance well.

EVELYN: It's only natural that you should.

CAROL: Oh no, it isn't.

EVELYN: You think there's some hope for me, after all, then?

CAROL: Now you're fishing.

EVELYN: It's cruel of you to snap me up like that.

CAROL: I'm sorry, Evie.

EVELYN: You'd find me a fearful bore after a bit, you know.

CAROL: Why should I?

EVELYN: I take things so damned seriously.

CAROL: That's refreshing! Most of the men I know don't take things seriously enough.

EVELYN: What an extraordinary woman you are!

CAROL: Why extraordinary?

EVELYN: Making me talk like this. I never have before.

CAROL: I shall take that as a compliment, whether you like it or not.

EVELYN: I mean it.

CAROL: Yes, I know you do.

EVELYN: I see now why your life's so hectic and why everyone runs after you so much.

CAROL (*smiling*): Why?

EVELYN: You've got the most amazing knack of drawing people out.

CAROL: Not always. Only people I like.

EVELYN: You've made me feel lonely for the first time in my life.

CAROL: How hateful of me!

EVELYN: It's not your fault; it's mine.

CAROL: In what way?

EVELYN: I ought to make more efforts and not be so boorish.

CAROL: You're not in the least boorish.

EVELYN: Yes, I am – utterly wrapped up in my own affairs, then suddenly someone like you comes along and makes me realise all in a minute what a lot I'm missing.

CAROL: You're not missing much, really. It's much better to remain yourself than try to be something you're not.

EVELYN: It's awfully sweet of you to say that.

CAROL: I mean it honestly. You never can guess how tired I get by having the same sort of things said to me always.

EVELYN: Do you really?

CAROL: Of course.

EVELYN: I wish you weren't dining out tonight.

CAROL: Why?

EVELYN: I'd like better than anything in the world for you to come and dine with me quietly.

CAROL: I'd adore to, Evie, but, you see —

EVELYN: Oh, I know you can't possibly; but it seems hard that the moment I begin to get to know you properly you're whisked out of sight again.

CAROL (*gently*): There are lots of other nights.

EVELYN: Yes, I suppose there are.

CAROL: I'm certainly not frightened of you any more now – you're an absolute baby.

EVELYN: Crying for the moon?

CAROL: I don't rate myself quite so high as that.

EVELYN: You're just as unattainable.

CAROL: Evie!

EVELYN: I'm sorry. I oughtn't to have said that.

CAROL (*after a slight pause*): I don't mind.

EVELYN: You are a dear.

CAROL: Am I?

EVELYN: May I ring you up tomorrow morning?

CAROL: Of course.

EVELYN: And perhaps – some time soon —?

CAROL (*with determination*): I'll dine with you tonight, Evie.

EVELYN: Carol!

CAROL: Yes. I can put off the Challoners. They bore me stiff, anyway. I'd much rather talk to you.

EVELYN: I say, it's most terribly sweet of you to take pity on me like this.

CAROL: Don't be silly. It'll be a mutual benefit. I'm bored and you're bored. Where shall we dine?

EVELYN: Anywhere you choose.

CAROL: The awful thing is I simply daren't go anywhere where I'm likely to be seen.

EVELYN: We could dine at the flat if you like, but it will be fearfully dull.

CAROL: Oh, *let's* do that. And we can creep out somewhere afterwards if we feel like it.

EVELYN: Are you sure that's all right?

CAROL: Positive. It will be divine being quiet for once.

EVELYN: Don't say anything to Edward.

CAROL (*quickly*): Why not?

EVELYN: Well, I got out of dining with him tonight. I wanted to be by myself, you see.

CAROL: Well, you're not going to be now.

EVELYN: I know. Isn't it damnable?

CAROL: Beastly. Will you fetch me?

EVELYN: Yes. What time?

CAROL: Latish – about nine.

EVELYN: Splendid —

> *Enter* EDWARD *in evening dress.*

CAROL: You have been quick.

EDWARD: I've hurried. I know how impatient Evie is. Are you quite determined about the Harringtons, Carol?

CAROL: *Quite!* I simply couldn't bear it.

EDWARD: Oh, all right, then. I'll apologise for you.

CAROL: Do, there's a dear. Goodbye, Evie. Come and see me again soon.

EVELYN: Thanks. I will.

EDWARD: Come on. I haven't got much time. Goodnight Carol.

CAROL: Goodnight, darling.

> EDWARD *and* EVELYN *go off.* CAROL *lights a cigarette and goes to the telephone.*

CAROL (*at telephone*): Mayfair 7065 please.... Yes. (*A pause.*) Hallo! Is that you, Fay.... Yes. Can I speak to Harry? Oh yes, rather. I'll hold on.... Harry.... Yes, it's me. Look here, I can't dine tonight, because I can't, I feel too tired. I may not have looked tired this afternoon, but I tell you I am now.... Don't be so annoying, Harry.... No, it isn't that at all. I'm going to dine in bed.... No, don't. I shall probably be asleep.... Well, of course, if you're going to talk like that.... I'm afraid you're developing into a bore, Harry. I'm so sorry! (*She bangs down the receiver.*) Silly fool!

> *She picks up her bag and gloves and goes off.*

CURTAIN

ACT II

The scene is EVELYN BATHURST'S *flat. It is a manly apartment, furnished with precision but no imagination. There is a door up L. opening into a small hall and thence to the front door. Up R. is* EVIE'S *bedroom and down L. a service door. Between these two is the fireplace, in front of which is a large sofa and a couple of armchairs. The windows occupy the right wall. The table, C., is laid for two.*

When the curtain rises, it is about 9.15 p.m. and BLACKWELL *is putting the finishing touches, which consist of a bowl of roses and a bottle of champagne in an ice bucket. He is regarding his handiwork pensively when there comes the sound of a key in the front door. After a moment* EVELYN *and* CAROL *enter.* EVELYN *is wearing a dinner jacket;* CAROL, *an elaborately simple dinner dress and cloak.*

CAROL: What a nice flat!

EVELYN: I've been here for years.

CAROL: It's all quite typical of you.

EVELYN: How do you know?

CAROL: Well, don't you think it is?

EVELYN: I've never thought about it much.

CAROL: Solid and rather austere.

EVELYN: That sounds beastly.

CAROL: No. I like it.

EVELYN: I'm glad. Let me take your cloak. (*He takes her cloak and lays it over a chair.*) Cocktails, please, Blackwell.

BLACKWELL: Yes sir. (*He goes off.*)

CAROL: I suppose he's been with you as long as the flat?

EVELYN: Longer, really; he was my batman when I was a raw subaltern.

CAROL (*smiling*): You must have been rather nice as a subaltern.

EVELYN: Oh no, I wasn't. You ask Edward.

CAROL: Edward adores you.

EVELYN: We're very old friends.

CAROL: It's always puzzled me. You're so very different from each other.

EVELYN: Edward's a damn sight cleverer.

CAROL: Now then —

EVELYN: But he is.

CAROL: You seem to have done very well at your job and you're always winning things.

EVELYN: I haven't done anything.

CAROL: Nonsense. (*She wanders round the room, looking at photographs*): Who's this?

EVELYN: Mary Liddle. I was engaged to her once.

CAROL: Oh, I see.

EVELYN: I suppose you want to know why nothing ever came of it.

CAROL: Of course.

EVELYN: She ran off with someone she hardly knew.

CAROL: What a shame!

EVELYN: I expect I bored her stiff —

CAROL: Were you very much in love with her?

EVELYN: Yes. I think I was.

CAROL: I can't imagine you in love.

EVELYN: It doesn't happen often.

CAROL (*smiling and patting his arm*): Never mind, Evie.

EVELYN: I don't. It's a relief really.

> BLACKWELL *enters with the cocktails; they both take them.*

Dinner please, Blackwell.

BLACKWELL: Very good, sir. (*He goes out.*)

CAROL (*at another photograph*): Is this your mother?

EVELYN: Yes.

CAROL: You're awfully like her.

EVELYN: It's the nose, I think.

CAROL: And the chin – so firm and unrelenting. I love firm chins.

EVELYN: They're awfully deceptive.

CAROL (*sipping her cocktail*): Are they, Evie?

EVELYN: Yes. I'm as weak as water, really.

CAROL: You'll have to prove it to me before I believe it.

EVELYN: I'd rather not.

> BLACKWELL *enters with caviare.*

Come and sit down.

CAROL (*sitting at table*): What divine roses!

EVELYN: They're in your honour.

CAROL: Thank you. I hoped they were. (BLACKWELL *helps her to caviare.*)

EVELYN (*opening champagne*): I feel awfully flattered at your being here.

CAROL: Why should you?

EVELYN: I just do.

CAROL: Don't be silly. (*He fills her glass and his own.*) Thanks.

EVELYN: I feel flattered because it's something I never thought possible.

CAROL: Me dining with you?

EVELYN: Yes.

CAROL: Idiot. (*She smiles.*)

EVELYN: I've always seen you as a frightfully dazzling creature – always in demand – always rushing about.

CAROL: Just because you feel flattered yourself, you mustn't begin to flatter me.

EVELYN: Is that flattery?

CAROL: Isn't it?

EVELYN: Well yes, and no.

CAROL: You mean you've never quite approved of me.

EVELYN: I didn't say that.

CAROL: I believe it's true, all the same.

EVELYN: I've wondered a bit what you were really like.

CAROL (*with subtle pathos*): I don't think I know, myself.

EVELYN: You haven't had much time to think, have you?

CAROL: No – I suppose not.

EVELYN (*sententiously*): We're all so different underneath.

CAROL (*laughing*): Oh, Evie!

EVELYN: What?

CAROL: You're awfully serious.

EVELYN: Don't laugh at me.

CAROL: I wasn't.

EVELYN: I don't mind, really; it shows that you're enjoying yourself.

CAROL: I am thoroughly.

EVELYN: I was terrified that you'd be bored.

CAROL: You're fishing again.

EVELYN: I wish you weren't so quick; it embarrasses me. (*He laughs.*)

CAROL: I'll try to be slower. (*She laughs too.*)

EVELYN: I'm the plodding sort, you know – gets there in the end, but takes a long time about it.

CAROL: Nonsense!

EVELYN: The British army doesn't specialise in wit.

CAROL: I won't hear a word against the British army.

EVELYN (*with jocularity*): Hurrah! (*They both laugh.*)

CAROL: You're like a schoolboy.

EVELYN: I feel one with you.

CAROL: Do I look so terribly old?

EVELYN: You know I didn't mean that.

CAROL: I'll let you off this time, but you mustn't do it again.

> BLACKWELL *enters with the soup; he takes away the caviare plates.*

EVELYN: How long is it since you dined quietly like this?

CAROL: Oh, ages.

EVELYN: I thought so.

CAROL: You're looking disapproving again.

> BLACKWELL *serves the soup and exits.*

EVELYN: I think I'm envious.

CAROL: Envious?

EVELYN: Yes.

CAROL: No, you're not, really.

EVELYN: Your life would never suit me, I know, but somehow it does sound rather fun, for a change.

CAROL: Let's make a bargain.

EVELYN: I know what you're going to say.

CAROL: Change over for a bit.

EVELYN: Temptress.

CAROL: You come out to a few theatres and parties with me —

EVELYN: I can't dance well enough.

CAROL: I'll soon teach you.

EVELYN: I'd drive you mad.

CAROL: Have you a gramophone here?

EVELYN: Yes.

CAROL: We'll start after dinner.

EVELYN: All right.

CAROL: And whenever I'm tired and sick of everything, I'll come here and dine quietly like this.

EVELYN: Will you, honestly?

CAROL: Of course, if you stick to your side of the compact.

EVELYN: I don't believe you'll have the patience to carry it through.

CAROL: You must despise me.

EVELYN: Despise you? Good heavens! Why?

CAROL: You're so untrusting.

EVELYN: No, I'm not; but it does look as though I were going to get more out of this than you.

CAROL: Not at all. It's a perfectly fair exchange. You've no idea how utterly weary I get every now and then.

EVELYN: Poor Carol.

CAROL: This is peace, absolute peace, and I'm tremendously grateful to you for it. (*They look at each other in silence for a moment.* EVELYN's *expression is faintly nonplussed.*)

EVELYN: The compact's on.

CAROL: Good! Shake hands.

EVELYN: Right you are. (*They shake hands across the table.* CAROL *allows hers to remain in his a shade more than is strictly necessary.*)

CAROL: Do you want to come to the first night of *Round Pegs* on Thursday?

EVELYN: What on earth's that?

CAROL: A new play by Burton Trask.

EVELYN: Who's he?

CAROL (*laughing*): Oh, Evie!

EVELYN: Well, how should I know?

CAROL: He's only the most talked of dramatist we've got.

EVELYN: Sorry.

CAROL: He wrote *The Sinful Spinster*.

EVELYN: Oh, the play all the fuss was about last year.

CAROL: Yes.

EVELYN: It sounded pretty hot stuff.

CAROL: It wasn't, really, but the woman in it fell in love with a man younger than herself and the Church of England didn't like it.

EVELYN: Oh, I see!

CAROL: You need educating badly.

EVELYN: I'm afraid I do.

   BLACKWELL *enters and takes away their soup plates.*

CAROL: Wasn't it funny us talking this afternoon and you asking me to dine all in a minute?

EVELYN: Awfully funny, but very lucky for me.

CAROL: You make me feel shy when you say things like that. It was just as lucky for me.

EVELYN (*with intensity*): Was it, honestly?

CAROL (*looking down*): Of course.

   BLACKWELL *enters with partridges and attendant vegetables. He serves them during the ensuing dialogue.*

EVELYN: Edward's looking awfully tired these days.

CAROL (*absently*): Is he? I haven't noticed it.

EVELYN: Why, you said so yourself this afternoon.

CAROL: So I did. I remember he looked very wan when I came in. By the way, what were you two discussing so intently. I felt as though I were interrupting a Masonic meeting.

EVELYN: Nothing particular.

CAROL: Me, by any chance?

EVELYN: Good heavens, no!

CAROL: There's no need to be so vehement about it; it wouldn't have mattered if you had been.

EVELYN: Have some more champagne.

CAROL: Thanks – just a little. (*She holds out her glass and he fills it, also his own.*)

EVELYN (*with great boldness*): Why did you think we were talking about you?

CAROL: You both looked so guilty.

EVELYN: Surely that proves we weren't.

CAROL: Very good, Evie.

EVELYN: You're embarrassing me dreadfully.

CAROL: Am I? Why?

EVELYN: Because we *were* discussing you.

CAROL: Ah!

EVELYN: I see it's useless to try and deceive you for a moment.

CAROL: What were you saying?

EVELYN: Must I tell you?

CAROL: Certainly.

EVELYN: You're terribly unrelenting.

CAROL: Come on – out with it.

EVELYN: I was lecturing Edward.

> BLACKWELL *goes out.*

CAROL: Lecturing him?

EVELYN: Yes. I said he was paying too much attention to his work and not enough to you.

CAROL: And do you think that's true?

EVELYN: Yes.

CAROL: It isn't; it's the other way round, really. I neglect Edward. You should have saved your lecture for me.

EVELYN: I'm sure it's his fault, really, he's so damned lackadaisical.

CAROL: It was nice of you, but a little interfering.

EVELYN: I'm sorry. I suppose I deserve to be snubbed.

CAROL: I'm not snubbing you, exactly, but I'm puzzled.

EVELYN: Why puzzled?

CAROL: It seems so strange that you should have taken up the cudgels on my side.

EVELYN: That was how I saw the situation.

CAROL: I never realised there was a situation.

EVELYN: There isn't, but there may be soon.

CAROL: How horrid of you!

EVELYN: I know Edward pretty well, you know.

CAROL: And me hardly at all.

EVELYN: Exactly. That's why I went to him, as I told you this afternoon. I always felt that you disliked me and thought me dull.

CAROL: How absurd!

EVELYN: You did, all the same. You'd have crushed me to the earth if I'd dared mention the subject to you.

CAROL: You must have thought me a prig.

EVELYN: Not in the least, I quite saw your point.

CAROL: And now —?

EVELYN: Now I'm muddled.

CAROL: Have I muddled you, Evie?

EVELYN: Yes, terribly.

CAROL: I'm so glad.

EVELYN: That's malicious of you.

CAROL: Go ahead with your lecture.

EVELYN: Certainly not.

CAROL: Whose fault do you consider this slight drifting apart –
Edward's or mine?

EVELYN: Edward's.

CAROL: I told you it was mine.

EVELYN: I don't believe you.

CAROL: Stubborn.

EVELYN: Is it yours?

CAROL: Yes.

EVELYN: Why?

CAROL (seriously): Oh, Evie —

EVELYN: Tell me.

CAROL: It's rather difficult.

EVELYN: I'm awfully sympathetic.

CAROL: I believe you are.

EVELYN: You love him still, don't you?

CAROL: Yes – in a way.

EVELYN: But not so much as you did?

CAROL: Not quite so much.

EVELYN: I suppose that's inevitable in married life, always.

CAROL: I expect it is.

EVELYN: It's sad, though.

CAROL: Not if one isn't sentimental about it.

EVELYN: Are you ever sentimental about anything?

CAROL (wistfully): Do I seem so hard?

EVELYN: A little, I think.

CAROL: I'm not, really.

EVELYN: I'm afraid Edward's unhappy.

CAROL: Not deep down inside.

EVELYN: Are you sure?

CAROL: He may think he is.

EVELYN: Poor Edward.

CAROL: He doesn't love me quite so much, either, you know.

EVELYN: Perhaps he wants to, but you won't let him.

CAROL: Evie, why are we talking like this?

EVELYN: I don't know.

CAROL: I can't bear to pretend about things.

EVELYN: You're quite right; it doesn't pay in the long run.

CAROL: But I don't want you to blame Edward and lecture him for something that's not entirely his fault.

EVELYN: I see.

CAROL: I'm awfully fond of him and I always shall be, but —

EVELYN: But what?

CAROL: Don't let's say any more about it.

EVELYN: All right. You're rather a dear, you know.

CAROL: Am I?

EVELYN: More than I ever suspected!

CAROL: Oh, Evie!

They look at each other for a moment, EVELYN *intently.* CAROL *with a faintly wistful smile.* BLACKWELL *enters to collect the plates and serve the sweet – pêche Melba – which he does during ensuing dialogue.*

EVELYN: You don't like Zoe St Merryn, do you?

CAROL: Why do you suddenly ask that?

EVELYN: I felt you didn't this afternoon.

CAROL: She's rather obvious, I think.

EVELYN: In what way?

CAROL: She tries to be clever.

EVELYN: I always thought she was clever.

CAROL: Yes, most men do, but very few women.

EVELYN: Why is that?

CAROL: Because they see through her. All that divorce business was a put-up job.

EVELYN: I say, Carol!

CAROL: Don't look so shocked. Of course it was. She's been so brave and defiant over it. Men love that.

EVELYN: Aren't you being a little hard on her?

CAROL: No, not really. I know her type so well.

EVELYN: She's an old friend of Edward's, isn't she?

CAROL: Yes, but that hasn't anything to do with it. She tried to marry him once.

EVELYN: He seems very fond of her.

CAROL: She flatters him terribly. He's an awful baby.

EVELYN: Thank heaven I haven't got your feminine intuition. It must complicate life dreadfully.

CAROL: It's very useful sometimes.

EVELYN: Do you size everyone up so mercilessly?

CAROL (laughing): Perhaps.

EVELYN: I'm trembling visibly.

CAROL: Nonsense! You're not frightened by anything, really.

EVELYN: You don't know!

    BLACKWELL goes out.

CAROL: Well, you shouldn't be, anyhow.

EVELYN: That's different.

CAROL: Why did you ask me not to tell Edward I was dining with you?

EVELYN (nonplussed): Did I?

CAROL: You know you did.

EVELYN: Perhaps I was afraid he'd think I was interfering again.

CAROL: Did he tell you that, too?

EVELYN: Yes.

CAROL (smiling): Never mind.

EVELYN: I don't. I'm used to Edward.

CAROL: So am I.

EVELYN: But when you tell me I'm interfering, I feel beastly.

CAROL: You are, you know.

EVELYN: There! You've done it again.

CAROL: People like Edward and me should be left to manage our own troubles.

EVELYN: All right. From now on I won't say a word.

CAROL: Cheer up.

EVELYN: I'm a blundering fool, anyhow.

CAROL (laughing): Yes.

EVELYN: And instead of making you like me, I've made you laugh at me.

CAROL: That's not quite true.

EVELYN: I'm afraid it is.

CAROL: You don't know a bit what I'm really like.

EVELYN: No.

CAROL: Do you want to?

EVELYN: Yes.

CAROL: I'm not sure that it's wise.

EVELYN: Why not?

CAROL: You might be shocked.

EVELYN: As bad as that?

CAROL: Yes – as bad as that.

EVELYN: I don't believe it.

CAROL: Good.

EVELYN: You're too sensitive to behave really badly.

CAROL: That's nonsense.

EVELYN: No, it isn't.

CAROL: Sensitiveness hasn't anything to do with it.

EVELYN: Yes, it has.

CAROL: Don't contradict me.

EVELYN (*with truculence*): Why shouldn't I?

CAROL: Because it infuriates me.

EVELYN (*slowly*): We're almost quarrelling.

CAROL: Yes.

EVELYN: I'm sorry.

CAROL: Antagonism is a bad sign.

EVELYN: What do you mean?

CAROL (*suddenly burying her face in her hands*): Oh, Evie!

EVELYN (*alarmed*): What on earth's the matter?

CAROL (*muffled*): Nothing.

EVELYN: Carol, don't – please — (*He gets up and comes to her.*)

CAROL: No, no. Sit down. Your man will be in in a moment.

EVELYN: Do tell me what's wrong.

CAROL: Sit down, please.

EVELYN: All right. (*He sits down.*)

CAROL: Give me my bag, will you? It's over there. I want to powder my nose.

> EVELYN *rises. When his back is towards her, an expression of extreme satisfaction flits across* CAROL's *face. By the time he has turned she is once again bravely melancholy.*

EVELYN: Here. (*He gives her her bag.*)

CAROL: Thank you.

> *She looks up at him with a weary smile.* BLACKWELL *enters and takes away the remains of the sweet.*

EVELYN: Serve the coffee at once, Blackwell; then I shan't want you any more.

BLACKWELL: Very good, sir. (*He goes out.*)

CAROL: I feel better now.

EVELYN: I don't suppose you'll ever want to dine with me again.

CAROL: Don't be silly. Of course I shall.

EVELYN: I seem to have depressed you terribly.

CAROL: No – it's not your fault, really.

EVELYN: I wish I understood you a bit better.

CAROL: I'm glad you don't.

> BLACKWELL *enters with coffee and liqueurs, which he places beside* EVELYN.

EVELYN: Thank you, Blackwell. Goodnight.

BLACKWELL: Goodnight, sir. (*He goes out.*)

EVELYN: Coffee?

CAROL: Yes, please.

EVELYN (*pouring it out*): Sugar?

CAROL: One.

EVELYN (*handing it to her*): There. Cointreau or brandy?

CAROL: Cointreau just a little.

EVELYN: The brandy's very good.

CAROL: All right. Brandy, then – you're so dominant.

EVELYN: Don't laugh me any more.

CAROL: I must a little.

EVELYN: Here you are. (*He gives her some brandy and takes some himself.*)

CAROL: Next time I come I'll try to be more amusing.

EVELYN: I don't want you to be amusing if you don't feel like it.

CAROL: You're awfully kind and gentle.

EVELYN: I want you to relax completely.

CAROL: I am relaxing completely.

EVELYN: I feel you need it.

CAROL: No one else has ever taken the trouble to feel that.

EVELYN: They're all too occupied in enjoying themselves.

CAROL: But I don't think they do, really.

EVELYN: That's true, but they wouldn't dare admit it.

CAROL: Put the gramophone on.

EVELYN: Now?

CAROL: Yes, please, or I shall cry again.

EVELYN (*rising*): What shall we have?

CAROL: Something blaring and noisy.

EVELYN: What a baby you are!

CAROL: Am I? (*He puts on a foxtrot and stands by the machine looking at her. After a pause she speaks.*) I love this tune.

EVELYN: It's not very new, I'm afraid. I must get some more of the latest ones.

CAROL: Are you ready for your lesson?

EVELYN: Lesson?

CAROL: Yes, your dancing lesson.

EVELYN: If you are.

CAROL: Of course I am! Come on. (*She rises.*)

EVELYN: I'll push the table back. (*He does so.*) There.

CAROL: Now then. (*They begin to dance.*)

EVELYN: Is the time all right?

CAROL: A scrap too fast.

EVELYN: Wait a minute. (*He stops for a second and regulates the time.*)

CAROL: That's better. (*They dance again.*)

EVELYN: I'm so sorry. Did I kick you?

CAROL: No.

EVELYN: I warned you, didn't I?

CAROL: Hold me a little tighter.

EVELYN: All right. (*They dance in silence for a moment.*)

CAROL: This is divine.

EVELYN: You're not teaching me a thing.

CAROL: You don't need it.

EVELYN: You're just being polite. I dance like an elephant.

CAROL: Don't be ridiculous. It would be terribly funny if anyone suddenly came in and found us.

EVELYN: There's not the least chance of it. (*They dance in silence for a little.*)

CAROL: Oh!

EVELYN: What is it?

CAROL: We nearly crashed into that chair.

EVELYN: I'm afraid I wasn't concentrating.

CAROL: That's very naughty of you. You must.

EVELYN: All right. (*The record comes to an end.*)

CAROL: Put on another.

EVELYN: Very well.

> *While he does so,* CAROL *looks at herself carefully in the glass over the mantelpiece.*

CAROL: I'm enjoying myself frightfully.

EVELYN: Are you, really?

CAROL: Aren't you?

EVELYN: You know I am. (*He takes her in his arms again.*)

CAROL: You really must hold me a little tighter – it's so much easier to follow.

EVELYN: Like that?

CAROL: Yes – like that.

> *They stand still, she surrendering herself to him, and holds up her face deliberately to be kissed.*

EVELYN (*softly*): Carol!

> *He kisses her. They stand tightly clasped for a moment; then he firmly disentangles himself and turns off the gramophone.*

CAROL (*sinking on to the sofa and passing her hand across her eyes*): Oh, Evie!

EVELYN (*in a different tone*): I thought so.

CAROL (*looking up quickly*): What do you mean?

EVELYN: It's unbelievable. (*He strides about a little.*)

CAROL (*alarmed*): What on earth are you talking about?

EVELYN: I was right. I knew it.

CAROL (*becoming exasperated*): Knew what?

EVELYN: I'm not quite such easy game as all that.

CAROL (*rising*): Evie!

EVELYN: What a little rotter you are.

CAROL (*outraged*): What!!

EVELYN: Yes, you may well look surprised. I, unfortunately, am *not* surprised.

CAROL (*after a pause*): I'm beginning to understand.

EVELYN: I'm glad.

CAROL: Very clever. I must congratulate Edward.

EVELYN: It's nothing to do with Edward.

CAROL: Liar! (*She goes and takes up her cloak.*)

EVELYN: You're not going yet.

CAROL: On the contrary, I'm going immediately.

EVELYN: Not until I choose.

CAROL: Don't speak to me like that.

EVELYN: I'm going to speak to you as you've never been spoken to before.

CAROL: Pompous ass!

> *She flings her cloak over her arm and goes towards the door.* EVELYN *stands between her and the door.*

EVELYN: You're going to stay here.

CAROL (*contemptuously*): Don't be so ridiculous.

EVELYN: I mean it.

CAROL: Are you quite mad?

EVELYN: No, not at all; I'm unflatteringly sane.

CAROL: Do you intend to use force to keep me here?

EVELYN: Yes, if necessary.

CAROL: Evie – what have you been reading? (*She flings down her cloak and returns to the sofa.*)

EVELYN: That's right.

CAROL (*helping herself to a cigarette*): I always thought you were a fool.

EVELYN: Thank you. I'm sorry I was less of a fool than you hoped.

CAROL: I didn't hope for much, whatever happened.

EVELYN: You'd forgotten I was Edward's best friend.

CAROL: You're very, very sure of yourself.

EVELYN: I can afford to be. I live decently.

CAROL: Rubbish!

EVELYN: And I've got a little honour left.

CAROL: Even after living decently.

EVELYN: You would say a thing like that.

CAROL: I did.

EVELYN: I should like to say one thing —

CAROL: Please do.

EVELYN: If you and I were alone on a desert island I wouldn't touch you.

CAROL: That would be very silly of you.

EVELYN (*rapidly losing his temper*): Haven't you any modesty or shame anywhere?

CAROL (*smiling*): Oh dear!

EVELYN: Stop being flippant; it's only a mask to cover your humiliation.

CAROL: How discerning you are!

EVELYN: I know you much better than you think I do.

CAROL: Idiot!

EVELYN: Flinging epithets at me won't help.

CAROL: Fatuous prig.

EVELYN: Shut up.

CAROL (*rising*): May I go now please?

EVELYN (*almost shouting*): No.

CAROL (*sitting down*): Very well.

EVELYN: I'm Edward's best friend.

CAROL: You've said that before.

EVELYN: And I'm damned if I'm going to stand by and see him cheapened and humiliated by you.

CAROL: You're insufferable.

EVELYN: That's beside the point.

CAROL (*suddenly furious*): It is *not* beside the point! How dare you behave like this! If you were Edward's Siamese twin you've no right to ask me here and insult me. You surely don't imagine that by talking until you're blue in the face you could ever alter my life one way or another. You've played a filthy second-rate trick on me and you think you did it for Edward's sake, but all the time it was only to prove to yourself how clever you are. You've got to let me go now – at once. Do you hear? If not I'll scream the place down. (*She rises and makes a dash for the door. He intercepts her. She struggles. He grasps her wrists.*) Let me go. Help! Help!

EVELYN: Shut up, you little fool! (*He puts his hand over her mouth and drags her back to the sofa, upon which she collapses, sobbing.*)

CAROL (*almost hysterical, in muffled tones*): How dare you! Oh, how dare you! It's outrageous. It's —

189

EVELYN: Do you want some brandy?

CAROL: Don't speak to me.

EVELYN (*with emphasis*): Do you want some brandy?

CAROL: No.

EVELYN: You'd better have some. Stay where you are. (*He goes over and pours out a glass of brandy and brings it to her.*) Here – sit up.

CAROL: Go away. Don't come near me.

EVELYN: You're hysterical. Drink this and pull yourself together.

> *He puts his arm round her to lift her up. She wriggles free of him, sits up quickly by herself, snatches the glass from his hand and flings it into the fireplace.*

CAROL: I don't want your filthy brandy.

EVELYN: That was childish.

CAROL: Why are you doing this to me? Why? Why? What have I ever done to you?

EVELYN: You're on the verge of ruining the life of one of the best men that ever lived.

CAROL (*tearfully*): How?

EVELYN: You know perfectly well how.

CAROL: It's no business of yours – what I do – ever.

EVELYN: I've made it my business. What you attempted tonight with me you've accomplished with other men – you've flirted and encouraged them to make love to you, and in many cases you've given yourself to them —

CAROL: Evie!

EVELYN: I don't want you to deny it or affirm it. I *know* it's true, but I don't think Edward does; he loves you too much to believe it possible, and my object in playing on you this second-rate trick, as you call it, is to make you realise what a hideous mess you're making both of his life and your own. (*During this speech* CAROL *is looking at* EVIE *intently. He begins to stride up and down while he talks.*) Edward's too sensitive and reserved to fight for his own rights. I've known for ages that he wasn't happy – that something was weighing on his mind. Today I asked him plump out and he admitted — (*He pauses.*)

CAROL: What did he admit?

EVELYN: That he was worried and miserable about you.

CAROL (*calmly*): And what did you advise him to do?

EVELYN: Give you hell.

CAROL: How crude of you!

EVELYN: Women of your sort require a little crudity occasionally.

CAROL: What do you mean 'women of my sort'?

EVELYN: Do you want me to tell you?

CAROL: No; I don't want you to say any more at all.

EVELYN: You have the soul of a harlot!

CAROL (*suddenly bursting out laughing*): Oh, Evie!

EVELYN (*losing control*): Don't laugh. Don't laugh.

CAROL (*continuing to laugh*): What do you expect me to do. You're so ridiculous —

EVELYN: I suppose you consider anyone with decent ideals ridiculous?

CAROL (*laughing helplessly*): Oh dear! Oh dear!

EVELYN (*working himself up more and more*): You think it funny that I should make an attempt to defend the honour of my best friend, who is too shamed by your utter wantonness to defend himself —

CAROL (*growing hysterical*): You're mad – quite, quite mad —

EVELYN: You're deliberately ruining his reputation and wrecking his happiness because you never make the slightest effort to control your rotten passions —

CAROL (*rising, trying to control her hysteria*): How dare you say that – how dare you —

EVELYN: Dare! I'll say it again and again. Rotten passions! All you live for, all you think of – women of your type can't exist without men – men – nothing but men all the time —

CAROL (*frantically*): Stop! Stop! You shan't say any more. (*She gives him a ringing slap on the face. He stands quite still.*) Cad! cad! unutterable cad! (*She gives him another slap between each word. He remains motionless. They stand facing each other.* CAROL *puts her hand to her head.*) I think – I think I'm going to be ill.

> She falls in a heap at his feet. He carries her back to the sofa. He deposits her there and rushes to get some more brandy. When his back is turned she lifts her head sharply and looks at him, then lets it drop attractively against the side of the sofa. He returns and ministers

the brandy. After a slight pause she opens her eyes and sits up and finishes the brandy.

EVELYN: Be careful. Don't spill it on your dress.

CAROL: I'm awfully sorry to be so stupid.

EVELYN: I didn't mean to make you ill.

CAROL (*meekly*): Please may I go home now?

EVELYN: You'd better wait a moment until you feel stronger. I won't say any more – I promise.

CAROL: My head aches.

EVELYN: Would you like some aspirin? I think I've got some somewhere.

CAROL: No, thanks.

EVELYN: It wasn't out of any personal spite, you know —

CAROL: It doesn't matter – it — (*She bursts into tears.*)

EVELYN: I say, don't cry – please.

CAROL: I can't help it. (*She cries a little more.*)

EVELYN: Please! Please!

CAROL: Leave me alone. I'll be all right in a minute.

EVELYN: I had no intention of losing my temper. I apologise.

CAROL (*with a fresh burst of tears*): It's all so – so horrible!

EVELYN: Carol – please, please don't!

CAROL (*sobbing bitterly*): I'd no idea – anyone could think of me like that.

EVELYN: I was only trying to show you, for Edward's sake —

CAROL: Don't – don't say any more. You promised.

EVELYN: All right, but you see I —

CAROL: I understand why you did it. It's not that I'm crying for. It's – it's — Oh God!

EVELYN (*appealingly*): Carol —

CAROL: I'm crying because I'm so bitterly ashamed —

EVELYN (*gently*): Carol —

CAROL: I don't want you to despise me utterly —

EVELYN: It's all right. Don't think any more about it.

CAROL: The things you've said to me are right – I have been shallow and cheap; but there's a reason that you don't know.

EVELYN: Reason?

CAROL: You've heard Edward's side of the story and you've

mixed yourself up in our lives – more than ever now. It's only
fair for you to hear my side, too —

EVELYN: Now look here, Carol. Don't let's say any more about it
at all.

CAROL: Do you mean that?

EVELYN: Yes.

CAROL (*rising*): Very well – I suppose I deserve it. Goodnight.
(*She walks sadly towards the door.*)

EVELYN: Carol —

CAROL (*turning*): Yes?

EVELYN: I'll hear your side if you want me to, but what's the use
of going on any further?

CAROL: Only that unless I explain now I can never look you in
the face again.

EVELYN: Carol, don't be so absurd.

CAROL: There are circumstances that justify me more than you
realise.

EVELYN: Come back, then, and sit down.

CAROL (*wearily returning*): I feel so horribly tired.

*She comes back to the sofa and leans against it, looking at him. Her
face is pale and she looks extremely sad and quite lovely.*

EVELYN: Do sit down.

CAROL: No, but I want you to. Sit here where you needn't look
at me.

EVELYN: Very well.

He sits down on the sofa and stares into the fire. CAROL *stands just
behind him with her hands resting on his shoulders. Both their faces
are half turned to the audience. She speaks very slowly.*

CAROL: You've been pretty brutal to me tonight and some of the
hard things you said I deserve, but not all of them. I'm selfish
and occasionally cheap and rather vain – and I have been
unfaithful to my husband, but not before he had been
unfaithful to me —

EVELYN (*starting*): What!

CAROL (*pressing him down*): Keep still, please. I'm telling you the
truth —

EVELYN: You mean that Edward —

CAROL: I mean exactly what I say. I was completely faithful to

Edward until eighteen months ago, when I discovered that he was having an affair with Zoe St Merryn —

EVELYN: Good God! (*He moves again, but she holds him firmly.*)

CAROL: That broke me up, rather.

EVELYN: I don't believe it.

CAROL: I can't help that; it's true, all the same.

EVELYN: How did you discover it? What proof have you?

CAROL: I suspected for a little while and said nothing until I could bear it no longer; then I asked Edward and he admitted it —

EVELYN (*twisting round*): I *must* look at you.

CAROL (*firmly, looking into his eyes*): He admitted it.

EVELYN: It's incredible.

CAROL: Why? Edward's awfully weak, and Zoe — (*She laughs sadly.*) Will you turn around again now, please. (EVELYN *does so and buries his face in his hands.*) Don't be upset about it, Evie – it's between Edward and me, really, and nobody knew – until now. I made him swear never to tell a soul, otherwise he'd have told you ages ago – he always tells you everything. I've behaved rather badly since then, I know, but something went dead, inside me and – well, it doesn't seem to matter much, does it?

EVELYN (*after a pause*): May I get up now and get a drink?

CAROL: There's nothing more to say, anyhow.

     EVELYN *goes over and pours himself out a drink. He turns suddenly.*

EVELYN: You wouldn't lie to me, would you?

CAROL (*with dignity*): Even I have a little decency left. (*She turns to go again.*)

EVELYN: Carol!

CAROL (*turning*): Yes.

EVELYN: What can I say to you?

CAROL: Nothing.

EVELYN: I'm desperately sorry.

CAROL: All right.

EVELYN: I've been an abject, blundering fool. It wasn't my business, anyhow.

CAROL (*with a wan smile*): Your motives were sound.

EVELYN: Can you forgive me?

CAROL: Yes, of course.

EVELYN: I mean really forgive me?

CAROL (*holding out her hand*): Completely.

EVELYN: You're very generous. (*He takes it.*)

CAROL: There's one more thing I want to clear up.

EVELYN: What?

CAROL: I came here tonight for one reason only.

EVELYN: Yes?

CAROL: I love you!

EVELYN (*dropping her hand*): Carol!

CAROL: It's all right – don't be afraid. I'm going now – but I didn't want you to think me too cheap – that's all.

EVELYN: I'm utterly bewildered.

CAROL: It hasn't been very easy for either of us, has it?

EVELYN: You can't mean what you say.

CAROL: You know I do – you've known it all along, subconsciously.

EVELYN: Carol – I'm dreadfully – horribly embarrassed.

CAROL: Poor old Evie.

EVELYN: I don't know what to do.

CAROL: We'll both laugh over tonight one day, won't we?

EVELYN: Will we?

CAROL (*with beautifully forced gaiety*): Yes – you see.

EVELYN: You are an extraordinary woman.

CAROL: Just rather silly, I'm afraid. Goodnight.

EVELYN: I'm going to see you home.

CAROL: No, please. I'd rather go alone. Please, I mean it, honestly.

EVELYN: But —

CAROL: It's only just round the corner.

EVELYN: I can't let you go alone.

CAROL (*with gentle firmness*): You must – please.

EVELYN (*looking down*): All right.

CAROL: We're friends, aren't we?

EVELYN (*still looking down*): Yes.

CAROL: In spite of everything?

EVELYN: Yes.

CAROL: Because of everything?

EVELYN: Oh, Carol!

CAROL: Goodnight, my dear. (*She comes to him and kisses him gently on the mouth. After a moment she disentangles herself.*) No, no! I didn't mean it, really. I'm not going to be cheap any more. Stand quite still where you are, not looking. I don't want you to move until I've gone.

She goes out quietly, leaving him standing stock-still. After a moment the front door slams. EVELYN *turns in the direction of the sound.*

EVELYN (*emotionally*): Carol – Oh God!

He goes over to the sofa and flings himself down on it, with his face buried in his hands. CAROL *comes softly in again. Her cloak is over her arm. She gives one look in his direction and then goes noiselessly into his bedroom, closing the door after her.*

CURTAIN

ACT III

The scene is the same as Act I. It is about twelve o'clock in the morning. One night has elapsed since Act II.

When the curtain rises the studio is empty. There is the sound of the front door bell ringing with some violence. BERRY *enters, R., and crosses over L. He exits and reappears in a moment, ushering in* EVELYN. EVELYN *is looking extremely white and strained.*

BERRY: Can I offer you anything to drink, sir?

EVELYN: No, thanks.

BERRY: The master's sure to be in soon, sir.

EVELYN: All right, thanks.

BERRY: He's only taking a walk in the Park.

EVELYN: I think I will have a drink, after all.

BERRY: Very good sir. Whisky and soda?

EVELYN: Yes, please.

> BERRY *goes out.* EVELYN *proceeds to pace up and down the room a little.* BERRY *returns with a whisky and soda.*

Oh, thanks. (*He takes it.*)

BERRY: Would you like the papers, sir, or have you seen them already?

EVELYN: I've seen them, thanks.

BERRY: Shall I tell Mrs Churt that you are here, sir?

EVELYN: No – no. Please don't disturb her.

BERRY: Very good, sir.

> *He goes out again.* EVELYN *once more proceeds to pace up and down with the whisky and soda in his hand. He is obviously extremely agitated. After a moment* CAROL *enters from R. She looks fresh and charming. She gives a slight start on seeing* EVELYN.

CAROL: Evie!

EVELYN (*jumping – he turns*): I've come to see Edward.

CAROL: What's the matter?

EVELYN: I've come to see Edward.

CAROL (*with faint apprehension*): I know – you just said so. Aren't you going to say good morning?

EVELYN: Good morning.

CAROL (*going over to him*): No more than that?

EVELYN: No – no more. (*He turns away.*)

CAROL (*biting her lip*): I see.

EVELYN: I want to see him alone.

CAROL (*putting her hand on his arm*): Evie, what's wrong?

EVELYN: You can seriously ask me that?

CAROL: Why are you behaving like this?

EVELYN (*turning away*): You're hopeless.

CAROL: You're not going to do anything foolish, are you?

EVELYN: I'm going to do the only thing possible.

CAROL (*swinging him round*): Evie!

EVELYN: Leave me alone.

CAROL: But listen —

EVELYN (*wrenching himself free from her*): Don't touch me, please.

CAROL (*pleading*): Evie – please – why are you being so horrid?

EVELYN: I don't want to look at you – or see you again ever!

CAROL: Why – why – what have I done?

EVELYN (*sinking into a chair with his face in his hands*): Leave me alone. Leave me alone.

CAROL: You don't love me at all, then?

EVELYN: For God's sake stop!

CAROL: You don't – you don't —

EVELYN: Shut up! Shut up!

CAROL: You coward! (*She goes over to the window.*)

EVELYN: Please go away. You'll only make everything much worse.

CAROL: Why have you come here this morning?

EVELYN: To tell Edward about last night.

CAROL: What will you tell him?

EVELYN: The truth.

CAROL: You're insane.

EVELYN: I was – but I'm not any more.

CAROL (*coming quickly back to him*): You can't mean this.

EVELYN: I do mean it.

CAROL: But why! Why!! Why!!!

EVELYN: I don't expect you to understand.

CAROL: Evie, listen. Be sensible for a moment.

EVELYN: It's no use going on like that. I've made up my mind.

CAROL: Evie —

EVELYN (*rising*): Go away! Go away!

CAROL (*following him*): I love you.

EVELYN: Be quiet.

CAROL: I love you – I love you. Tell what you like – shout it from the housetops. I love you!

EVELYN (*catching hold of her*): Shut up – you must. Someone will hear.

CAROL: I don't care.

EVELYN: You don't love me – you never did for a moment – it was all a trick.

CAROL (*outraged*): Evie!

EVELYN: I can see it all now – I can see it all.

CAROL: You're talking nonsense.

EVELYN: For God's sake go away from me.

CAROL (*helplessly*): I don't know what to do.

EVELYN: Leave me alone. I've got to tell Edward the truth.

CAROL: In heaven's name, why?

EVELYN: Can't you see why?

CAROL: No. What good will it do?

EVELYN: I've betrayed him.

CAROL: That's no reason for you to betray me as well.

EVELYN: He trusted me – completely.

CAROL: Well, why not let him go on trusting you?

EVELYN: Because I'm unworthy of it for ever.

CAROL: And what about me?

EVELYN: It was your fault.

CAROL: How chivalrous.

EVELYN: You lied to me.

CAROL (*firmly*): I did *not* lie to you.

EVELYN: You said you came last night because you loved me.

CAROL: So I did!

EVELYN: You came out of curiosity and stayed out of revenge.

CAROL: What a fool you are!

EVELYN: You determined to get even with me.

CAROL: Evie!

EVELYN: It's true – it's true – you know it is.

CAROL: Why have you built up this ridiculous story in your mind?

EVELYN: It's true.

CAROL (*with great firmness*): It's nothing of the sort, and if you calm yourself and think seriously for a moment, you'll realise the complete absurdity of it. You must be sensible. Do you hear – you *must* be sensible. You're on the verge of wrecking everything out of sheer hysteria.

EVELYN: Everything is wrecked already. I've got nothing left – no honour, no decency —

CAROL (*quietly*): I gave myself to you last night, Evie —

EVELYN: Don't – don't —

CAROL: I gave myself to you completely and for one reason only – I loved you. I love you now.

EVELYN: Carol, please —

CAROL: If you tell Edward – I shall go away and never see either of you again.

EVELYN: I can't help it. I —

CAROL: You *can* help it. What you're contemplating is utterly without reason. If you're trying to vindicate your honour, you can't seriously achieve it by betraying mine. We've both behaved abominably, I admit. We've both been weak and uncontrolled and given way completely and we shall suffer for it accordingly, you needn't doubt that for a minute. We're in a terrible mess, but we're in it together and together we must remain —

EVELYN: I shall never be able to look Edward in the face again.

CAROL: Will you be able to face him any better after you've told him?

EVELYN: Yes.

CAROL: Why?

EVELYN: Because I shall have done the only decent thing left to me.

CAROL: You'll only succeed in making him suffer as well as yourself and me. Can't you see the uselessness of it?

EVELYN: I can't see him and talk to him with this shame between us.

CAROL: You must – so must I. It's the just penalty for what we've done. You said just now you never wanted to see me again. Well, I promise you you never shall – alone. You at least can go away. I can't – I've got to stay and get through the next few months as best I can —

There comes a ring at the front door bell.

EVELYN (*pacing the room*): O God! what am I to do?

CAROL (*quickly*): Nothing – nothing yet, anyhow. Think sensibly and quietly – everything depends on your keeping calm —

BERRY *enters and crosses over L. and exits.*

EVELYN: Is that Edward?

CAROL: Yes, I expect so. He's always forgetting his key.

EVELYN (*terribly undecided*): Carol, I —

CAROL: Promise you'll do nothing yet.

EVELYN: I can't – I —

CAROL (*whispering violently*): Promise me – wait a little – promise me. Will you promise me?

EVELYN (*helplessly*): Yes.

BERRY *re-enters.*

BERRY (*announcing*): Mrs St Merryn.

ZOE *enters briskly.*

ZOE: Good morning, Carol. I haven't seen you for months. How are you?

CAROL (*as they kiss*): Splendid. I heard you were back.

ZOE: Hallo, Evie!

EVELYN (*coldly*): Good morning.

ZOE: I gather that Edward is expected?

CAROL: Yes, he'll be back at any minute.

EVELYN: Goodbye.

He goes out abruptly.

ZOE (*surprised*): That was one of the most sudden exits I've ever seen.

CAROL (*carelessly*): I think Evie's upset about something.

ZOE: I didn't think he was capable of it.

CAROL (*conventionally*): Are you glad to be back?

ZOE: Delighted. London's looking so pretty with all the roads up.

CAROL (*absently*): Are they? I hadn't noticed.

ZOE: I don't see how you could fail to unless you travel exclusively in the underground.

CAROL: Where are you staying?

ZOE: Claridge's.

CAROL: Oh!

ZOE: It's so beautifully austere.

CAROL: What?

ZOE (*patiently*): I said it was so beautifully austere.

CAROL: Oh yes, it is.

ZOE: You're looking awfully well.

CAROL: I am, frightfully well.

ZOE: Don't you think I'm looking frightfully well?

CAROL: Yes, you certainly are. Travelling obviously agrees with you.

ZOE: It's so comforting to know that we both look so awfully well. Can I have a cigarette?

CAROL: Yes, of course. I'm so sorry. Here — (*She hands her a box open.*)

ZOE: Thank you, dear. There aren't any in this box, but it doesn't matter.

CAROL: How annoying! Wait a minute. (*She takes another box off a table, L.*) Here —

ZOE (*taking one*): You seem a little distrait this morning, if I may say so.

CAROL: I've got rather a headache.

ZOE: I'm so sorry. You don't look very well.

CAROL: I think, if you'll forgive me, I'll go and take some aspirin.

ZOE: Of course. I should lie down until lunch if I were you.

CAROL: Perhaps I will. Edward's certain to be in soon.

ZOE: I'll be perfectly happy waiting.

CAROL: You must come and dine one night.

ZOE: I'd adore to.

CAROL: Goodbye for the present, dear. (*She kisses her.*)

ZOE: Goodbye. I'm sorry you're so seedy. I'm afraid you've been overdoing it lately.

CAROL (*irritatedly*): Overdoing what?

ZOE (*vaguely*): Oh, everything.

CAROL: No, I haven't.

ZOE: I'm so glad.

> CAROL *goes out.* ZOE *wanders round the room, smiling to herself, examining various portraits, etc. After a moment* EDWARD *enters.*

EDWARD: Zoe! How long have you been here?

ZOE: Only a few minutes.

EDWARD: I've been out in the Park.

ZOE: I didn't know it was still there.

EDWARD: I'm afraid you're finding the old town sadly changed.

ZOE: I'm sure it's much more hygienic now.

EDWARD: Have you seen Carol?

ZOE: Yes. She's just gone to bed.

EDWARD: Gone to bed?

ZOE: She said she had a headache.

EDWARD: How do you think she's looking?

ZOE (*laughing*): Awfully well.

EDWARD: What are you laughing at?

ZOE: Carol always makes me laugh.

EDWARD: Why?

ZOE: She's so consistent.

EDWARD: Are you lunching with me?

ZOE: If you like. I've got to go to Sloane Street first and look at Mary Phillip's house. She wants to let it to me.

EDWARD: Pick me up here on the way back.

ZOE: I really came to ask you to dine tonight and go to a play.

EDWARD: I'd love to. What do you want to see?

ZOE: A nice clean play, please, Edward.

EDWARD: Splendid. We shan't have any trouble getting seats.

ZOE: I'm so old-fashioned – I like love stories without the slightest suggestion of sex.

EDWARD: You ought to be a critic.

ZOE: You're an awfully nice person to come back to!

EDWARD (*smiling*): Am I?

ZOE: Yes. One picks up the threads exactly where they were dropped.

EDWARD: They were never dropped.

ZOE: Carol's an awful fool.

EDWARD: Why?

ZOE: She could hold you if she wanted to.

EDWARD: Don't be tiresome, Zoe.

ZOE: What are you going to do about it?

EDWARD: About what?

ZOE: Do you really want me to be explicit?

EDWARD: No. I know perfectly well what you mean.

ZOE: You're wasting time.

EDWARD: Not at all. I'm working hard.

ZOE: You said that yesterday and it was no more convincing then than it is now.

EDWARD: It's true.

ZOE: Perhaps, but rather beside the point.

EDWARD: What is the point?

ZOE: Your happiness.

EDWARD: What beautiful thoughts you have, Zoe.

ZOE: Don't be flippant.

EDWARD: Flippancy alleviates my boredom with the whole subject.

ZOE: Are you sure you're not confusing boredom with lack of moral courage?

EDWARD: Possibly.

ZOE: Well, don't.

EDWARD: I refuse to be dominated, Zoe – even by you!

ZOE (*smiling*): That's right, dear.

EDWARD: And don't laugh at me.

ZOE: I always have. I fail to see why I should stop now.

EDWARD: I resent it bitterly.

ZOE: Dear Edward.

EDWARD: What do you expect me to do?

ZOE: Deliver an ultimatum.

EDWARD: That would be stepping out of my character.

ZOE: Nonsense!

EDWARD: I am essentially a weak-minded man.

ZOE: Nothing of the sort – you're a lazy idealist.

EDWARD: That sounds delightful.

ZOE: So it is in theory; in practice it's sterility personified.

EDWARD: You're terribly didactic.

ZOE: I'm trying to rouse you.

EDWARD: Why?

ZOE: Because you're discontented and unhappy.

EDWARD: I never said so.

ZOE: You don't need to – it's written all over you.

EDWARD: You think I'd be happier if I bashed about making scenes and delivering ultimatums?

ZOE: Certainly – you at least might achieve something.

EDWARD: What, for instance?

ZOE: Freedom!

EDWARD: That's a myth.

ZOE: Oh no, it isn't.

EDWARD: In this case it's impossible.

ZOE: Why?

EDWARD (*turning away*): Oh, don't let's discuss it any more.

ZOE: You *are* annoying, Edward.

EDWARD: Evie went on like that for hours yesterday.

ZOE: Evie?

EDWARD: Yes. He seemed to advocate violence as being the best method.

ZOE: He would.

EDWARD: He even offered to teach Carol a lesson.

ZOE: What sort of lesson?

EDWARD: He didn't explain.

ZOE: Poor Evie.

EDWARD: You needn't despise him so utterly. He's a good sort.

ZOE: He's the quintessence of masculine complacency.

EDWARD: I'm sure it's a great comfort to him. I wish I was.

ZOE: Evie will get into trouble one of these days. He's too worldly.

EDWARD: If I were free, Zoe, would you marry me?

ZOE: Edward!

EDWARD: I suddenly thought of it.

ZOE (*laughing*): This is terribly sudden.

EDWARD: Don't be silly.

ZOE: You must give me time to think.

EDWARD: Do shut up and be serious.

ZOE: I have a vague feeling that your proposal is a little previous.

EDWARD: It wasn't a proposal – just an idea.

ZOE: Not exactly an original one. We discussed it all ages ago.

EDWARD: And whose fault was it that it never came off?

ZOE (*promptly*): Yours.

EDWARD: Zoe, how can you? It was entirely yours.

ZOE: Nonsense! I was dead set on it.

EDWARD: You refused me and rushed off to Africa.

ZOE: You can't call Algiers Africa.

EDWARD: It is, all the same.

ZOE: If you'd loved me enough, you'd have followed me.

EDWARD: I was waiting for you to come back.

ZOE: Let's stop talking about it – it's rather painful.

EDWARD: We weren't in love, really, anyhow.

ZOE: Weren't we?

EDWARD: I don't know.

ZOE: It's all very difficult.

EDWARD: Yes.

ZOE: I think I shall go away again soon.

EDWARD: Oh, Zoe, please don't!

ZOE: It's going to be awkward if I stay.

EDWARD: No, it isn't.

ZOE: We're both on rather dangerous ground.

EDWARD: I don't see why.

ZOE: Yes, you do, perfectly.

EDWARD: I do not.

ZOE: If I stay, we shall probably fall in love properly – we're both at a perilous age.

EDWARD: What if we do?

ZOE: It would be too horrible, with all this Carol business going on and everything.

EDWARD: You're crossing your bridges before you come to them.

ZOE: I shall go, all the same.

EDWARD: That is rank cowardice.

ZOE: No, it isn't; it's sound sense.

EDWARD: It will be beastly for me.

ZOE: Not so beastly as if I stayed, really – in the long run.

EDWARD: What could happen?

ZOE: Oh, the usual thing, I suppose – we should have an affair and spoil everything.

EDWARD: I don't see why.

ZOE: You're being very obstinate this morning.

EDWARD: If I were in love with you at all, it would be in a very nice, restrained way.

ZOE: We should both tire of that very quickly.

EDWARD: Zoe, how can you be so unpleasant?

ZOE: I'm only facing facts.

EDWARD: We've been together a good deal in the past.

ZOE: I know.

EDWARD: And everything was above reproach.

ZOE: Entirely.

EDWARD: Well, why can't we go on like that?

ZOE: Because even if we do, people will say we don't.

EDWARD: What does that matter?

ZOE: It matters a lot. I've had enough squalor in the past few years to last me for life.

EDWARD: Yes, but I don't see —

ZOE: Also I have a strange aversion to coming between man and wife.

EDWARD: Oh, shut up, Zoe.

ZOE: It's true. I suffer from a pre-war conscience.

EDWARD: There's no question of that, really.

ZOE: Don't be silly. Of course there is.

EDWARD: Carol wouldn't care.

ZOE: What difference does that make? Really, Edward, you're being horribly flaccid over the whole thing!

EDWARD: Don't let's argue about it.

ZOE: All right.

EDWARD: But please don't go away again – just yet.

ZOE: I'll think it over, Edward.

EDWARD: You've depressed me terribly.

ZOE: I'm sorry.

EDWARD: It's all such a hopeless muddle.

ZOE: It needn't be.

EDWARD: I'd no idea you were so designing.

ZOE: What a horrid thing to say!

EDWARD: It's true though, isn't it?

ZOE: Absolutely.

EDWARD: Oh, Zoe —

ZOE: I must go.

EDWARD: Remember lunch.

ZOE: I'll pick you up here.

EDWARD: No, don't – I'll meet you.

ZOE: Where?

EDWARD: Berkeley – one o'clock.

ZOE: I'm sure to be late.

EDWARD: So am I.

ZOE: Goodbye, dear. (*She goes up to him and kisses him lightly.*)

EDWARD: Zoe!

ZOE: That was part of the design!

> *She goes out.* EDWARD *walks up and down irritably for a moment, then lights a cigarette and flings himself into an armchair. The telephone rings. He gives an exclamation of annoyance and rises to answer it.*

EDWARD (*at telephone*): Hallo! ... Yes – yes ... Who is it speaking? ... No, I'm afraid you can't. She isn't very well —

> CAROL *enters in time to catch the last sentence.*

CAROL: Who is it?

EDWARD: Oh. ... hold on, please. ... Harry Challoner. (*He hands her the telephone curtly and goes over to the window.*)

CAROL (*at telephone*): Hallo! ... Yes, it's me. ... No – no, I can't. I'm sorry. ... All right, if you like. ... I'll be in between six and seven. ... Yes. ... Goodbye.

> *She hangs up the receiver and looks towards* EDWARD *who has his back turned. She is about to go out again, when he turns.*

EDWARD: Carol.

CAROL: Yes?

EDWARD: I want to talk to you.

CAROL: Is anything the matter?

EDWARD: Yes. Sit down, will you?

CAROL (*sitting*): If you like.

EDWARD: I want to get things settled.

CAROL: Get things settled?

EDWARD: Yes.

CAROL: What sort of things?

EDWARD: Our exact relationship.

CAROL: What *do* you mean?

EDWARD: Just that.

CAROL: I don't understand.

EDWARD: I think you do.

CAROL (*by now extremely apprehensive*): I don't Edward, honestly.

EDWARD: Do you intend to pursue your present course indefinitely?

CAROL: What are you talking about?

EDWARD: Infidelity.

CAROL: Are you insinuating that I —

EDWARD: I'm insinuating nothing. I'm stating that you have been unfaithful to me.

CAROL (*rising*): Edward!

EDWARD (*firmly*): Sit down. This is not a scene – it's a process of readjustment. Please let us keep it as brief as possible.

CAROL (*sinking down*): How can you be so horrible!

EDWARD: Do you deny it?

CAROL: Of course I do.

EDWARD: Carol, let me disillusion you. I'm not bluffing. I *know*. I've known for ages. It's no use wasting time denying and arguing. We must decide what's to be done about it.

CAROL: How can you be so foul!

EDWARD (*wearily*): Oh, Carol, do stop acting.

CAROL: You're insufferable.

EDWARD: Once and for all will you be sensible?

CAROL: I hate you.

EDWARD: That would be beautifully definite if you weren't so unreliable.

CAROL: Do you want me to hate you?

EDWARD: To be honest with you, I really don't mind.

CAROL (*outraged*): Edward!

EDWARD: Don't be a fool, Carol.

CAROL: How dare you! How dare you!

EDWARD: We will face facts, please.

CAROL (*rising*): I'm not going to stay here and be insulted.

EDWARD: You're not being insulted – it's I who have been

insulted. You've been publicly underrating my intelligence for months.

CAROL: That's what's upsetting you, is it?

EDWARD: Certainly it is. I wish you'd sit down.

CAROL: I'm going to my room.

EDWARD: You're only temporarily evading the issues by doing that.

CAROL: What's the object of all this?

EDWARD: The object, as I said before, is to get our relationship satisfactorily defined.

CAROL (*with grandeur*): It's satisfactorily defined now as far as I am concerned.

EDWARD: I would prefer the satisfaction to be mutual.

CAROL: You think you're very clever, don't you?

EDWARD: What a common remark! You'll be sticking your tongue out at me in a minute.

CAROL: I suppose Zoe has been putting you up to this.

EDWARD: Meaning that I have no initiative of my own anyhow?

CAROL: Exactly.

EDWARD: That's charming of you – and fits in beautifully with your behaviour during the last year.

CAROL: Are you in love with me still?

EDWARD: Do you expect me to be?

CAROL: Are you?

EDWARD: No, Carol.

CAROL: I see.

EDWARD: All of which is beside the point.

CAROL: No, it isn't. If you loved me you'd never say such things to me.

EDWARD: I admit that it would be more comfortable for you if I just suffered and suffered in silence.

CAROL: You're too unemotional to be capable of any suffering.

EDWARD: Do you imagine you're putting up a good defence for yourself?

CAROL: I'm not attempting to.

EDWARD: That brings us to my ultimatum.

CAROL (*with a forced laugh*): Ultimatum! Really Edward!

EDWARD: You've been unfaithful to me three times during the

past year – Maurice Verney, Geoffrey Poole, and now Harry Challoner!

CAROL (*blanching slightly*): Edward!

EDWARD: All three married men, which adds considerably to the general sordidness of the whole business.

CAROL (*losing control*): I will *not* be spoken to like this!

EDWARD (*with sudden force*): Be quiet! Do you still deny it?

CAROL (*more dimly*): No.

EDWARD: That's better.

CAROL (*sullenly*): I'm sorry.

EDWARD: That's too sudden to be convincing.

CAROL (*breaking up slightly; after a long pause*): What are you going to do?

EDWARD: Wait until next time.

CAROL: Next time?

EDWARD: Yes.

CAROL: And what then?

EDWARD: I shall divorce you.

CAROL: Edward!

EDWARD: I mean it. Whether the man happens to be married or single will not make the slightest difference.

CAROL (*looking down*): I see.

EDWARD: Is that quite clear?

CAROL: Quite.

EDWARD: Incidentally, I wish you to give up Harry Challoner entirely. I object to you even being seen with such a second-rate bounder.

CAROL (*looking at him*): Very well.

EDWARD: We'll both do our best to forget the whole thing. We can get along perfectly well together with a little effort.

CAROL: There's no more, is there?

EDWARD: No, that's all.

> CAROL *goes slowly towards the door in silence. Her expression is very thoughtful. When she reaches the door she turns.*

CAROL (*in a different voice*): Edward.

EDWARD: Yes?

CAROL: Please forgive me.

EDWARD: Forgiveness in this case is surely rather unimportant.

CAROL: Oh, please, please — (*She bursts into tears and goes towards him.*)

EDWARD: Now then, Carol —

CAROL (*standing in front of him weeping*): You must forgive me – you must!

EDWARD: All right.

CAROL: I didn't love any of them – I swear I didn't.

EDWARD (*turning away irritably*): Oh, Carol —

CAROL: You've been utterly indifferent to me for ages.

EDWARD: Naturally.

CAROL: No, but before – I mean before – last year you stopped loving me.

EDWARD: Please don't go on like this.

CAROL: It's true – it's true. I was lonely.

EDWARD: Don't talk such utter nonsense.

CAROL (*working herself up*): It isn't nonsense – it's you I love really all the time. I hate Harry Challoner, really. I've been trying to break with him for ages. I made a vow weeks ago that I'd never be unfaithful to you again – honestly I did, I swear it. I'm sick of everybody. I wanted to ask you to take me away abroad somewhere, but I didn't dare – you had so much work to do – and you were so cold and horrid. Edward – Edward – you've got to love me again – you must. I shall go mad if you don't. Please – Edward darling. (*She flings herself into his arms.*)

EDWARD (*gently disentangling himself*): There now – it's all right. Do stop. (*He kisses her dutifully.*)

CAROL: I feel so bitterly ashamed.

EDWARD: Stop crying.

CAROL: I swear I'll be good. I swear I will.

EDWARD: That's right. Now control yourself.

CAROL: I'll never see Harry again.

EDWARD: Very well. For heaven's sake stop crying.

CAROL: I do love you really, you know. That's what makes it so awful.

EDWARD: Pull yourself together.

CAROL (*dabbing her eyes*): I'll try.

EDWARD: Go and lie down and take something.

CAROL: What shall I take?

EDWARD: Aspirin, I should think.

CAROL: I had some just now.

EDWARD: Have some more.

CAROL: All right. Oh, God!

> *She goes out slowly, still half sobbing.* EDWARD *heaves a sigh of mingled relief and irritation, he again flings himself into an armchair. Then comes the sound of the front door bell. He groans.* BERRY *enters from R.*

EDWARD: Whoever it is, Berry, I'm out.

BERRY: Very good, sir. (*He goes out L. After a moment he re-enters.*) I'm very sorry, sir; it's Major Bathurst. The porter downstairs told him you'd just come in; he's called already this morning.

EDWARD: Nobody told me. You'd better show him in.

BERRY: Yes, sir. (*He goes out and returns, announcing*) Major Bathurst.

> EVELYN *comes in. He looks more harassed than ever.* BERRY *goes out.*

EDWARD: Hallo, Evie!

EVELYN (*haltingly*): Edward – I – I've come to say goodbye.

EDWARD (*surprised*): Goodbye?

EVELYN: Yes. I came earlier this morning, but you were out.

EDWARD: But where on earth are you going?

EVELYN: Australia.

EDWARD: Why Australia?

EVELYN (*weakly*): I've always wanted to go to Australia.

EDWARD: What *do* you mean?

EVELYN: I mean I've got to go there on business.

EDWARD: It's very sudden, isn't it?

EVELYN: Yes. I had a wire from my brother.

EDWARD: I didn't know he was in Australia.

EVELYN: He isn't. He's in Cheltenham, but he sent me a wire saying I ought to go out there at once.

EDWARD: What's the matter with you, Evie?

EVELYN: Nothing.

EDWARD: You're not only telling me extremely fatuous lies, but you look like death.

EVELYN: They're not lies. I —

EDWARD: Don't be an ass. Have a drink.

EVELYN: No – I don't want a drink.

EDWARD: What's wrong?

EVELYN: There's nothing wrong.

EDWARD: You'd better tell me, you know.

EVELYN: I want to tell you.

EDWARD: Come on, then.

EVELYN: I've got to tell you.

EDWARD: Out with it.

EVELYN: But I can't.

EDWARD: Surely that's rather silly.

EVELYN: I tried to shoot myself this morning.

EDWARD: You what!!!

EVELYN: Tried to shoot myself.

EDWARD (*alarmed*): In God's name, why?

EVELYN (*brokenly*): Oh, Edward!

EDWARD: Evie, what *has* happened?

EVELYN: I'm the filthiest cad in the world.

EDWARD: Don't be ridiculous.

EVELYN: Our friendship is over for ever.

EDWARD (*with irritation*): Do stop all this melodrama, Evie, and tell me what's the matter.

EVELYN: I've betrayed you, utterly.

EDWARD (*in great astonishment*): Betrayed *me*?

EVELYN (*looking down*): Yes.

EDWARD: How?

EVELYN (*brokenly*): Carol!

EDWARD: Carol! Well, what about her?

EVELYN: Carol dined with me last night.

EDWARD: Oh, did she?

EVELYN: And – and – O my God! (*He sinks into a chair by the table and leans his head on his arms.*)

EDWARD (*in amazement*): You don't seriously mean to tell me —

EVELYN (*in muffled tones*): Yes.

EDWARD: You and Carol!

EVELYN: Yes.

EDWARD: This is too much! (*He bursts out laughing.*)

EVELYN (*looking up astounded*): Edward!

EDWARD: I can't bear it. (*He laughs louder.*)

EVELYN (*rising*): Edward – old man – please —

EDWARD (*helplessly*): It's unbelievable – incredible. Oh dear! (*He collapses on the window seat.*)

EVELYN (*approaching him*): Edward – for God's sake —

EDWARD (*weakly*): Don't come near me. I shall be all right in a minute.

EVELYN (*with growing anger*): You must be mad.

EDWARD: I certainly feel very strange. (*He goes into fits of laughter again.*)

EVELYN (*outraged*): Edward – do you realise what I've just told you?

EDWARD (*trying to control himself*): Yes – perfectly.

EVELYN: And you can laugh!

EDWARD: Will you hand me a cigarette, please?

EVELYN (*irately*): Look here, Edward —

EDWARD (*with sudden firmness*): Will you hand me a cigarette, please.

EVELYN: Here. (*He offers him his case.*)

EDWARD: Thanks. (*He takes one.*) Light.

EVELYN: Here. (*He strikes a match.*)

EDWARD: Thanks. I feel better now.

EVELYN: Well! What are you going to do about it?

EDWARD: Ring that bell, will you? By the door.

EVELYN: I can find my own way out.

EDWARD (*firmly*): You're not going yet. Ring the bell, please.

EVELYN *looks at him and then goes and rings the bell.*

EVELYN: Look here, Edward, I came here this morning because I felt I owed it to our friendship, to confess the truth to you —

EDWARD: You're out of your depth, Evie – far, far out of your depth.

EVELYN: I don't know what you mean.

EDWARD: This is reality, not fiction.

BERRY *enters.*

BERRY: You rang, sir?

EDWARD: Will you ask your mistress to come down immediately, please, Berry? It's very important.

BERRY: Yes, sir. (*He goes out.*)

EVELYN (*panic-stricken*): Edward, this is not fair of you.

EDWARD (*unceremoniously*): Shut up.

EVELYN: This is between us.

EDWARD: The three of us, Evie – what's known, I believe, as the eternal triangle.

EVELYN: Let me tell you one thing – what happened was not deliberate.

EDWARD: You prefer to be thought a fool rather than a cad!

EVELYN: Yes, if you like to put it that way.

EDWARD: How typical!

EVELYN: I only asked Carol to dine, in the first place, for your sake.

EDWARD: For my sake?

EVELYN: Yes, I intended to teach her a lesson.

EDWARD: And she ended up by teaching you one.

EVELYN (*utterly shocked*): Edward!

EDWARD: Men of your sort should stick to athletics and not attempt physiology.

EVELYN: I deserve that.

EDWARD (*agreeably*): Fully.

CAROL *enters from* R. *She starts visibly on seeing* EVELYN.

CAROL: What's the matter?

EDWARD: Don't look so surprised, Carol. It's terribly irritating.

CAROL: I don't understand.

EDWARD: I gather that you and Evie —

EVELYN (*wounded by such frankness*): Edward!

CAROL (*looking at* EVELYN): You cad!

EDWARD: It was very unpleasant of you, Carol —

CAROL (*appealingly*): Edward, please —

EDWARD: I should like to know how it all happened.

EVELYN: I told you – I —

EDWARD: Carol, will you explain, please?

CAROL: Certainly not.

EDWARD: Very well. You must allow me to reconstruct it for myself.

EVELYN: Surely this is unnecessary.

EDWARD: That is entirely for me to decide.

CAROL: You're being unbelievably cheap.

EDWARD (*mildly*): Really, Carol – keep a slight grip on your values.

EVELYN: Say what you like. I don't care.

EDWARD: It wouldn't make the slightest difference if you did.

EVELYN: Damned ungenerous.

EDWARD: Shut up and don't be an ass. You and Carol have brought about this abominable situation. It's up to you to keep quiet and let me straighten it out in my own way.

EVELYN (*turning away*): Very well.

EDWARD: Thank you. Now then – Evie, you asked Carol to dine with you alone at your flat?

EVELYN: Yes.

EDWARD: Why?

EVELYN: I told you.

EDWARD: In order to teach her a lesson.

CAROL: Oh, this is insufferable.

EDWARD: You're perfectly right, it is. I gather that the first part of the lesson, Evie, necessitated you making love to her. Am I right?

EVELYN (*impatiently*): Oh yes —

EDWARD: And then what? (*Turning.*)

EVELYN: Look here, Edward, I'm damned if I'm going to listen to this any longer —

CAROL: Neither am I!

EDWARD: Tell me the truth, then, Carol. It will simplify matters considerably. Do you love Evie?

CAROL: No.

EDWARD: Then why, if it's not an indelicate question, did you —

CAROL (*violently*): Because he insulted me and tried to humiliate me and I determined to show him that he wasn't as clever as he thought he was.

EDWARD: Admirable. You, Evie, had the ineffable conceit to pit your meagre experience of the world against an extremely attractive and obviously unscrupulous woman. You then give in to her completely despite the fact that she is the wife of your friend, and not content with that, you turn on her afterwards, work yourself up into a frenzy of false melodramatic values, rush round here and blurt it out to me doubtless under the delusion that by uncovering the whole shameful business you are vindicating your own honour! Oh, Evie, what a pitiful fool you are!

EVELYN: It's no use blackguarding me any more, is it? What are you going to do about it?

EDWARD: I don't quite know yet.

CAROL: There's nothing to be done.

EDWARD: You're too sure of yourself, Carol – you always have been.

EVELYN: I wish to God I had shot myself.

EDWARD: It's a little late to think of that now.

EVELYN: You're being unnecessarily cruel, Edward.

EDWARD: I'm afraid I'm a bitter disappointment to you both. You see emotionally I'm unmoved. The capacity for feeling very deeply over Carol died a long while ago.

EVELYN: I should have thought that for the sake of our friendship —

EDWARD: That's sheer cant. You've considerably over-estimated our friendship for years. If you care to analyse it honestly you'll discover that we both bore one another stiff and always have. We were at school together – in different forms – since when we've dined together on an average of once a month. We've confided our troubles superficially for the want of something to talk about. We're poles apart mentally and physically; we've built up this so-called great friendship on a basis of false tradition, and the only reason I realised it first is because my brain functions quicker than yours —

EVELYN (*shattered*): Edward!

EDWARD: And I should like to add – having naturally a more acute sense of sex psychology than you – that the reason you took such a fatal interest in Carol's morals was not on my account at all, but because she'd snubbed you severely several times and you were probably very much attracted to her.

EVELYN: It's not true. You're disgusting.

EDWARD: Be that as it may, the solution to the whole thing is obvious.

EVELYN: What do you mean?

EDWARD: I'll tell you. Carol you must go away immediately.

CAROL (*horrified*): Edward —

EVELYN (*stricken*): But – I – I —

EDWARD: Wait a moment. Let me explain. Carol, you and I have no longer the slightest justification for living together. If you go away abroad somewhere I will make it perfectly easy for you to divorce me. If you don't agree to this, I shall file a petition against you at once, naming Evie as co-respondent. That's the second ultimatum I've delivered this morning and I'm feeling extremely tired. (*He sits down.*)

CAROL: Edward, you can't mean this – you can't.

EDWARD: I do. I mean it more than I've ever meant anything in my life.

CAROL (*bursting into tears of rage*): I won't stand it. I won't!

EDWARD: You're not being very polite to Evie.

EVELYN: You think you're being damned clever.

EDWARD: That's been hurled at me so often just lately that I'm honestly beginning to believe I am.

CAROL: You utter beast.

EDWARD: Well – what's the decision?

CAROL (*wailing*): I'll never speak to you again – never – never – never.

EDWARD (*rising*): Evie?

EVELYN (*gruffly*): You'd better give us time to think.

EDWARD: What is the time now, anyhow?

EVELYN (*looking at his watch*): Twenty-past one.

EDWARD: My God! I knew I should be late. I'll be at the Berkeley if you want me.

> EDWARD *goes out.* EVELYN *and* CAROL *look after him and then at each other.* CAROL *after a pause walks over and sits next to* EVIE.

CAROL: Evie.

EVELYN: What?

CAROL (*sweetly*): There's still time for you to shoot yourself!

CURTAIN

If you enjoy the work of 'The Master', why not join
the Noël Coward Society? Members meet on the
anniversary of Coward's birthday at the Theatre Royal,
Drury Lane to see flowers laid on his statue by
a star such as Sir John Mills, Alan Rickman or
Vanessa Redgrave. Groups go to Coward productions,
places of interest and celebrity meals.

Members receive a free copy of our regular colour
magazine, *Home Chat*, as well as discounts on
theatre tickets, books and CDs. All are welcome to join –
serious students, professional and amateur performers,
collectors of memorabilia or simply fans.

Visit our regularly updated website: www.noelcoward.net
for a membership form
or write to the Membership Secretary:

Noël Coward Society
29 Waldemar Avenue
Hellesdon
Norwich NR6 6TB
UK